D0853490

CRIME AND JUVENILE DELINQUENCY

Published under the auspices of

The National Council on Crime and Delinquency
New York

and

The Institute for the Study and Treatment
of Delinquency
London

CRIME and JUVENILE DELINQUENCY

A Rational Approach to Penal Problems

by

SOL RUBIN

Counsel, The National Council
on Crime and Delinquency

Revised Third Edition

1970

OCEANA PUBLICATIONS, INC.
DOBBS FERRY, NEW YORK

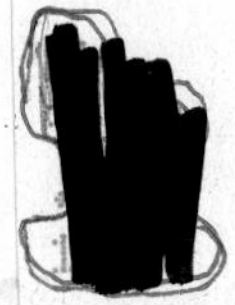

First Edition 1958

Revised Second Edition 1961

Second Printing 1966

Revised Third Edition 1970

Library of Congress Catalog Card Number: 61-8524
Standard Book Number: 379-00452-6

MANUFACTURED IN THE UNITED STATES OF AMERICA

Contents

Foreword to First Edition

Ever since the revealing and inspiring course on criminal law given by Professor Sayre at Harvard Law School which I took in the early twenties, I have proudly and consistently allied myself with the ever increasing group of socially minded lawyers. Today, some 35 years since those halcyon student days, I am more convinced than ever that the law has always been, is today, and will continue to be—to an even greater and more effective degree than at present—one of our strongest forces in achieving a more complete human well-being.

Hence it gives me a very special satisfaction and pleasure to be privileged to offer this foreword. Sol Rubin, the author of *Crime and Juvenile Delinquency,* belongs to the revered company of those, headed by Holmes, Brandeis, Cardozo, Pound, Sayre, who have given the law humane and living strength.

It has been clear for over half a century that sound public policy in the correctional field must be based on the insights and orientations provided by law, sociology, and social work. For almost as long a period, the potential contributions of psychology, psychiatry, and modern social administration have also been manifest. Yet publication lists and professional journals still suffer from a paucity of works with a sophisticated integration of these dimensions relevant to the vital issues facing the correctional field.

No reader of the present volume will feel that it suffers from narrowness of background. Drawing with outstanding competence on his legal and social science training, as well as on his exposure to social work philosophy and practice, Mr. Rubin has, in fact, demonstrated an ability to think deeply but not narrowly, and thus encourages those who see such a broad approach as prerequisite to the further progress of science and practice in correction.

Perhaps the key to the author's work is his view that we can be scientific about human behavior provided we "reckon with the complexities of human ethics, social ethics, with the special values inherent in people," and that "in the human sciences, to be scientific is to be humanitarian." He does not, however, substitute sentiment for science or ad hoc improvisations for legal scholarship. The reader will find in these pages a creative demonstration of how rigorous sociological and legal thinking may serve, rather than betray, the interests of the individual.

As a member of the bar and a former judge, I feel called upon to remind my colleagues in the law that we have had before us for a long time the teachings of Roscoe Pound and others who have pioneered in sociological jurisprudence. Their influence has been felt in children's courts, in some youth courts, in probation and parole, and in some family courts, but often far too superficially and incompletely. Mr. Rubin has explored some of the ramifications of further socialization of the law and raises provocative questions. His approach at times suggests solutions other than those which have been traditional; for example, he takes a stand for the sharing of presentence reports with defendants. Legal educators should find great value in these chapters; their students will discover in these pages that many stereotypes do not hold true, that many implications of the new approach are yet to be worked out.

As the Dean of a graduate school of social work, I must hasten to add that while we are making reasonable progress in aligning the field of correction with social work practice, there are large tasks still before us. I refer not only to the problems of recruitment, adequate field training opportunities, civil service requirements and the like, but also to the content of educational efforts. Recent thinking reflects a heightened awareness of the importance of social science. In the recent past only psychiatric or psychological concepts governed our ideas on case evaluation, treatment, and administration. Sociological and social psychological insights, in particular, have shown the way to modifications in our definition of the practitioner's role, as well as in agency policy.

Having reached this point, if we are to build soundly it now becomes important to add the still missing legal dimension. Some social work educational programs have always contained appropriate legal content, but others have suffered from the extreme scarcity of appropriate written material and teaching talent. Here, too, Mr. Rubin's book fills an important need. I recommend it to social work educators as a volume which marshals legal concepts clearly and effectively around issues of concern to students and to practitioners.

Not that any group of lawyers, sociologists, or social workers is necessarily expected to agree with all of Mr. Rubin's views, any more than the author of a foreword need endorse all of them. The author is original; he is hard-hitting, and he is a man of great integrity. He does not hesitate to call a whitewash just that. If his reasoning brings him to a minority position, as on pre-sentence reports, he outlines his position effectively but indicates that the majority hold another view. What more could one ask of a scholar, or of a humanitarian, or of a reasonable man? Let it be said, finally, that almost every page of this work is intellectually stimulating and, to the student in this field, exciting. The logic is tight, the arguments well reasoned, and the point of view fresh and independent. Mr. Rubin has rendered a valuable service in giving us *Crime and Juvenile Delinquency*.

Kenneth D. Johnson, Dean
New York School of Social Work
Columbia University

1958

Foreword to Second Edition

As an American penologist and, in particular, as counsel to the National Council on Crime and Delinquency (formerly the National Probation and Parole Association) Mr. Rubin is primarily concerned with the correctional problems of his own country, and he also takes a critical look at its legislation and court procedure. Non-American readers will, naturally, want to know how far his book can be of theoretical or practical interest to them. In the United States the machinery of legislation often works differently from that of other countries. "Model Acts" are increasingly drafted by public spirited private bodies of high repute and great influence such as the American Law Institute, the National Council on Crime and Delinquency, or the National Conference of Commissioners on Uniform State Laws, and presented to the individual states of the U.S.A. for adoption.

In the drafting of these Model Acts and in the public discussions following their publication the author has taken an important part, and his views on them are reproduced on this sector of the American lawmaking machine. The Standard Juvenile Court Act, the Standard Probation and Parole Act, the Model Sentencing Act, and others, which are here critically examined, present outstanding examples of the kind. Through these Model Acts the federal and state legislatures are in no way deprived of their constitutional powers, but their tasks are made easier through the well-informed guidance which they receive.

Is there not a danger, however, the author asks, that this guidance, emanating from intellectual centres of the highest standards, may prove to be too unrealistic and theoretical to cope with the grim realities of life as legislators and administrators in remote states may have to face them? In particular, is such model legislation not likely to require for its practical working a judicial and administrative personnel of a calibre not easily found in daily life? In his Introduction, the author shows himself well aware of this risk, but he thinks it can be avoided by encouraging the selection of better trained personnel and by providing controls to protect the recipients of the services concerned against the effects of bad administration. A third indispensable requirement, he stresses, is the existence of a scientific, and at the same time, humanitarian criminology to provide the basic factual material for the draftsmen of this model legislation, a criminology producing research which, in the author's words, never indulges in mere "whitewashing" of the shortcomings of administration, nor "deals with people as fragments" or "loses sight of their lives in statistics." Surely, these are problems of very general interest and application.

His humanitarian approach leads Mr. Rubin to occasional bitter criticisms of American treatment policies. He rightly denounces the tendency towards excessively long prison sentences, contrasting it unfavourably with the more lenient British sentencing policy. He also denounces the view, so often in recent years heard in this country as well, that "everything has been tried—so we must turn to punishment," meaning punishment of a retributive nature. In fact, he thinks, "rehabilitative methods, even today, usually get token support, at best." In this connection he suggests that probation could be used far more than at present—a recommendation which certain courts in this country, too, might well take to heart. On the other hand, some of the practices or trends he fights against are hardly worth bothering about in this country, for example, punishment of the parents of juvenile delinquents, but even so it is good to see the case against it so forcefully argued, and the same applies to the American tendency to use excessively loose and vague definitions of "juvenile delinquency," a tendency against which the recent Report of the Ingleby Committee has come out very clearly. In the present edition, Mr. Rubin is able to report that the latest version of the Standard Juvenile Court Act, in so far going beyond the previous one, declares only acts which are violations of the criminal law to constitute juvenile delinquency, which brings the Act somewhat nearer to English law. Altogether, it will be interesting for readers in this country and the Commonwealth to look at their juvenile and family court systems in the light of Mr. Rubin's comments on American developments.

Some of the crucial chapters of the book deal with the American sentencing practice for adult and adolescent offenders, and it is this subject that is perhaps nearest to the author's heart. He is not altogether satisfied with the proposals in the American Law Institute's draft Model Penal Code, which seem to him to be too much in line with the present policy of very long prison sentences. The "Youth Authority Plan" he regards as a "movement of considerable value, despite its lack of a unique pattern," but not wholly without reason he also sees in it the danger that it might increase the frequency and length of commitments to institutions. There are, nevertheless, features in the various American Youth Authority programs which may repay further study.

The author offers penetrating critcism of the indeterminate sentence. Contrary to the prevailing trend in the United States and in some of the literature on the subject, he dislikes this form of sentencing because, as he demonstrates statistically, it is likely to increase the length of the periods actually served by the offender. "I suspect that often the indeterminate sentence has been adopted not only for the reasons advanced by the original theorists who advocated it, but precisely because it was known to the legislators that its effect was to increase the terms of imprisonment." Outside the United States there has been no widespread desire in recent years to use the indeterminate sentence indiscriminately. In this country even the length of the sentences of preventive detention and corrective training is fixed by the courts, and where relatively indeterminate sentences are used as in the Borstal System the margin of discretion left to the administration is, by American standards, narrow. The Criminal Justice Bill, 1960, proposes to make such relatively indeterminate sentences more widely applicable for young adults, but on the other hand their maximum length will be reduced. On the whole, the movement in favor of indeterminate sentences seems to have spent most of its force, and those who wish to advocate its further extension should take note of Mr. Rubin's observations.

One of the outstanding lessons of this book seems to be that it is wrong and futile for legislators to spend much time and energy on technicalities and on devising over-elaborate prescriptions for sentencing. Apart from definite guidance, which is indispensable, on the philosophy and fundamental principles of the matter, the courts are better left to their own discretion, and further guidance should be provided by better training of judges and magistrates, coupled with whatever enlightenment can be derived from scientific research on the pattern and effect of the various categories of sentences. If Mr. Rubin's book should convey this message to readers outside his own country, the publication of this edition in England as well as the U. S. A. will have served its purpose.

HERMANN MANNHEIM

London

Foreword to Third Edition

Revising *Crime and Juvenile Delinquency* in 1969 involved not only a reexamination of old and traditional concepts, some of which must be and are being changed, but doing so in a period when the deceptive phrase "law and order" was a political issue of national importance.

In this period ghetto riots in many cities have involved widespread arson and looting, mass crimes, in contrast to the individual crimes with which this book deals. These were protest crimes, in some respects similar to the college youths and various other protesting groups involved in confrontations with the police. Often these resulted in violence which could only be called (as one investigating body did) a "police riot."

What then is the relevancy of the old standards in such a time? It seem to me that they are more relevant than ever. If we are ever to overcome the spirit of violence among us, it will only be through decency and legality in the law enforcement process, and through improved methods of treating convicted offenders, not in violent or illegal law enforcement, not in indifferent and calloused treatment methods for offenders.

The recent years have seen some but very limited improvements in juvenile courts, probation and parole services and their legal procedures. The concepts set forth here provide, I hope, the next goals toward which we have to reach.

I want to pay tribute to Charles L. Chute, first director of NCCD and the man who organized it as a national service agency, a devoted, creative and independent man, with whom I was privileged to work for a number of years until he died in 1953. I have gained much from working with the two men who succeeded him, able and creative individuals under whom the work and scope of NCCD has broadened and enlarged considerably—Will C. Turnbladh, director until 1959, when he left to become the first commissioner of Minnesota's consolidated Department of Corrections, and Milton G. Rector, who, first as assistant director, guided the pioneer efforts of the Citizen Action Program of NCCD. These men have notably contributed to and continue to increase a new spirit of understanding and a consciousness of treatment responsibility and professionalization in the correctional field and in the public mind.

I acknowledge with appreciation to the editors of the following journals permission to use articles originally published in their journals: *Federal Probation* (Administrative Office of the United States Courts); *The Annals of the American Academy of Political and Social Science; The Journal of Criminal Law, Criminology, and Police Science* (Northwestern University School of Law); *The American Journal of Sociology;* and the NCCD publications, *Focus* and the *Journal* (quarterly).

December 1969

Sol Rubin

Preface

In May, 1960, after some fifty-three years, the familiar name *National Probation and Parole Association* was changed to *The National Council on Crime and Delinquency.* The step was the product of a long process of broadening the scope of the Association's work and goals, recognized by the membership, which formally proposed the new name at the annual meeting in 1959. This grass roots movement had drawn strength, maturity and solidarity from the annual Institute on Crime and Delinquency, begun in 1954, and held jointly with regional and state correctional and probation and parole associations in all sections of the country.

The new name was therefore inevitable, it would seem. The old NPPA had never represented a dogmatic approach to the crime and delinquency problem. Rather, its program and staff were sensitive to varying needs of court, correctional, and community services, gained from hundreds of survey and consultation visits in all states. Dynamic as it was, it was bound to grow in scope with increasing knowledge and confidence in the nature of the social engineering needed.

It is still abundantly clear to us, clearer than ever, in fact, with the completion of the three-year demonstration in Saginaw, Michigan, that probation, its increased use, the presentence investigation as a tool in sentencing, are fundamental in dealing with offenders. Parole offers the safest and sanest means for returning offenders to the community. But crime and delinquency stem from forces that are cummunity-wide, and efforts in prevention and correction must be broad, flexible, and varied. We have learned that citizen leadership is essential to any sustained effort in this field, and place great faith in our Citizen Action Program as the beginning of a dynamic citizen movement for more effective prevention and correction; the judges are at the fulcrum of law enforcement and correctional services, and we have found judges everywhere responsive to the leadership of the Council of Judges of NCCD and our other advisory groups, continue to work for the improved quality of services and practices.

Sol Rubin has been a vital influence in all of these deevlopments. In this book he examines some fundamental ideas and procedures, applying to them the tests of objective but humane inquiry, subjects theories to facts, and uses facts in reaching for new theories of criminal and administrative behavior. There are no sacred cows in his view, nor should there be, if we are to advance, as he says, rationally.

Milton G. Rector
Director, National Council on Crime and Delinquency

Part I

INTRODUCTORY

Chapter 1

Point of View

Disease in man is not one problem but many. There are many forms of illness, and many roads to prevention, cure, and health. The same is true of crime and juvenile delinquency. They are not one problem, but many. Crime and delinquency have different meanings in their different forms, both to the individual and to society. They have many different aspects—prevention; treatment; public attitude; legislative control; administrative practice which, as in most other enterprises, suffers a constant menace from insufficient resources and chronic bureaucracy.

It is not surprising that the problems raised by crime and delinquency, being many-sided, elicit different and conflicting views. There are divergent views as to what should be done, though it is often agreed that what is done is inadequate or unsucccessful. On these many issues, how do we—individuals, organizations, officials and official bodies—arrive at the stands we take?

John Dewey wrote that "differences in theory . . . grow out of conflicting elements in a genuine problem—a problem which is genuine just because the elements, taken as they stand, are conflicting. Any significant problem involves conditions that for the moment contradict each other."

Crime and delinquency, like other problems in society, at point after point, present questions of understanding, of social policy, and of social action, which are made up of conflicting elements. These are, as Dewey says, *genuine* problems, *significant* problems. The issue of capital punishment involves elements of vengeance, fear, hope, of deterrence, the fallibility of judgment, respect for life, and the striving for a better ethic. A rational, objective and scientific approach is necessary to the solution of this and the many other issues in the interest of sound social policy.

Solutions arrived at are frequently not scientific because the conflicting elements in the problems are not seen, or are disregarded, perhaps partly because the problems are not seen as subject to scientific approaches. Social decisions result from a mixture of many pressures, although inertia and passivity also play a part. All the greater is the need to muster the forces of reason in tackling the problems of crime and delinquency.

How does one do this? "Solution comes," continues Dewey, "only by getting away from the meaning of terms that is already fixed upon and coming to see the conditions from any other point of view, and hence in a fresh light. But this reconstruction means travail of thought. Easier than thinking with surrender of already formed ideas and detachment from facts already learned is just to stick by what is already said, looking about for something with which to buttress it against attack. Thus sects arise: schools of opinion. Each selects that set of conditions that appeals to it; and then erects them into a complete and independent truth, instead of treating them as a factor in a problem, needing adjustment."

I have tried to see the issues in the crime problem as "genuine" in Dewey's sense; and in part perhaps I have used the suggested technique of "getting away from the meaning of terms that is already fixed upon and coming to see the conditions from another point of view." My point of view in searching for solutions can best be explained as a particular attitude toward, first, law; second, administration; third, science; fourth, humanity; and last, responsibility.

Dynamic Law

One of the documents prepared for the Midcentury White House Conference on Children and Youth (unfortunately one which was not printed) was a symposium on "Law and its Relation to Healthy Personality Development." It declared that law, "considered as an institution, or as one of the basic sciences, or as a philosophy, has a direct and vital bearing upon the opportunities of children and youth for healthy personality development. . . . In giving consideration to the influence of the environment upon children and youth, due consideration has to be given to the law, both as it conditions that environment and as it itself constitutes an integral part of that environment." Comments substantiating and illustrating this view came from such people as A. Delafield Smith (assistant general counsel, Federal Security Agency), Professor Max Rheinstein (University of Chicago), and numerous other contributors.

Law, of course, defines crime and delinquency, and sets the framework of attempts to control them. The laws declare what is criminal and what is not; crime is a violation of the law; delinquency (as pointed out in chapter 3) is what the law says it is. By the law I mean those constitutional provisions, statutes, and court decisions which determine the consequences of crime and specify the resources for dealing with criminals.

But the law does much more than merely define crimes and set up the structure of treatment services. Rather, the law itself accomplishes a great deal by what it can express and do. For example, seen narrowly, a probation law authorizes a court to use, as a disposition in a criminal case, a judgment which allows the defendant to remain in the community under certain conditions and subject to resentence if they are violated or if he commits a new crime. During the term fixed the probationer is subject to the supervision of the court, exercised through probation officers.

Seen dynamically, a probation law does much more. First, it establishes certain rights. Although the judge must act to give the defendant the status of a probationer, he does so by bringing the law into play. It is the law itself, however, which defines the status. In doing so the law can accomplish a great deal. It imposes on a convicted offender a considerably less condemnation than does a sentence to prison, and it is obviously less destructive, the individual being allowed to remain free. (In fact the power of this status is such that many have the misconception that a person on probation or suspended sentence has not suffered a conviction.) As stated by a psychologist: "The immense social value of probation comes from the fact that it protects the offender from the ego-shattering experience of incarceration. The person on probation is not stigmatized by the term 'jailbird,' 'ex-con,' 'inmate,' or any of the other terms which are so damaging to his sense of self-respect. He does not need to look at himself as a person who has done time. He is protected from being identified with the prison population. If probation did only this, it would still be worth its cost."[1]

Such laws add to the dignity and self-esteem of individuals. Thus of *itself* the law may be said to have a rehabilitative effect by subtly altering the public's attitude toward the offender, and his own attitude toward himself and the law. Seen in this way the law assumes increased importance in the scheme of correctional services. It is not only a framework for action; it is itself a force. Accordingly one looks at the writing of probation laws (a subject discussed in chapter 10) with a view to having the law serve as more than a mere vehicle or enabling tool for the judge. One can try to write the same kind of force into laws governing juvenile delinquency (chapter 3), juvenile courts (chapter 5), the sentencing of youths (chapters 6 and 7) or adults (chapter 8).

In America, as in England and Canada, a great struggle exists over the issue of capital punishment (discussed only briefly in chapter 6). The struggle to abolish the death penalty is a struggle over an ethical as well as a legal and penological issue, as is true of many penological issues. The debate itself is significant, and influences men's minds. The effort to get the abolition law passed has, in fact, some of the impact of the law itself, by its educational and psychological impact on the public and officials. A state in which the effort to abolish the death penalty becomes strong is a state which is likely to have fewer executions, somehow, whether by reduction of a charge, or jury action, or executive clemency, or in recent years, legal action by abolition and civil liberties groups.

Law has another positive effect. It is a great educational tool, declaring or implying standards of conduct in a highly authoritative way. People incline to defend the things that are theirs, whether their own foibles, those of members of their families, or the laws they live under. Before probation laws were as widespread as they are now judges often opposed their passage, sometimes on such grounds as a fear of lessened judicial independence, or some other rationalization.

Those who come in as judges under systems with a fair history of probation seldom question its rightness. Indeed, any attempt to tamper with the probation system is deemed by them to be a threat to judicial independence! Confirmation of this point may be found in the fact that today most judges are served by probation department woefully inadequate in numbers of personnel. Many judges (perhaps most) hardly ever question their existing staff level, and would oppose any effort to change exactly that degree of inadequacy in their departments!

But of course it is true that judges came to support probation not only because it was part of the law and part of their accustomed existence, but because it worked ,and worked well. This, too, is a part of the viewpoint one may have toward law: law is an experiment. It is not sacred because it is law, but only if it is good. And if a law is bad, we have to be independent enough to say so, and to labor for its repeal. There are illustrations in this book of such laws, too.

If seen in this way, as a positive educational and rehabilitative force, the law and its instruments take on increased respect and value. If we think of courts as positive, constructive resources, we turn to them for what they can do when they can do it best, rather than wait until a situation becomes desperate, perhaps beyond recovery, and then turn to the courts to acknowledge a hopeless situation. The same positive attitude as opposed to distrust of the law would enable us to make better use of correctional services. But this can be most true if the court or correctional resources receive adequate financial support.

Lastly, the law has a profound effect on administration. There is no doubt that many communities lag behind in their treatment of people accused or convicted of crime or delinquency because of archaic or inadequate laws. Law determines the forms of organizational structure; it may encourage or prevent selection of highly qualified personnel; and it greatly influences the procedures of agencies.

Progressive Administration

The lagal basis of correctional treatment has models in the "Standard Acts," drafted by the leaders in the field for adoption (with necessary adaptations) by the legislatures of the various states and jurisdictions. (Chapter 5 discusses the Standard Juvenile Court and the Standard Family Court Acts; chapter 8 the

Model Sentencing Act; chapter 10 the Standard Probation and Parole Act.) Of course the form and substance of social institutions are determined by the whole complex of factors constituting the culture, not only law, although law is a highly important factor, especially so in a field like criminal correction. Yet within the framework of any institution, there is a great deal of room for decision and initiative by administration, by which we mean the governing persons through whom the particular social institution functions. Probably administration is as important as the nature of the institution itself. Administration can have a large measure of independent development, aside from law and personnel.

Administration is sometimes equated with the rank and file personnel; that is, it is said that the effectiveness of a program depends on little more than the quality of the people functioning in the court, correctional institution, or department. There is considerable truth in this viewpoint. But it is important to realize that the leadership of an organization puts it unmistakable stamp on the character of the organization, and vitally affects the performance of all personnel.

If the Standard Acts are to be "models" of systems, legislatively and administratively, is there the danger of writing a law in contemplation of the high, or highest personnel standard (the model acts incorporate provisions to obtain the best personnel)? We know that for various reasons we cannot count on the personnel being the best. There are not enough professionally trained people for the court and correctional services. These services frequently lose out in competition for qualified people. Often the failure traces back to lack of appropriations, so that there is not provision for enough people, trained or not. And for the people on the job, a bureaucratic setting or a setting of political favors and favoritism may prevent their doing their best work.

Do we not then face the danger of having an instrument designed for use by fine hands, applied instead by poorly trained or untrained workers who carry grossly excessive workloads? Progressive administration, like progressive law, is realistic. It must deal with this dilemma; how? How is drafting a "model" act justified when it must operate in the real world, which is so far from model?

The dilemma is more apparent than real. The solution lies in writing law which establishes or encourages administration to seek a high level, yet provides necessary controls and limitations, to protect the recipient of the service against the effects of bad administration.

The second element of the solution is as important as the first—protecting the *recipient of the service* against bad administration. We can illustrate this by what happened with one state's parole law. The state had a law that conformed well to the recommended standards. It was flexible, in that it permitted parole release at any time, provided for a parole board made up of members serving full time, had a civil service staff, and so on. Somehow, political rot set in and, in time, paroles were commonly granted for political influence or money. When the situation blew open, the legislature stepped in with a revision of the law.

One revision restricted parole eligibility to the prisoner who had served one-third of his term. There was no such limitation in the previous law. That is, the new law "corrected" the rotten administration by penalizing the prisoners! The peculiar thing is that the release of parolees by political influence or purchase did not lead to a crime wave, mainly because, as we know, parole suffers not from too liberal use, but from the opposite.

Of course this legislation did not ease the job of administration. Potentially it threatened to worsen the state's prison problem by requiring prisoners to stay longer before parole; and perhaps it also deceived the public into thinking that a corrupt situation had been cured by the new law. Such experiences are not uncommon; another similar situation is described at page 208; and the observations (at page 191) on the judge who feels 'safer" with a commitment than with probation.

What other course might have been taken? Although law is important in its substance, its administration is a separate, independent effort. It is good that it is, because laws are often not models, and yet under poor laws administration can be better or worse, depending on its own measure. This state needed to strengthen and improve administration, in part by law (but the opposite was done); and more—by erasing the political corruption that corroded a potentially good system, by sufficient financial and moral support for competent personnel, and by improving procedures.

Somehow we become more distraught at corruption than we do at mediocrity or inferiority in administration. Yet these, which are so prevalent, are more harmful even than corruption. This is hardly a plea to keep hands off corruption. But hamstringing administration is not an answer. Corruption in administration must be fought in many ways, including support of competent personnel and sound procedures.

But perhaps the central lesson in this parole experience is that administration in correction performs best when it keeps its eye on the people in its care. In that way it serves the public best. It must not lose its focus even in the face of inadequate facilities and indifferent support.

If administration is to have its own development, it is also necessary that, like law, it be imaginative and flexible. An illustration is the creation, in one probation department, of a special caseload to deal with the most difficult cases, probationers with deep-rooted psychological problems. In this department the caseload, not exceeding 30, was assigned to an officer with psychiatric casework training and experience.

The device proved successful, a tribute to the officer assigned, but also to the administrative device. The other officers found time to spread supervision more profitably over their regular loads without time-consuming interruptions from the few "problem cases"; the problem cases had the opportunity to obtain psychiatrically-oriented guidance, flexibility in their supervision, and understanding of their problems; and it helped in interpretation to the court. Routine handling of difficult cases was avoided because the administrative device prevented these cases from being lost in the bulk of the entire caseload.[2]

Applying Science to Behavior

It is evident that the problems of criminal behavior and its control are difficult and complex. Law and administration also offer problems of complexity. It must be said that mere common sense, by which we mean the opinion of the relatively uninformed, is more likely to be wrong than right, as in other fields of comparable complexity and difficulty.

Instead, it is necessary to apply scientific thought to these things, by which we mean the constant pursuit of facts, and the constant effort to understand them better. (This subject is dealt with specifically in chapter 14, "Research.")

There are those who say we cannot have a science of human behavior. It is said that in trying to deal rationally with human beings, we are beset by special factors which endanger our ability to be scientific—emotions, especially in criminal correction, of fear (anxiety), and anger (hostility). But of course this was true of the natural sciences, which arose in the battles against the most rabid superstition.

Most people sense that we can be scientific in criminology. The question is like, "Can we do casework in correctional treatment?" (See chapter 11 on conditions of probation and parole.) A brief, and I think valid answer is—we *can* practice casework methods in this field, because it involves human relationships, in which the attempt is made to affect behavior and attitude. Is any field more ripe for casework? It is a matter of saying correction is a field of casework if we attain the level at which we do, in fact, practice casework at a professional level of competence.

So, of scientific criminology. This, or any other field of human conduct, can be scientific if we deal with it scientifically. But the fact is that at present criminology differs from other fields of scientific work in the extent to which governing decisions are made by laymen. Unlike medicine, engineering, and so on, in criminal and correctional treatment enormous roles are played by laymen.

First, a great deal of control is exercised by legislators, who are rarely trained or experienced in this work. In turn they are influenced mainly by another lay source—the press. It is true that from time to time, mainly in a minority of newspapers, and occasionally in periodicals, articles appear which are accurately informative and interpretive. But the back page doesn't know what the front page is doing. The educational articles are a puny weight compared to the daily splashing of melodrama which supports a philosophy of punishment and fear, and gives a false picture of the nature of crime and criminals.

The effects are illustrated over and over again—for example, in the drive to punish parents for delinquency (chapter 2), in the severe punishment of youthful offenders (chapter 6), and of offenders generally (chapter 8).

The layman's view of crime and punishment is not without its apparent logic. That is, it is a common sense approach, as one must grant, because reasonable people come to it readily. I speak in detail about science in criminology later (chapter 14); but perhaps the most relevant brief comment on the lay view is that it has not profited from the experience of the human race in dealing with crime. We cannot unduly disparage common sense. In science it is a big part of the invaluable ingredient of *intuition*. But common sense, or intuition, is not reliable unless proved so by test. If a common sense notion is disproved, it is no longer common sense to believe the intuitive notion. A principal ingredient in science is the use of experience, successful and unsuccessful, in arriving at a better, clearer, more accurate grasp of reality.

Finally, the life of reason is the life of action, too. Where experience teaches that a mode of law or administration is unsuccessful, it is wise to turn to better forms which reason develops. This, too, is illustrated over and over in this book.

To Be Rational Is to Respect Others

It is true of course that we cannot deal with people as we do with things. But that does not mean that we cannot be scientific about human behavior. What it does mean is that the sciences of human behavior must reckon with the complexities of human ethics, social ethics, and with the special values inherent in people. An individual blocked in his study of people by a contempt for them, cannot be a scientist in psychology, medicine, or criminology.

In the previous editions of this book I said at this point—"In brief, in the human sciences, to be scientific one must be humanitarian; to be anti-humanitarian is to be unscientific." I must change "humanitarian" to "respecting others." Under the guise of treatment (humanitarian), drug law violators, so-called sexual psychopaths, and others, are "civilly committed" under the pretext of "treating" them. But the words are false, and the deprivation of liberty under the guise of treatment is worse than a criminal conviction.

Before one decides on treating a person, even a convicted criminal, one must consider whether leaving him alone may not be better, better for him and for society. If we are sincere about "treatment" of criminals on the medical model, we should abide by the doctor's precept, *primum non nocere*—"first, no harm to the patient." Imprisonment is punishment, not treatment, and can be justified only where it is needed to protect society—but it cannot be justified by arguing that the person needs "treatment" which will be given while we deprive him of liberty, or otherwise disrespect his person or psyche.

There is a book (its identity better forgotten) in which the authors declared that they could not decide whether the third degree—which is illegal physical or psychological coercion by police to obtain a statement by a prisoner—exerted a "positive or a negative influence upon potential offenders," and hence were not prepared to condemn or endorse. The authors could not condemn corporal and capital punishment; "It is irrelevant," they said, "to defend such proposals [to abolish] by reference to the greater humanity of the proposed methods." They feel the same about police courts (generally in disrepute), or the characteristics of jails (the most disgraceful of our penal institutions). This is the worst kind of status quo-ism; and is the application of so narrow a test that the most brutal practices can find justification. Fortunately, most of the administrative justice is guided by legality and humanity, and the search for better forms of treatment.

Again: *The Prison World* several years ago published a report of a study of the phenomenon of self-mutilation by prisoners, which has occurred in the institutions of certain states in which prison labor is imposed in an especially brutal way. Under these circumstances many prisoners had recourse to actually smashing their legs or severing their Achilles tendons to avoid the labor requirement. They also used the method of slitting their skin and placing lye in the slit, to slowly burn away the skin and make an open sore which healed slowly. One man cut off his foot. Obviously such action calls for a study of the prison administration, and especially its methods of prison labor. Instead the writer of the article—an academically well-trained official of a prison system under which hundreds of prisoners had mutilated themselves—conducted his study by comparing 100 mutilators and 100 non-mutilators as to their social background, psychological makeup, and social situations in prison life. Seasonal changes in mutilation rates were noted.

The study found such things as—the mutilators had 37 relatives with criminal records, the non-mutilators had 19; 68 per cent of the mutilators showed frequent changes of home and community environment, as against 50 per cent of the non-mutilators. It was thought to be "significant that only 10 per cent of the mutilators were exposed to the stabilizing environment of a rural community or small town, while 60 per cent were products of urban areas "whereas . . . of the non-mutilators, 42 per cent were urban, 15 per cent rural, 28 per cent of small-town origin, and 15 per cent residentially unstable." There was more of this.

It was assumed by the researcher that the prisoner's behavior could be understood by searching out their assumed special inadequacies. And so the conclusion was inevitable. It was concluded that "the group studied are young, emotionally unstable psychopaths, whose attitude and behavior is characterized by hostility and aggression toward authority and organized society. In addition to the tremendous ego appeal that comes with the publicity and their names in the newspaper, further satisfaction is gained through status with other inmates, as well as the sympathizers on the outside who are maudlin in their attitudes toward the treatment of prisoners."[3]

The plain word for this is, whitewash. Obviously the sensible "control" was not other prisoners, but other institutions in which mutilations did not occur. When, more recently, the public came to knowledge of an equally brutal prison in another state, with hundreds of prisoners mutilating themselves, they also heard the director of the state department of correction report that his investigation showed the incidents to be "motivated by self-pity," and the convicts to be seekers after publicity. Like the other illustration, the research is silly, and of course unscientific, despite the "control group" approach, because the research lacked a belief in humanity, including criminals.

Fortunately the two illustrations of criminological thought given are in fact rare, at least in such gross forms, although in less obvious forms perhaps the same loss of touch with humane values is present. The revision of the parole law referred to above is likewise an illustration of this point.

In chapter 13 I urge that when investigation is made prior to a defendant being sentenced, and the judge renders his sentence on the basis of the investigation report, the defendant should have the right to see and if necessary controvert any part of the report. This, as I explain, is a minority view. A strong argument on behalf of a right to disclosure is the interest of the defendant in an accurate report; whereas denying the right to the report may well be based, in part, on the obvious administrative convenience in a rule which avoids challenge of the report by a defendant. I prefer to trust the position that respects the defendant and his civil rights.

In the human sciences, to be rational one must respect people; this is not sentiment, but science. To illustrate: we have discussed administration, and have found that the guide to sound administration is never to lose sight of the service to the people whose behavior or care is the responsibility of the agency. The responsibility to them cannot safely be sacrificed to any form of administrative interest, or anything else. The interesting thing is that the penology that respects people is the one best protective of the public.

In the discussion of research in criminology (chapter 14), the approach suggested is people, their life histories, the impact of the community upon them. In a suggested approach to research in correctional services, the measure of the service is the impact on the people. There can be no other, but we are not always clear about it. In chapter 15, I discuss a study which dealt with people as fragments, lost sight of their lives in statistics, and (the chapter declares) turns out to be erroneous in findings and analysis as a result.

There is an even broader, more leavening thought about criminals. It is that almost all of us are criminals; that is, we violate criminal laws. The prisons are occupied mainly by certain limited types of criminals, those who committed aggressive personal crimes (assault, homicide), or aggressive property crimes (theft, burglary), and were caught. But law enforcement overlooks far more than it finds. Probably the vastest criminal area is "white-collar" crime, so-called, crime committed in the course of business.

Few bussinesses or businessmen have not violated one or many criminal laws—in the filing of personal or business tax returns, fraud ("sharp business"), short weight, adulteration, kickback, etc. Congressional reports in recent years (as other reports in other eras) have documented a fabulous world of rackets and graft, almost completely untroubled by prosecution. Government is probably not freer of crime than business, these reports show. In some instances, the law enforcers themselves, the police, operate their own rackets, and connive in those that exist. It is an oft-demonstrated truism that no racket can long continue without police indulgence, which must be paid for. Few of us indeed (the Kinsey reports showed) have not committed sex crimes, that is, violations of laws. Adultery, for example, is a crime; so is the broadly defined crime of sodomy.

Many books could be written about these things, and they have been.[4] This is probably the sternest application of the maxim, "There but for the grace of God go I." It is not "I am luckier to be better than the criminal," but "he was unfortunate enough to get caught," or, "he committed the kind of crime which is much riskier than mine." The studies show (see page 209) that physically, mentally, and psychologically, the criminal population (as we understand the term in popular usage) does not differ from the rest of us.

Another Point of View

The point of view thus far expressed is not the only one. If it were there would be no need to elaborate it as has been done; and the book would not have been written. But there is another one, a view strongly held by many, and influential in public policy. The view is that the needed policy to counter the crime problem is severity in the criminal law and its enforcement. I have called it above the layman's or common sense point of view, but it is also true of some specialists in the field of criminology. It is this view which considers that punishment of parents is an effective way of dealing with juvenile delinquency; it considers that harsh, repressive treatment of convicted persons is a good way to deal with criminals and that youthful offenders should not be dealt with differently. In the late 1960's, the political platforms and the governors and mayors are profuse in calling for "law and order," by which is meant violent police action, the attack at the same time on the Supreme Court and due process of law having its own clear implication that laws restricting the police are too burdensome to be borne by them.

In the chapters that follow I have analyzed particular applications of this other point of view from what I hope is an objective consideration based on experience. The entire experience of correction through the ages is that severe punishment does not work. When in England, not many generations ago, the death penalty was used against thousands every year, even for petty crime, and even against very young children, it is well known that the ultimate penalty did not deter crime. Pickpockets, who if caught were subject to hanging, plied their trade in the very mobs that watched the public executions.

British penal policy changed, until today it is far less punitive than ours (page 110). The change did not come about because capital punishment or lengthy imprisonment were effective in deterring crime; they were not effective. If they were effective the policies would have been retained, not only in law but in practice. Rather, as Sutherland points out, the change occurred not because of a reduction in the general crime rate, but because of changes in penal policy.[5] No doubt the change in the penology further contributed to a more humane, less brutal culture, itself a factor in bringing down the crime rate. (See page 131.)

Again, in the early history of the American prison movement, labor, generally in the form not of productive work but of punishment, sometimes in grossly cruel forms, was the rule. With solitary confinement it produced insanity in large numbers of prisoners. This is generally changed in today's prisons. Cruel, unproductive labor is no longer the rule, although we still have many examples of it (especially the "rockpile" where prisoners are kept at the aimless task of breaking big rocks into smaller ones), and deliberate brutality as prison policy has by no means vanished.[6]

But more pervasive damage is the result of today's common form of destructive punishment, prolonged imprisonment, today even longer than it used to be (page 119). After several years in prison, during which the prisoner's life is rigidly uniform, all physical wants being taken care of, but initiative, responsibility, individuality being altogether suppressed, the prisoner acquires a prison stupor, may become "stir-crazy," and becomes more or less unfit for ordinary living.

We condemn these practices because they are not effective either in reforming criminals or deterring others from crime. No juvenile court judge can contribute to a solution of the juvenile delinquency problem by what he does to children before him, or to their parents. Whatever produces crime in the culture will continue to do so. But the judge can help the delinquent before him by his understanding of the child's and family's problems, and helping to solve them through his own policy and the court's services.[7]

Today we have alternatives to punishment, developed through the years—probation, parole, casework, clinical services and psychiatry. These rely on discipline rather than punishment; on enabling people to carry responsibility successfully. And the judge can further help in the problem by his leadership in raising community standards in correctional treatment, furthering the modern forms and reducing the outmoded punishments.

The two contrasting views, which can be summarized as punishment versus rehabilitation, are sometimes recognized by the punishment-minded in a somewhat subtle form. They say that "everything has been tried—now we must turn to punishment." The view is pitifully misinformed. About the only device that has been thoroughly tried has been punishment. Rehabilitative methods, even today, usually get token support, at best.

For example, probation can be used far more than it is at present, with benefits to the offender, his family, and the public. But although probation service to an individual defendant costs approximately one-tenth the cost of imprisonment, we have the most meager support for probation departments in most places.

Those who are responsible for dealing with criminals and delinquents do not hesitate to acknowledge and have no interest in denying the shortcomings of their services. In fact the part of wisdom and public service is to make the true facts known. The existing state of affairs as an argument for repudiating programs of correctional treatment is false and a disservice to public security. The public cannot serve as a whipping boy. As urgent as is the need for mature public understanding of criminal behavior and treatment, the public cannot be blamed for the failures of law enforcement and criminal administration. The blame lies with those who have the power to discharge their duties well or badly—the legislators, the police and the prosecutors, the judges, the administrators of institutions and probation and parole services, the press. Too often the administrator talks out of two sides of his mouth, a progressive side, for public consumption, and a repressive side, for his staff and those in his care. He cannot blame the public. The public must come to blame those who have the responsibility, the failing administrator, legislature, press, and others, and to force the necessary corrective steps.

Responsibility

The approach suggested in this chapter is obviously not mine alone. It is a reflection, a verbalization, one of many, of practices and expressions frequently found in the field of correctional treatment. It is a satisfaction to realize that there are many who adhere to and try to implement such views. Punishment *per se* is clearly recognized by the correctional field as futile and destructive.

"The true story of prisons lies not in charts and statistics but in the tragedy and heartbreak they represent to the prisoner, the wasted years that can never be recaptured, and, to society, the loss of precious human resources and talent. Each year, the courts send thousands of people to prison. They come from all walks of life and are of all types. Some are professional, calculating criminals against whom must be marshalled the full force of society's organized authority; many are hostile, impulsive, and psychopathic individuals, who, for the safety of others, must be confined; but mostly, those who enter prison are confused, frustrated, and inadequate people caught in the web of some unfortunate circumstance, or pushed down the blind alley of criminality by some impulsive action. These need redirection, training, understanding and guidance." This was written not by a starry-eyed romanticist in an ivory tower; it is from the 1956 report of the Federal Bureau of Prisons, generally acknowledged to be one of the soundest and most forward looking prison systems in the country.

Notes

[1] "The Prisoner and Self-Respect," by O. G. Johnson (*Federal Probation,* September, 1957, p. 56).

[2] "Probation Supervision of a Specialized Caseload," by Milton Nechemias (*Federal Probation,* June, 1957).

[3] North Carolina reacted to such prisoner behavior by passing laws in 1959 making it a felony punishable by up to ten years imprisonment for a prisoner to inflict a self-injury incapacitating him to perform his prison assignment, or to aid or abet another inmate in such an offense; and authorizing the local health director to withhold consent to treatment if the prisoner refuses to consent to treatment. Unfortunately, more recent studies have been no better. North Carolina simply confimed its prior study in one made in 1967, "Self-Mutilation and Dynamics of Imprisonment,"by Dr. Ben E. Britt (North Carolina Prison Department).

[4] *The Black Market,* by Marshall B. Clinard (Rinehart & Company, 1952), and its extensive bibliography. *Crime Is a Business,* by Estes Kefauver (Doubleday, 1951). *Our Sovereign State and Our Fair City,* edited by Robert S. Allen (The Vanguard Press, Inc., 1949). *History of the Great American Fortunes,* by Gustavus Myers (The Modern Library, 1936).

[5] Edwin H. Sutherland, "The Decreasing Prison Population of England," in *The Sutherland Papers,* edited by Albert Cohen, Alfred Lindesmith, Karl Schuessler (Indiana University Press, 1956).

[6] Mabel A. Elliott, *Coercian in Penal Treatment: Past and Present* (Pacifist Research Bureau, Ithaca, New York, 1947).

[7] A particularly notable organization of judges exercising leadership in judicial work in criminal correction, juvenile and family courts, is the Council of Judges of the National Council on Crime and Delinquency. It has produced *Guides for Sentencing,* and *Guides for Juvenile Court Judges,* and other books distributed widely to judges and others, and it sponsored *The Law of Criminal Correction,* the first legal treatise on the law of sentences.

References

There are many excellent textbook on criminology, bringing together a vast knowledge of crime, criminology, and penal treatment. Among them are: *New Horizons in Criminology,* by Harry Elmer Barnes and Negley K. Teeters (Prentice-Hall, Inc., third edition, 1959). *Criminology,* by Donald R. Taft and Ralph W. England (Macmillan, 4th ed., 1964). *Man, Crime and Society,* by Herbert A. Bloch and Gilbert Geis (Random House, 1962). *Principles of Criminology,* by Edwin H. Sutherland and Donald R. Cressey (Lippincott, 6th ed., 1960).

The Prison World, cited in the chapter, was published by the American Prison Association, now the American Correctional Association, in New York; and the periodical is now *The American Journal of Correction.* The other principal correctional journals in the United States are *Crime and Delinquency* (formerly *NPPA Journal,* and up to 1953, *Focus*) published by the National Council on Crime and Delinquency; *Federal Probation,* quarterly, published by the Administrative Office of the U.S. Courts; *The Journal of Criminal Law, Criminology and Police Science,* published by the School of Law, Northwestern University. The main British journals are *The British Journal of Criminology,* quarterly, published by the Institute for the Study and Treatment of Delinquency, London; *Probation,* quarterly, journal of the National Association of Probation Officers; *The Howard Journal,* annual, published by The Howard League for Penal Reform. The Canadian Corrections Association, Ottawa, publishes *The Canadian Journal of Corrections,* a quarterly. The United Nations publishes a quarterly, *International Review of Criminal Policy.*

Part II

JUVENILE DELINQUENCY

Chapter 2

Are Parents Responsible for Juvenile Delinquency?

There are those who think that there is a certain simple cure for juvenile delinquency. Since delinquency starts in the home (they say) and parents are responsible for the quality of home life (evidently), one should make the parents responsible in law, and hence punishable if the home causes or fails to prevent a child's delinquency. Such punishment, or its threat, will deter delinquency. The more frantic approach to the same recourse is to declare that although the causes of delinquency may be more complex than just stated, nevertheless the whole thing can be attributed to the parents anyway. I have seen reports in the newspaper of claims that such laws reduce delinquency by 50 or 75 per cent. Unfortunately investigation shows them to be not remotely true.

A study was made several years ago of the way legislatures responded to newspaper scare stories of sex criminals by passing new, punitive laws. At least equal interest should be devoted to studying the way there arises, spasmodically, a hue and cry that parents are responsible for juvenile delinquency, and that something—generally in the form of punishment—should be done about it.

This theory of criminal responsibility and causation climbs upwards in popularity every now and then. When it has its effect we have increased punishment, including imprisonment, of parents of delinquent children.

Testing Belief

Is this allegation sound? Or is it a cliché, based on little more than repeated assertion and the evident truth that as long as we have had delinquency we have had parents? The most comprehensive study of the merit of "punishing parents" was made in 1947 by Judge Paul W. Alexander, of the Toledo, Ohio, Domestic Relations and Juvenile Court. Judge Alexander, who had been "punishing parents," examined the records of his court for the years 1937 to 1946, inclusive. He found that in that ten-year year period there had been over a thousand cases of *contributing to delinquency*—the statute used for prosecution of parents and other adults. Half of the defendants were parents; most of these were mothers. Three-quarters of the parents pleaded guilty or were found guilty.

One out of four of the convicted parents was sentenced to prison, where each served, on the average, almost a year. The others received suspended sentences. What effect did this have on juvenile delinquency in Toledo? No noticeable effect at all. With increasing war preparations and war, the delinquency rate rose sharply, reaching a peak in 1943, and then declined. The rise in delinquency was not counterbalanced or affected by the prosecutions of parents, and the decline was in no way attributable to those prosecutions. This was pretty much the course of the incidence of delinquency elsewhere in the country, including places where parents were punished and places where they were not punished.

In 1937, the start of the ten-year period, only seven parents were arrested in Toledo for "contributing." During the first three years, the juvenile delinquency rate was comparatively stationary. The number of prosecutions of parents steadily increased (as the popularity of the idea gained ground), reaching 118 in 1946. Judge Alexander found no evidence that punishing parents had any effect whatsoever on curbing delinquency.

Application of Statutes

Almost every state has a statute defining the crime of contributing to delinquency or neglect. If the statutes were strictly enforced only perfect parents in favorable circumstances would be exempt from prosecution. The statutes read something like this: A parent or guardian or other person who omits to exercise reasonable diligence in the control of his child to prevent him from becoming delinquent or neglected or truant, or who permits the child to associate with immoral persons, or to wander about the streets at night, or to enter any gambling place, etc., etc., or who knowingly is responsible for, or encourages, aids, causes, or connives at, or does any act to produce, promote, or contribute to the conditions which cause the child to be delinquent or neglected, etc., etc., is guilty of a crime. Under some statutes the parents can be convicted without the child being adjudicated a delinquent.

This statute is used against persons other than parents. However, in such cases it is almost invariably used as a substitute for another, more appropriate statute. Frequently it is used against adults who indulge in sexual behavior, generally short of rape, with children. The most apppropriate offense in the penal code is "impairing the morals of a minor." A prosecution on that charge would be conducted in the criminal court, whereas in most states the charge of contributing to delinquency is heard in the juvenile court. The contributing statute is not essential to the proper prosecution of such cases, or any other in which it is used against adults other than parents.

Of course a simple statutory provision could place cases of adult offenses against children in the juvenile court, as in many states now. If it is desirable to have adult cases heard in the juvenile court, the sensible thing is to so provide, rather than use an inappropriate classification of crime (contributing to delinquency) simply because juvenile courts now have such jurisdiction.

It is likewise true that where parents commit crimes against their children, they are sometimes prosecuted for "contributing" instead of for the specific, and possibly more serious, offense. Some judges will not proceed with a contributing charge unless some other crime has been committed. But most judges do not insist on this. Generally the parent prosecuted for contributing to delinquency is *guilty of no other crime.*

A Test Case

During World War II the resulting social dislocations were pointed to as the big factor in delinquency. With the war's end, the parental-responsibility notion took the center of the stage. The New York City Police Department was one of many which grasped this means to "suppress" delinquency. It heralded a drive against delinquency by prosecution of parents, and proceeded, in a test, to arrest the mother of a boy who had been committed as a delinquent. A good deal of publicity was given to the case. On the radio the judge who convicted the mother advocated severe penalties for parents.

But the prosecution backfired and the drive proved a fiasco. Public-spirited citizens came to the support of the mother and obtained counsel for her. On appeal the conviction was reversed: the appellate court found that the eager judge had admitted improper testimony.

But the most illuminating aspect of the case was that the mother was found to be mentally defective, therefore not criminally responsible. Instead of being kept in prison, she was committed to a mental institution for treatment. In other words, the appellate court found the reason for her failure as a parent, and the intelligent consequence was treatment of a defect, rather than punishment.

The mother had not been prosecuted and imprisoned for *doing* anything. The complaint, typical of many such cases, charged her with being "indifferent and irresponsible" and with "failing in her responsibility" as a parent. That constituted the crime. She did fail as a parent, just as other parents fail. Not all parents who fail are mentally defective; few are. More prevalent is emotional disturbance in parents, which not only handicaps them but may have the added effect of encouraging emotional difficulty in the children. As obviously as the mentally defective parent, these other parents need help—not *punishment,* which only adds to their trouble.

Flogging a Dead Horse

Many parents of delinquents are normal, but are swamped by environmental circumstances. Juvenile delinquency is a result of failure to satisfy the basic needs of children for security, status, and the opportunity for a full, normal life. The immediate responsibility for meeting these needs rests in the home, upon the parents. But the existence of severe handicaps in many normal parents in their efforts to meet this challenge cannot be denied.

Perhaps there is a "causal relationship" between a parent and the child's delinquency. Does it call for punishment of the parent? Delinquency is a symptom of trouble, exhibited by a troubled child and a family in trouble. If a parent has not been able to provide properly for his children, if he has not been able to supervise the children adequately, clearly that family needs help. Perhaps the juvenile court's staff of probation officers can help, either directly or by referring the family to clinical facilities of various kinds. Public or private social service agencies offering treatment or help should be available. Punishment increases the family's problems and burdens the court and institutions.

Of the factors making for delinquency, parental inadequacy is only one of many; others are the high cost of living, poor standards of education, inadequate recreation, and slums, to name only a few. But the only one of these at hand for punishment is the parents. We cannot imprison poor housing; we cannot catch "inadequate child guidance." We *can* catch the parents and charge them, perhaps truly, with failure—but we can no more correct them by punishment than we can correct the contributing social conditions by cursing them.

But it is also true that parents of delinquents may not be failing at all, so far as anyone can see. Many parents of delinquents are providing all of the child's needs, material, ethical and psychological. Other children of the same parents are not delinquent. Juvenile delinquency (see chapter 15) is not easily traceable. A reliable answer still eludes the researchers, but certainly much of the causative influence comes from outside the home.

Weird Logic

Other logical and sociological dilemmas confront us. Which parent is chargeable, the father, because he can pay a fine? The mother, because she can be imprisoned without impairing the breadwinner's job? If we punish the parent as the one responsible for the delinquency, should we also punish the child for the delinquency itself? If the child is truant, should we punish the teacher, who may be incompetent, or underpaid, and may as logically be called a "cause" of truancy? Should we punish the superintendent of schools, who is responsible for the teacher? Should the mayor be prosecuted?

Delinquency is only one way in which a child may fail. For the sake of consistency should we not punish as criminals those parents whose children fail in other ways—for example, parents whose children fail academically, or fail socially, or who are sexually ignorant and maladjusted, or who are neurotic? How wonderfully busy our courts would be!

Parents at lower economic levels have greater difficulty in providing the physical attributes of a sound home environment. This may well contribute to difficulty in inter-personal relationships within the family. The greatest difficulties they have should conceivably be weighed in the balance to *lessen* the legal responsibility of lower level parents. Instead, we find that most of the parents subjected to prosecution for contributing come from lower economic levels.

The definition of delinquency is limited by an artificial age bracket. In some states, the age limit of juvenile court jurisdiction is sixteen; in others, it is eighteen. A minor over the juvenile court age limit—and occasionally one who is below it—is prosecuted in the criminal court. This produces something of a paradox so far as parental responsibility is concerned. A parent is prosecuted for having contributed to delinquency, but he is *not* prosecuted if the child's offense is so serious that the child is tried in the criminal court for a *crime!* In other words, as the law now stands, the parent's responsibility is in inverse proportion to the gravity of the child's offense. In New York, for example, if a fifteen-year-old child is an habitual truant, the parent may be held legally responsible; if the same child kills someone, the parent is not held legally responsible. Strange logic indeed.

Other inconsistencies are involved. It is frequently said that the "broken home" is an important factor contributing to delinquency. For that reason courts make earnest efforts to keep families together. A good court works with a family, bringing in not only its own staff but social agencies which have the needed facilities. If a parent is sufficiently incompetent or bad, the child may have to be placed elsewhere. Even in such case, removing the parent via imprisonment is a contradictory expedient. It should be condemned not only as vengeance rather than rehabilitation, but as further contributing to delinquency, this time by act of the court in breaking up the home.

Practical Results

Does punishing parents reform the parents who are punished? Judge Alexander's study shows that punishment does not reform the parents. Of parents imprisoned by him, he writes, "We . . . broke up their home for a year, supported their children in foster homes, gave them the stigma of having 'jail-bird' parents, caused the father to lose his job, and set the family back at least a year economically." Nor was there any deterrent effect on other families.

Does punishing the parent help reform the delinquent child? Punishment of the parent makes clear to the child that if he has done something bad he has done only what his parent has done, something for which the parent is being punished. Perhaps in the child's mind, punishment of the parents absolves the child of blame. Suppose the *parent* is the *victim* of the child's delinquency—an attempted homicide, let us say, or stealing from the parent because the child resents his parent's stinginess or discipline. Does the fact that the parent is guilty of causing the delinquency provide a defense for the child's act? If, then, the child has a defense and is not delinquent, is the parent in turn legally absolved from responsibility? Needless to say, the courts which interpret parental responsibility as meaning punishment of parents do not acquit the child.

Whatever logic there is going behind parental failure in delinquency, the same logic even more importantly leads further—to the community's responsibility to afford sound conditions for normal living and, where delinquency occurs, to treat it constructively. If we punish the parent for the child, why not punish the parent's parents? In more than only a symbolic sense, the community is the parent of the parents and of the child as well. The home is only part of the child's environment.

The use of the statutes defining the crime of contributing to delinquency is spotty. Whether it is used or not used depends on the policy of a particular place at a particular time. Either these statutes make good sense and ought to be used, or they ought to be taken out of the laws to avoid their abuse, to avoid the *punishment of parents and the accusation of parents as scapegoats for delinquency*. The existence of these statutes would be warranted only if punishment of parents were found to be helpful in solving the delinquency problem.

As long as "contributing" statutes are on the books, the danger exists that they will be used, and when they are used, the danger exists—is almost inevitable—that they will be abused. It would be the better part of wisdom for the legislatures to repeal these laws, for they cannot be safely regarded as statutes which are harmless and may be ignored.

But are there not some exceptional cases where the statute might be used? Perhaps. One answer to such a defense of the law is that it is a peculiar kind of penal law that is used only when convenient. We think of crimes as acts that should be suppressed and punished consistently and equally. Another answer is that for every case of proper use there are numerous cases of improper use.

There is a further answer. Aside from the statute dealing with the crime of contributing to delinquency, there remain in the penal laws numerous statutes that may be used in serious cases. In fact, in serious cases, parents and others are prosecuted under the specific statute rather than for contributing. One objectionable aspect of the contributing statutes is that their definition of criminal responsibility is flimsy when compared with the definition of other crimes in other statutes.

Until the 1949 edition the Standard Juvenile Court Act contained a "model" section on contributing to delinquency. The 1949 Act dropped it, and the 1959 Act likewise omits it. The comment to the Act states on this point: "The efficacy of the 'contributing' laws, which are frequently directed against parents, has been doubted in many quarters. It seems more desirable, from both a legal and social point of view, to prosecute in such cases under a definite criminal code provision, such as assault, impairing the morals of a minor, or any of the varied statutes in existence."

Financial Responsibility Acts

In the last few years another form of attack upon parents of delinquents has come up. It has passed in many states, and has been defeated in a number. These acts provide that the parents of delinquents may be required to pay for the damage caused by the delinquent act (usually up to $300), whether there was any fault on the parents' part or not. No new law is needed if there is fault on the part of the parents, or such neglect or carlessness that they are reasonably chargeable with responsibility.

This law is part of the same school of thought as the contributing statutes we have been discussing. Yet if anything, it pulls away that last shred of reason one might look for in the contributing acts. The older laws say—punish the parents because they are responsible. This one says—punish the parents even if they aren't responsible, because that will teach them to be responsible! (Under the ordinary rules of negligence a parent may be responsible if in some way he was charged with advance knowledge of the child's act and could have prevented it, or was constructively charged with knowledge, that is, he should have known. But these acts are in derogation of the common law, imposing liability without fault. Such laws have been upheld where strict liability is imposed upon those who are in a position to control persons, activities, or things—for example, in controlling animals or motor vehicles. But even there the obligation of care must be reasonably within the power of the person to be charged with liability.)

There are other grounds for opposing such laws. The juvenile court is not principally concerned with restoration of property to the victims (any more than a criminal court is). This is a police problem, or a problem for civil action. The function of the juvenile court is to help children before the court and to protect the community. If people resorted to the criminal courts, or to the juvenile courts, to obtain restitution, the guiding principles of the judges in the courts, the guiding principles developed in the field of correction, would certainly be confused and distorted. The courts and litigants would be preoccupied with punishment instead of the basic function of seeking to understand the cause of the delinquency or neglect and the means of rehabilitation.

Within this framework of treatment, there is still room for restitution, and it is a fairly common practice for restitution to be ordered in juvenile or criminal court proceedings.

Repeals Are in Order

The main reason to oppose the contributing acts and the responsibility-at-peril laws is that they cannot work, that is, they cannot work to reduce delinquency, or to make parents more responsible—better parents. Repealing the laws would be clear affirmation that the community is not going to pass the buck of responsibility for delinquency from itself to the parents. We don't punish a car when it breaks down: we fix it or junk it. We can't junk parents. Under these statutes parental responsibility becomes a vague catch-all eminently suited to abuse. If there is to be substance to "parental responsibility," parents must be enabled to carry out their duties successfully.

There is no repealer movement of any proportions detectable. The newer form of law—which would impose liability on parents without any fault on their part being established—is making some headway, although considerable opposition is alert to the danger. Probably one reason why the laws are not on their way out is that they are enforced only sporadically. If they were persistently enforced their unjustified harshness would convince many that the laws should be repealed. But we are not sure how much the laws are enforced. There are no national statistics, and the Toledo court does not include the information in its latest reports.

Just as we shall note in the next chapter that the laws defining juvenile deliquency are inordinately broad, so also these laws impose on parents of delinquents obligations, enforceable by criminal sanctions, that go beyond the requirements of the penal codes for other people, and go beyond the bounds of reason.

As Reuben Hill said to the Midcentury White House Conference, "For too long American families have been called upon to take up the slack in a poorly integrated social order." To deal with the problem of delinquency requires effort in many directions—improved social facilities, realistic sex education, improvement in social conditions—however best these generalizations may be implemented. Wherever the concept takes hold that parents who fail should be punished, it should be exposed as a delusion; wherever it is put into practice, it should be attacked as spurious.

References

The United States Children's Bureau has published "Parents and Delinquency," a report of a conference (Children's Bureau Publication No. 349). Judge Justine Wise Polier, of the New York Domestic Relations Court, is the author of an outstanding pamphlet, "Back to What Woodshed?" published by Public Affairs Press. The article by Judge Alexander appeared in *Federal Probation,* March 1948. *The Journal of Social Therapy* (April, 1955), published "On Penalizing Parents for Children's Deviant Behavior," by Lewis J. Siegal. A good antidote to the tiresome repetition that children today are worse than they used to be "when we were children" is the report "Teacher Opinion on Pupil Behavior," a survey published by the National Education Association, Washington, D.C. The present chapter is based in part on an article that appeared originally in *Focus* (National Council on Crime and Delinquency) in March, 1955, with several others on related aspects of the problem.

Chapter 3

What Is Juvenile Delinquency?

The underlying purposes of the juvenile court movement were two-fold—one, to remove child offenders from the ordinary criminal courts to courts specially adapted for dealing with children not as criminals, but affording treatment as needed; and two, to have this specialized court render protection and treatment to other children needing them.

With regard to the first purpose, it was considered that, for children in any event, the ordinary procedure obtaining in a criminal court was objectionable. The adversary process between defendants and the state has produced an intricate, highly formalized procedure, the specific purpose of which is to determine the responsiblity of the individual defendant for his act.

Instead the development of juvenile courts utilized a type of proceeding for which there was already some precedent. For juveniles such a procedure was in time established in all states, although not applicable to all juveniles—informal, not limited to a particular act as in the criminal court, and whose functions of treatment and prevention were widely asserted as the guiding principle of the court.

With regard to the second purpose of the juvenile court—to render special assistance to children needing protection—juvenile courts generally included in their jurisdiction not only delinquent children but also children who were dependent and neglected, and those said to be incorrigible or wayward.

However, the juvenile courts never reached their full expectations, for reasons which were well known but minimized. A generation ago in *The Annals* they were summarized in an attack on the court entitled "The Juvenile Court at the Bar," by J. Prentice

Murphy, then executive secretary of the Children's Bureau in Philadelphia. In brief, the inadequacies of the court were inadequate personnel standards—the caliber of the judge, the training and education of the probation staff, and their sufficiency in numbers; inadequate treatment resources, and disregard of legal rights.

Finally, in two cases decided by the Supreme Court of the United States the criticism was acknowledged not only on a high level but by means that promised a new effort to achieve the promise of the juvenile court—a better deal for children. These cases—Kent vs. United States (1966) and In the Application of Gault (1967) decided that the juvenile courts could not be allowed a procedure so informal that the legal rights of children and parents were disregarded. It said in the Kent case that "there is evidence, in fact, that . . . the child receives the worst of both worlds: that he gets neither the protections accorded to adults nor the solicitous care and regenerative treatment postulated for children."

But these cases touch only part of the problem. They do not examine the definition of delinquency, and leave it untouched.

What Is Juvenile Delinquency?

The following description of what happened at an international congress on the prevention of crime and treatment of offenders, held in 1955, may describe a discussion that was comical or profound, or not quite necessary: "For the first three or four days of the congress, there was endless discussion on the point of defining juvenile delinquency. For example, it was held by some that juvenile delinquency does not exist until after some kind of infraction or offense is committed and there is an adjudication of guilt. By others it was felt that juvenile delinquency needs to be dealt with before an adjudication, particularly since the agenda called for a consideration of the prevention of juvenile delinquency. . . . As the days passed, there was growing concern on the part of the Steering Committee of the congress and it was finally decided that the interminable discussion would have to be halted and that the meetings would be limited to the discussion of certain aspects of the problem; to wit the community, the family, the school, social services including health agencies," etc.

Astounding! But perhaps not so. A social worker wrote that delinquency consisted of "socially unacceptable acts"; a psychiatrist suggested that delinquent behavior "is activity which deviates from the normal." Accordingly it is expected that a lawyer will write, as I do, that *juvenile delinquency is what the law says it is,* just as it is the law that says what a contract is.

The psychiatrist just quoted should be quoted more fully; he said delinquency was activity "which deviates from the normal and is prohibited by the laws and sanctions of our society." That gets closer to home. "Juvenile delinquency" is a legal concept, upon which is based a particular kind of court (a juvenile court) and the special procedures applicable, by law, in the court. Does the legal definition of delinquency coincide with what "deviates from the normal"? Of course not. Psychiatrists could hardly give a definition of normality practical enough to a law. Is the legal definition of delinquency to be equated with "socially unacceptable behavior," as the social worker suggested? No; social workers and others could not agree on that; and they *would* agree that what is socially acceptable to one group may not be acceptable to another—but it is the legislature that decides.

Legislatures revise laws, including definitions of juvenile delinquency. It is absurd to consider that such revisions accord with sudden changes in basic concepts of normality or social unacceptability. The psychiatrist would agree that children properly adjudicated delinquent by juvenile courts include normal and abnormal; and the social worker would agree that they include acts socially acceptable to some groups. As to the question—does an act constitute delinquency before adjudication?—of course; just as murder is murder, whether a court convicts anyone of it or not. And if a court convicts an innocent man of murder, or a child of delinquency, that does not make the innocent act guilty, although someone may be punished for it.

A Loose Concept

Juvenile delinquency is what the law says it is. It is a legal and sociological concept, not psychological. When psychologists and psychiatrists use the term, they use it in the legal sense, or more loosely as a sociological concept.[1]

As indicated, a chief purpose of the juvenile court is to take

child offenders out of the criminal court and protect them from criminal procedure and its effects. We therefore find in the juvenile court acts that every definition of delinquency includes violations of laws and ordinances by children, although in a number of states the court does *not* have exclusive jurisdiction, and children *may* be prosecuted in criminal courts.

The definition of delinquency does not, however, stop with law violations, but *starts* there. The list of other acts or conditions which may bring a child within the jurisdiction of the juvenile courts as a delinquent is painstakingly long. The following is a list of abbreviated definitions of acts or conditions included under the heading of delinquency in the juvenile court laws of the United States:

Violates any law or ordinance
Immoral or indecent conduct
Immoral conduct around school
Engages in illegal occupation
Associates with vicious or immoral persons
Growing up in idleness or crime
Enters, visits house of ill repute
Patronizes, visit policy shop or gaming place
Patronizes saloon or dram house where intoxicating liquor is sold
Patronizes public poolroom or bucket shops
Wanders in streets at night, not on lawful business (curfew)
Wanders about railroad yards or tracks
Jumps train or enters car or engine without authority
Habitually truant from school
Incorrigible
Uses vile, obscene or vulgar language (in public place)
Absents self from home without consent
Loiters, sleeps in alleys
Refuses to obey parent, guardian
Uses intoxicating liquors
Is found in place for permitting which adult may be punished
Deports self so as to injure self or others
Smokes cigarettes (around public place)
In occupation or situation dangerous to self or others
Begging or receiving alms (or in streets for purpose of)

Of course not every state, nor any state, has all these items in its definition of delinquency. However, many laws average eight or nine items in addition to violations of law. The most impor-

tant of these is "incorrigible" or "wayward" behavior, or being beyond control of the child's parents.

Nor are these jurisdictional possibilities neglected. The national statistics of juvenile delinquency prepared by the United States Children's Bureau, inform us that "ungovernable" was the reason for reference to juvenile courts in nine per cent of the cases, and running away in another nine per cent—18 per cent of the total delinquency cases. Some of these possibly could have been represented as some violation of the law. But undoubtedly many of these cases represented no violation of a penal law. Twenty per cent of the cases were referred for "acts of carelessness or mischief." Very likely many of these were not violations of penal law. Some would be torts rather than crimes if committed by adults. In the latest U. S. Children's Bureau report containing the information (1964) the figure is higher—27 per cent of delinquency cases are running away from home, ungovernable, truancy, curfew, etc.

As we have already said, the juvenile court laws go far beyond the purpose of taking child offenders out of the criminal courts. The juvenile courts have a proper function beyond delinquency jurisdiction. This question is present, however: Does inclusion in the court's jurisdiction of children who are not offenders complicate the concepts of the juvenile court? Does it confuse them? Does it contradict them?

When the court goes beyond violators of the penal code, and takes in children who are not subject to the jurisdiction of a criminal court, the test of its value should be exacting. It must then be established that the juvenile court, by bringing into court children designated as delinquents who could not be criminals under the penal laws of the state, is making a positive contribution to the well-being of the children and the community. Does the juvenile court by means of this widely inclusive delinquency definition lessen delinquency, or does it contribute to the solution of other problems of children and the community?

We must face the question of quality in the administration and practice of juvenile courts. It being recognized that probation staffs are inadequate in many courts, and that judges are inadequate in many courts, is it wise to augment the definition of delinquency as broadly as is done? Where the staff is not adequate, such augmentation may not only fail to help children who do not violate laws, but may impede the proper handling of children who are offenders against the penal law.

Furthermore, the extravagant expansion of the definition of delinquency may have a retrograde effect on jurisdiction ove child offenders. At present the jurisdiction of some juvenile court is severely limited as to child offenders. Although the age juri diction goes as high as eighteen in a majority of the states, several states jurisdiction stops at sixteen. In a number of sta the juvenile court is not given exclusive jurisdiction, and ma child offenders are tried in the criminal court. In some st certain offenses are *exclusively* the province of the *criminal co*

The result is that although the juvenile courts everywher beyond the concept of a court only for child offenders, in n states they have not been given complete jurisdiction to f their function to taking child offenders out of the criminal courts, and in some states the court has lost jurisdiction originally given to it.

It is in keeping with the present state of development of juvenile courts that jurisdiction be made most complete over child offenders before shaping delinquency definitions that include standards of conduct which go far beyond the prohibitions of the penal code.

Standards of Conduct for Children

Aside from the argument that as a matter of proper development of the juvenile court the delinquency definition ought not to be greatly expanded until well-nigh all child offenders have been taken out of the criminal courts, the problem of how comprehensive the definition of delinquency ought to be requires a sociopsychological examination. Do these parts of the delinquency definitions establish standards of conduct for children which are to be preferred rather than required?

It is relevant to look to the penal codes not as standards of child behavior, but as guides to what the community considers dangerous and intolerable. A child who associates with immoral persons is doing nothing which in an adult would be considered criminal. Of course such a child requires community attention;

but we are talking here of *delinquency* definitions and court jurisdiction. A child who absents himself from home without consent is doing nothing which in an adult would be deemed criminal.

Children and adolescents coming within the age jurisdiction of the juvenile courts are in process of continuous growth, experimentation, and development. Stringent rules of conduct are not realistic. Yet the adult is not so closely bound by the penal code as the child is by the standards of juvenile court laws.

Perhaps we do not like children to smoke or drink. But there is no proof that children who smoke or drink are likely to become criminal offenders. Using vile or obscene language is not nice. Nor is it nor should it be criminal or delinquent. Including in a delinquency definition such provisions as patronizing poolrooms or bucket shops is simply out of date.

It is clear from a reading of the various items that go into delinquency definitions that standards of conduct are applied to children which are not applied to adults, at least so far as the penal laws are concerned. Since we are greatly concerned with the wide incidence of delinquency, since the very finding of delinquency is popularly, and in practice, considered to be only a lesser evil than a conviction for crime, since, furthermore, training schools generally are—like prisons—schools of crime. The broad delinquency definitions should be carefully examined to give these adverse factors full weight. It is a matter to which far less attention has been given than the problem deserves.

The Standard Juvenile Court Act, recognized widely as representing the best available model, in its latest (sixth) edition, published in 1959, declares that only violations of law constitute delinquency. In this it goes further than the previous, 1949, edition, and existing juvenile court laws. From what has been said above, it is a sound advance. The Standard Act does not actually use the term "delinquency," for reasons to be discussed in a moment, but it clearly separates the law violators by the structure of the jurisdiction and decree sections.

Standard Act section 8, subdivision 1, gives the juvenile court exclusive jurisdiction over children who violate the law. Section 8, subdivision 2, gives it jurisdiction over neglected children. Section 24, subdivision 1, authorizes disposition of children under 8, subdivision 1, law violators; and subdivision 2 over neglected children. The authorized dispositions are not identical, as they were under previous Standard Acts. Under the 1959 Act only law violators (i.e., those usually termed "delinquents") may be committed to a training school.

It is worthwhile to look at the neglect subdivision of section 8. The court is given jurisdiction over any child " (a) who is neglected as to proper or necessary support, or education as required by law, or as to medical or other care necessary for his well-being, or who is abandoned by his parent or other custodian; or (b) whose environment is injurious to his welfare, or whose behavior is injurious to his own or other's welfare; or (c) who is beyond the control of his parent or other custodian."

Most juvenile court laws categorize truancy as delinquency. But it is universally recognized that truancy is a mere symptom of more basic maladjustment. As we shall see in the next chapter, modern school authorities wish to rely as little as possible on juvenile court proceedings in handling truancy.

The "Ungovernable" Child

What about the child who is "beyond the control of his parent"? Under many acts such a child is deemed a delinquent, and may be—often is—committed to the training school, among children who are predominantly law violators. Under the Standard Juvenile Court Act this may not be done, but the child may still be committed, to other institutions.

But why should he be committed under either category? He has broken no law; and in fact a wayward child is generally *not* neglected, that is, is not suffering from want of adequate food, shelter, clothing, etc. The so-called wayward or incorrigible child is behaving in ways his parents do not approve, and cannot control. But the behavior may not be destructive at all, and often it reflects a super-anxious parent, a highly puritanical one, or a parent who for one reason or another is venting wrath on a particular child.

Juvenile courts should not have jurisdiction over "incorrigible," or "wayward" children, or should have no jurisdiction in such a case *unless a condition of neglect actually exists.* That is, if the child, despite the family conflict, despite being beyond control of his parents (how much is "beyond control"?), is attending school, has his needs taken care of—why should a court take jurisdiction?

Where the result of the child's behavior does reach a point where he is truant, ill, etc., then he is, in fact, neglected under the concept of neglect jurisdiction which all juvenile courts have. I suggest that the foregoing approach will protect many children against needless court procedures and adjudication without inhibiting the authority of the court where the situation is serious enough to warrant its intervention.

With the broad delinquency definitions in most juvenile court laws added to the vague concept of waywardness, a vast population of children, particularly children in slum areas, could be adjudicated delinquent (or neglected). It would be hard to justify such a concept, just as it is hard to explain away the experience in California where a judge closed a juvenile institution because he was disgusted with the absence of sound treatment. The children had been neglected and abused in the institution. Most were simply sent home by the judge, some were placed in foster homes. The police predicted a crime wave; it never came. Six months later, out of 140 children taken out of the institution, only ten were in trouble again.

Avoiding the Delinquency Tag

We have referred to the delinquency category in the Standard Juvenile Court Act. The Standard Act, however, does not define delinquncy, but merely describes situations and classifications of children over which the court has jurisdiction. Thus in the Standard Act a child who violates the law is not called a delinquent. About ten juvenile court acts similarly avoid the delinquency tag.

What is the purpose of avoiding the delinquency tag? It is to support the underlying philosophy that in a juvenile court a child is being protected and helped and not being categorized as antisocial. Avoiding the delinquency tag thus implements the common legislative declaration of policy that a juvenile court proceeding is noncriminal. It requires, in turn, administrative and community implementation. However, it is clearly an advantage, although the same result should obtain where the delinquency tag *is* used, since the effect of an adjudication of delinquency is likewise noncriminal.

Does avoiding the delinquency tag have any other advantage? None is apparent.

An incidental advantage in the *use* of categories is facility in statistical reporting (although more is required than mere existence of the categories before statistics of delinquency can attain reliability). There are more important advantages in the use of the categories.

Where the categories of children within the jurisdiction of the juvenile court are separated into delinquent, dependent, and neglected, it is frequently provided that only the delinquent children may be committed to the training school or other institution for delinquent children. Although under the new Standard Act provision it would not be possible, under the existing juvenile court laws in which the categories are not used (as under the previous Standard Act), a danger exists in the legal possibility that *any* child within the jurisdiction of the court, including dependent and neglected children, may be committed to the institution for delinquents. Possibly there are rare cases where a child not adjudicated delinquent would benefit from commitment to the training school. It would seem, however, that the lost opportunity of placing in the training school children who are not delinquent is more than compensated for by lessening the danger of improper commitments of this kind.

There is also the danger, where the categories are not used, that the thinking of a court may become too vague for the proper protection of the child. A court without categories may engage in deciding that a child before it might benefit from the court facilities, without concerning itself with a clear legal test of jurisdiction and proof. With the categories, the court has to decide that the child is either neglected or delinquent, and not merely that the court finds the child to be within its very generally described jurisdictional sections. If the distinction between delinquency and neglect is not always clear, the difficulty is not overcome by avoiding the terms. Avoiding the use of the terms "delinquency" and "neglect" does not avoid the use of categories, but merely avoids naming them.

Of course the terms "delinquency" and "neglect" are not complete or necessarily sound psychological descriptions. But they do make a generally accurate distinction in gross terms, between two categories that are in fact psychologically distinguishable. Is avoiding the term, and calling both delinquent and neglected children "wards of the court" more accurate, more definitive, or is it not less so? But besides that, the use of the terms is not so much to have a legal definition which is psychologically precise, but rather one which affords greater protection to children.

We stress the need to *individualize* children. The use of the tags ("delinquency," "neglect") is part of the identification not only of the legal basis for referral to court, but the actual difference in the condition of the child which brought him to court. Judge Justine Wise Polier (of the New York City Family Court) wrote, "Sectarian and private institutions are generally subdivided into those for neglected and those for delinquent children. The recognition that dependent and rejected children should not be treated as delinquents registered a forward step in institutional child care. A less custodial and disciplinary attitude toward neglected children marked distinct progress. The protection of children in this group from contamination by known delinquents was, and still is, a factor to be considered."[2]

Age Floor for Delinquency

Again, bearing in mind the inadequacies of many courts and juvenile institutions and the need for the most careful selection in institutional commitments, means of controlling commitments should be welcomed. Where the delinquency tag is used, it is possible to place an age floor on delinquency, therefore on children committable to the training schools.

The common law rule and the most common statutory rule is that a child under seven is conclusively presumed to be incapable of committing crime. A child between seven and fourteen is presumed incapable of committing crime. In a criminal proceeding the state must prove affirmatively that such a child has sufficient capacity to entertain a criminal intent (*doli capax*). In a juvenile court, these presumptions against responsibility of children do not exist. In several of the states the penal law provides that a child under a particular age—twelve years, or ten—may not be convicted of *crime*. In these states, however, a child under the specified age *may* be found delinquent for an act prohibited by the penal law. Children under seven years of age are sometimes adjudicated delinquents.

Is not the reason fo the rule exempting children from criminal responsibility applicable to delinquency? Accordingly, in some juvenile court acts the provision appears that a child under a stated age cannot be a delinquent, therefore cannot be committed as delinquent. In Mississippi and Texas, for example, a child under ten cannot be adjudicated a delinquent. New York has an age floor of seven. By far most juvenile court laws have no floor; the definition applies to "children under 18" or whatever the upper age limit may be.

Retaining the delinquency tag permits a definition of delinquency to be applicable to a specifically limited age group, thus keeping the younger children out of the training schools. The same effect might be obtained in the noncategorized laws by providing that any one of the defined situations shall apply to children of a particular age. Thus the Standard Act in its decree section authorizes training school commitments only for law violators—and, if it were deemed a desirable policy, the decree section could also limit training school commitments to those over a certain age. The same effect might also be obtained by suitable provisions governing the institutions.

Not all expert opinion is that training school commitments should be limited to law violators, i.e., delinquents. It is the position of the Standard Act. To this writer it seems the sounder position, more desirable in the long run. Its rationale is that law violators call for separate treatment, not only for the distinctive nature of their behavioral experience, but also for the protection of other children who have not violated the law. This rationale also supports the idea of separating the very young group, even if law violators, from the older delinquents.

A Choice of Juvenile Court Concepts

Juvenile courts, like other social institutions, are in a continuous state of change. Some of our juvenile courts do not go far beyond the function of taking child offenders out of the criminal courts, and by having a comprehensive and exclusive jurisdiction they fulfill this function. Other juvenile courts perform this function rather poorly, leaving a wide jurisdiction over the child offenders in the criminal court. Many juvenile courts operate under the laws which are concerned with special standards of conduct on the part of children, special standards which are not established as related to crime prevention or community protection.

Despite the growth of the juvenile courts, they are still beset with difficulties on all sides. It is suggested that it is the part of wisdom for the juvenile courts to go slow, to achieve important although limited purposes before embarking upon projects of doubtful utility. The juvenile court law should not attempt to govern child behavior with special standards of conduct until—and this has not happened—child behavior experts agree that these standards are necessary for children or the community. At this time it would seem that the most effective course of development is that of the new Standard Act, by which no child is a delinquent unless he has violated the law. Furthermore, with the natural limitations on social services for problem individuals, it helps neither the child nor the court to increase the scope of the delinquency definition. But we would differ with the Standard Act in including children beyond control of their parents as "neglected," just as we criticize all the juvenile courts that designate them as delinquent. Perhaps the family needs help; but they should get it voluntarily, out of court.

Notes

1 Fritz Schmidl comments, "We hear psychiatrists make a distinction between 'neurotic' and 'delinquent' behavior. [But] we have searched in vain for a definition of the term 'delinquent' in the psychiatric literature." ("The Rorschach Test in Juvenile Delinquency Research," *American Journal of Orthopsychiatry,* January, 1947).

2 Justine Wise Polier, *Everyone's Children, Nobody's Child* (Charles Scribner, 1941).

References

Part of the present chapter appeared as an article in the January, 1949, issue of the *Annals* of the American Academy of Political and Social Science, devoted entirely to the subject of juvenile delinquency. Commenting on the article when first published, Roscoe Pound, *dean emeritus,* Harvard Law School, referred to it as urging "that the juvenile court should not attempt more than its original function and that in trying to be an agency of preventive justice as well as one of treatment of the individual before the court, the court is likely to fall down between two tasks." He continued: "There is no doubt much to be said for this point. It is never wise to impair the doing well of whatever an institution has been set up to do and has learned to do well, by trying at the same time to do also something else which it has not been set up to do and has yet to learn how to do or even whether it can do it.

I am looking at social control as an integrated whole and at the view of that whole as giving the end and spirit and guiding method to each of its agencies. The juvenile court should not impair its usefulness by seeking to do what it cannot well do. But it can make the most of its usefulness by the fullest realization of the task of prevention which confronts all institutions and agencies having to do with delinquency and the fullest exercise of its powers in cooperation with and by utilizing the help of those other institutions and agencies." ("The Juvenile Court in the Service State," NCCD *Yearbook,* 1949, p. 33.)

There are a number of good textbooks on juvenile courts and material on the nature of juvenile delinquency, including: *Crime, Courts, and Probation,* by Charles L. Chute and Marjorie Bell (Macmillan, 1956). *Justice for the Child: The Juvenile Court in Transition,* ed. by Margaret K. Rosenheim (Free Press, 1962). *The Challenge of Delinquency,* by Negley K. Teeters and John O. Reinemann (Prentice-Hall, 1950).

Chapter 4

The Child in Juvenile Court

Those who bespeak harsh treatment for children who misbehave, or delinquent children, are the most vociferous critics of the juvenile court. They decry what they consider to be leniency in the juvenile courts, and declare such a policy to be an encouragement to delinquent children and neglectful parents.

Although often the juvenile courts are indeed more "lenient"—less punitive—toward children before them than the criminal courts would be to the same children, yet the facts are not altogether one way. As pointed out in the previous chapter, many children are brought into juvenile court for acts which are not violations of the criminal laws, and thus are acts for which they could not be brought into criminal court, whether a juvenile court existed or not.

Furthermore, some procedural protections afforded to defendants in criminal courts are not available to children in juvenile courts. Children's hearings are not before a jury. Hearsay evidence, not admissible on a criminal trial, is admissible in many juvenile court hearings. A criminal may not be convicted unless his guilt is established beyond a reasonable doubt, but a child may be adjudicated delinquent in juvenile court by a far less stringent test, usually a "preponderance of the evidence."

The result is what we should expect, that in many cases children are adjudicated delinquents upon evidence on which they would have to be discharged if they were before a criminal court. Although the same critics call for the age jurisdiction of juvenile courts to be lowered, and they wish juvenile courts to have less power to retain cases, the fact is that often when a case of an older juvenile is transferred to criminal court instead of his receiving severe treatment there, the case is dismissed. In some cases a child is committed for a minor violation that would bring a fine or a few days in jail in an adult criminal court.

It is anomalous that there are others, whose motivation is quite different from the first kind of critic, who nevertheless supplement the attack from another side. This group is represented by certain juvenile court judges whose extreme informality amounts to a substantial disregard of the rights of parents and children. They may be well-meaning, but being highly authoritarian in a court out of the public eye, it is their kind of court that from time to time calls forth the protest against the "star chamber."

The Authority of the Court

The first half century of the juvenile court movement in the United States saw the extension of juvenile court laws to all of the states. This progress has been noted with a general feeling of great achievement in the national acceptance of an idea which has become an integral part of the community's program for the protection of special groups of children.[1] The acclaim given this historic development has not been unmixed with acknowledgment that much remains to be accomplished for the ideal standards of the court to be realized. Under the challenging title, "Most Courts Have to be Substandard!", Lowell Juilliard Carr writes that outside of the 200-odd "big city" counties (counties with cities of 50,000 or over) "the juvenile court in its dealings with children is actually a kind of legal fiction. It has the name, it has a presiding officer—probate judge, common pleas clerk, or what-have-you—chosen without regard to his understanding of children. It has sundry sketchy documents called case records compiled, of course, without benefit of any trained caseworkers, and sometimes not even compiled."[2] But big city courts, with their hurried procedure, overworked staffs, assembly line hearings, may be no better.

The challenge is one that many communities are striving to meet, recognizing the need for specially qualified judges, competent, trained probation staffs, and necessary related facilities. The materials of the court are needed and are being sought. Meanwhile, and indeed, particularly while these inadequacies exist, is the work of philosophical and legal creation complete? Have the Gault and Kent cases, decided by the Supreme Court in recent years (and discussed above in chapter 3) brought the juvenile court legal situation to maturity? Although welcome, they are only a limited step, and further steps are needed, both by courts and legislatures.

That there is a continuing problem of legal creation is the significance of the periodic revisions of the Standard Juvenile Court Act.[3] It is worth noting that the 1959 Standard Juvenile Court Act called for practically everything the Supreme Court decided in the Gault and Kent cases, right to counsel, and assigned counsel if indigent; a hearing before a case is referred to criminal court; due notice of a charge; notification of one's legal rights.[4]

What should be the direction of further legal development? The motivation and justification of the court is that it is a superior agency for the *protection* of children, specifically, superior, for children, to a criminal court and its criminal procedure. On behalf of this purpose a great deal of power has been given to the court which in itself has raised problems. It is not enough to say—"The more power to the court, the better it can deal with the problems brought to it." We must stop to consider that the power of the juvenile court is over the *child,* for the most part, rather than over the things affecting the child.

We may exercise that power to protect the community against the child, at times, as we do with adult criminals. The court is justified, however, not so much as an agency with authority over the child, but as an agency which has been given authority in order to carry out its responsibility to protect the child. This protective role is in fact the constitutional basis of the juvenile court. The juvenile court disposition is non-criminal—the court exists to protect the child from the condemnation of a criminal conviction. Constitutionally the juvenile court law stands or falls turning on whether the child within the jurisdiction of the court may be punished as a criminal. If he may, the court is a criminal court and the rights of the defendants in a criminal court must be applied.

The proceeding, the statutes declare, is to be entitled not *against* the child, but on *behalf* of the child.[5] But we do not pretend that the constitutional validity of the court and its social validity are one and the same.

The increased flexibility of the court, its informality, have been achieved principally by the sacrifice for the child of rights which a defendant in a criminal court has. It becomes doubly necessary, therefore, to protect the child from abuse of the authority of the court itself. Roscoe Pound writes, "Child placement involves administrative authority over one of the most intimate and cherished of human relations. The powers of the Star Chamber were a trifle in comparison with those of our juvenile courts and courts of domestic relations. . . . It is well known that too often the placing of a child in a home or even in an institution is done casually or perfunctorily, or even arbitrarily. . . . *Even with the most superior personnel, these tribunals call for legal checks.*"[6]

The problem of further legal development must include, then, the seeking of the best means of protecting the child in the juvenile court. Evidently the work of legal creation is not complete with the grant of authority to the courts. The power of the court must be examined; is it in fact the best protection to the child, or are limitations to be sought, which would provide a better protection? Can this protection be provided without obstructing the treatment process of the court, which is also a protection to the child?

Wih these considerations we examine the jurisdiction of the court, detention of children before the court, the procedure, and finally the treatment process, to point out existing provisions which require stressing, and to suggest others which would provide additional protection to the child in the juvenile court.

Jurisdiction

The basic jurisdiction of juvenile courts is a taking over of cases which would otherwise belong to the criminal court. We shall turn to this presently. Meanwhile we find that the jurisdiction of the juvenile court has become much broader than this, to include cases of dependency (in some courts) and neglect (in almost all courts). Here we find dangers to be guarded against. The child who is neglected or dependent has done nothing requiring judicial action, nor does his condition require any more than the providing of aid. Yet courts whose jurisdiction includes dependency and neglect are given legal authorization, as we have seen, to *commit* such children to the same training schools to which delinquent children are committed, subject to release in the same manner as delinquents. Neglected and even dependent children are to be found in our training schools, in small numbers, to be sure.

Can legal protection to the child be provided to guard against abuse of dependency and neglect jurisdiction? The 1949 revision of the *Standard Juvenile Court Act* moved specifically against dependency jurisdiction in juvenile courts. In contrast to earlier editions of the Act, the 1949 and 1959 editions recommend that dependency jurisdiction should not be given to the juvenile court. The explanatory comment to the jurisdiction section reads: "The court should intervene only where authoritative action is required with respect to a child or the adults responsible for his care, or condition. Cases of dependency without an element of neglect, or where no change of custody is involved, should be dealt with by administrative agencies without court action." Probably there is little disagreement concerning the position of the Standard Act on dependency, but many acts include this jurisdiction.

Neglect jurisdiction too requires close examination. In some juvenile court acts, as formerly under the Standard Juvenile Court Act, no legal distinction whatever is made as between the disposition available for delinquent and neglected children. This is true in those jurisdictions which, like the Standard Act, principally to avoid the stigma of a delinquency adjudication, do not attach the terms "delinquency" or "neglect" to the different categories of jurisdiction. It is also true in jurisdictions which, although using the terms "delinquent," "neglected" and "dependent," authorize all the same types of disposition of any case.

Perhaps the simplest protection to the neglected child in juvenile court would be to exclude training school commitments from dispositions available in such cases. In some states this result is obtained by simply authorizing training school commitments for delinquent children, and not for neglected children. It can also be done in acts which do not use the labels "delinquent" or "neglected" by nevertheless limiting the types of disposition as to the cases which are in fact neglect cases without being so tagged. This is the position taken in the 1959 Standard Juvenile Court

Act. (In fact, although the Standard Act does not define "delinquency," the term "neglect" is necessarily identified; the definition has been quoted in the previous chapter.)

The justification for taking jurisdiction in neglect cases is that authoritarian judicial action is needed against a culpable parent or other custodian. The fact is, however, that the juvenile court proceedings in neglect cases are not against parents, but the children themselves are subject to the order of the court, are subject to probation and commitment. The legal necessity for this is that the neglectful parent may be deprived of custody over the child. Nevertheless the authority goes to the *child* when he is committed or placed away from home, rather than to the parent. And when probation is used, often the legal form is placing the *child* on probation.

The problem is to avoid action against the child while still intervening to overcome the neglect. Action may be needed to coerce the parent to cease his neglect. In such a case should not the order run against the parents? Most juvenile court laws do not so provide, except in prosecutions against parents under "contributing to delinquency and neglect" statutes,[7] and direct actions against parents to enforce support.[8]

The *Standard Juvenile Court Act* suggests the following: "In support of any order or decree under Section 8, subdivision one or two, the court may require the parents or other persons having the custody of the child, or any other person who has been found by the court to be encouraging, causing, or contribution to the acts or conditions which bring the child within the purview of this Act and who are parties to the proceeding, to do or to omit doing any acts required or forbidden by law, when the judge deems this requirement necessary for the welfare of the child. If such persons fail to comply with the requirement, the court may proceed against them for contempt of court."[9]

But the action against the parent may be ineffective or inadequate. Often the court must see that care is provided by other than parental means. What power does the court have in such cases? In neglect cases judges often have a feeling of helplessness because the tools of the court—authority and casework—are not the solution. *Facilities* are needed, placement facilities, or assistance of one kind or another for the family, and the community may not have them. The judge's only recourse is to do what he can with the family and perhaps console himself with the thought that the legal definition of neglect is ultimately governed by what support the community gives to families in trouble—the juvenile court law standard of neglect cannot be on a such higher plane than community facilities. It is no triumph for the court to substitute court neglect, or community neglect, for parental neglect.[10]

If the community does not have the means of curing the neglect of the child, and the court tools are merely those of coercion and casework for the parents, the court is frequently faced with the choice of becoming a punitive agency or returning the child to an unsatisfactory home. In either way the neglect is not cured; in either case the neglect jurisdiction is not useful. If the community *does* have the means of curing the neglect, organization of its facilities on a welfare basis should enable the court neglect jurisdiction to fall into relative disuse. Perhaps we should have in mind also that, as Dorothy Hutchinson commented, "Sometimes the neglect is one that offends the community more than it hurts the child."[11]

It is particularly neglect and dependency jurisdiction that more and more in recent years brings criticism upon the role of the juvenile court. Martha Branscombe, for example, points out that "at the time the juvenile court idea was developed, the only public administrative agent was the poor relief official. It is, therefore, understandable historically that the courts became one of the first specialized public services for children." But "in the past three decades, the development of public child welfare services throughout the country, together with the recognition of the inherent limitation of the court as a casework agency, have given rise to difficult jurisdictional questions. Today, however, it is essential to recognize the principle established by our tradition that distinguishes between judicial functions, which are the responsibility of courts of competent jurisdiction, and those of an administrative nature, which must be performed by an appropriate administrative agency. It is clear that legal questions relevant to compulsory commitment or removal of the child from his parents, and those affecting the status of the child, must be decided by a court. In the light of our experience, however, we should not continue to expect the court to decide what should be done beyond resolving the legal problem, or to provide the service for the child requiring not legal but social services or other treatment."[12]

Two studies of truancy[13] and the court may be used as illustrations, one in which the court jurisdiction was used, one in which it was avoided by the use instead of highly developed administrative facilities. A study by Herbert A. Landry of the effect of court process on attendance rates indicates that "for the great majority of children, court action does not seem to accomplish the purposes for which it was established."[14] Landry concluded that the attack on the truancy problem should emphasize prior responsibility in the school.

The second study is a report of remarkable success by a school system (Gary, Indiana) which accepted this prior responsibility. Mark Roser reports that an experimental group of chronic truants, children with poor attendance records, and children with serious behavior problems, were placed in small classes, held for only half time, and emphasis was placed upon giving them a feeling of some success each day. The setting of the separate school centers was made as permissive as possible; casework counseling was provided for the parents. After two years truancy in this group completely disappeared. At the present time, Roser states, "The Gary school system does not use the juvenile court for problems of truancy. As facilities have been increased and trained staff made available, referral of truants to the juvenile court has been reduced from an average of 350 cases per year out of an enrollment of 23,000, to zero. . . . Insofar as we can determine, the rates of school attendance have not been lowered."[15]

Such views and experience may foretell a decline in the use of neglect jurisdiction by juvenile courts, but not its disappearance, since court authority will always be needed where neglect is such that a change in custody is necessary for the welfare of the child. Court authority is also called for in neglect where some positive action for curing the neglect is needed, such as the ordering of urgent medical care, [16] or a court's making mandatory what was originally a voluntary welfare placement, but where the parents are no longer cooperating. Probably the statute could be drafted to spell out these criteria with some precision.

We return to delinquency jurisdiction. We noted in the previous chapter that some delinquency definitions, including such things as waywardness (being beyond the control of parent or guardian), have the effect not of taking children out of the criminal court, but of bringing into the juvenile court children who should not be in any court. This jurisdiction is not explained by the purpose of providing a more sympathetic, less punitive forum than the criminal court for children who would otherwise be tried criminally. Presumably it can be explained only on the basis of the court as a preventive or protective agency. It is a survival of ancient, and archaic, provisions. Judicial authority for such activity, like dependecy and neglect jurisdiction, can be questioned.

Conversely, many juvenile court laws leave large loopholes, permitting criminal prosecution of children. For example, some juvenile courts are excluded from taking jurisdiction where certain felonies are involved; others permit the criminal court to take jurisdiction; others provide for transfer of cases from juvenile court at the discretion of the juvenile court judge. The Standard Act excepts only, at the discretion of the juvenile court judge, cases of felonies committed by children 16 and over.

This provision also establishes the exclusive jurisdiction of the juvenile court, one of the most basic elements in the Standard Juvenile Court Act. To the degree that the court's exclusive jurisdiction is compromised, and exceptions exist, it is not protecting certain classes of children from criminal procedure. In addition, a danger in the existence of concurrent jurisdiction in juvenile and criminal court is that instead of juvenile court being a refuge for the child, it becomes, with its lesser evidentiary rules, its dropping of constitutional safeguards of the defendant, the recourse of the weak case. A California crime study commission recently wrote :"It is hoped that the law enforcement officers will be alerted to prepare their cases as they would for a trial in the criminal court since it could no longer be assumed that the case would routinely be processed by the juvenile court [the juvenile court having authority to transfer cases to criminal court]. In cases which appear to law enforcement officers to be unfit for juvenile court adjudication they would have an incentive to retain evidence and preserve their records as for a criminal trial.

This would *reduce the number of occasions when for lack of evidence to convict in a criminal court, cases acknowledged to be unfit for juvenile court procedure have, nevertheless, been retained in juvenile court, or on being remanded to the criminal court have been dismissed for lack of evidence*."[17]

Detention

The breadth of juvenile court jurisdiction has important consequences, and must be considered in connection with other aspects of juvenile court functioning. Along with the purpose of removing children from the criminal courts by means of the juvenile court, has been the effort to remove from the jails, the most notoriously inadequate of our penal institutions, children who are before these courts.

The goal is to prevent *any* such children from being incarcerated in jails. The Standard Juvenile Court Act therefore provides that "No child shall at any time be detained in any police station, lockup, jail, or prison, except that, by the judge's order in which the reasons therefor shall be specified, a child sixteen years of age or older whose conduct or condition endangers the safety of others in the detention facility for children may be placed in some other place of confinement that the judge considers proper, including a jail or any other place of detention for adults."

Several detention realities may be noted. First, there is a substantial use of jails for children before the juvenile court. A survey of children detained in 1965, made for the President's Commission on Law Enforcement and the Administration of Justice, found that 22 per cent of delinquent children were detained in jail, and an additional number were held in police lockups. Much of this jail detention is, incidentally, in violation of juvenile court law.

Second, there may be excessive use of detention facilities other than jail, and frequently these are no great improvement over jails, having no diagnostic or treatment service, being custodial merely, and sometimes being run in a punitive and brutal fashion. Again citing the President's Commission, two-thirds of all juveniles apprehended were detained, a percentage enormously and unnecessarily high.

Furthermore, it must be recalled that detention is used in neglect and even dependency cases also, cases in which under *no* circumstances—without the juvenile court law—would the child be detained in a jail. These children in detention are housed with children with delinquency patterns. And having in mind the broad delinquency definitions, it may be observed that many children are detained as delinquents who would never—without the juvenile court law—be detained in a jail. These are the children whose delinquency is based on behavior or circumstances other than violation of a criminal law.

These considerations are especially significant inasmuch as children detained by juvenile court, in most jurisdictions, do not have, as does a defendant in a criminal court, the right to release on bail. This is because the right to bail is an accompaniment of criminal court procedure. It is, however, a *right* of the criminal defendant. In eliminating it as a right of the child in juvenile court, we are obligated to protect the child from unnecessary detention, and from detention in inadequate and improper facilities.

In complying with this obligation we must rely on the facilities afforded, the policy of the law, and the policy of the court. As we have noted, the Standard Act, and many juvenile court laws, prohibit jail detention. That the law is often violated is an attribute of a failure to provide suitable other facilities, as well as a policy of over-detention by the courts. Standards of detention facilities and court policy are available.

Probably the most important control would come from jurisdiction. Eliminating dependency jurisdiction (as the Standard Act does) eliminates dependent children from the detention homes. So far as the child is concerned, a neglected child is no different from a dependent child. Why then should not the juvenile court laws prohibit detention of neglected children? Their care is a shelter problem—a welfare responsibility—not a detention problem, not a problem of custody, not a court problem.[18] The 1959 Standard Act does define, for the first time, "detention" and "shelter." Detention "means the temporary care of children who require secure custody for their own or the community's protection in physically restricting facilities pending court disposition." Shelter "means the temporary care of children in physically unrestricting facilities pending court disposition." Although the definitions are useful in pointing out the distinction in the kinds of temporary care facilities, the Act does not utilize the definitions for any mandatory separation of delinquent and neglected children.

Delinquency jurisdiction too may be more limited than it generally is today, as already pointed out,[19] and such limitations would automatically limit detention.

Procedure

The characteristic procedural tool in a juvenile court is its informality, in contrast to the highly developed formalities of a criminal court. The criminal court trial is public, governed by strict rules of evidence and procedure, and attended by a number of constitutional limitations and requirements; whereas the juvenile court proceeding is private, informal and free of limitatons on its procedure.

The merit of informal juvenile court procedure is that it is gentler in its impact on the people in the court, less dramatic, less threatening. It replaces a public trial which is heavily laden with authoritative individuals as well as authoritative law. At the same time, however, the informality is achieved at the expense of a formality which is also protective. The juvenile court has the responsibility of using its formality as a protective device, to compensate for the loss of the procedural protections given to the defendant in the criminal court.

The most markedly informal procedure in juvenile court is the practice, now being used in about half of the cases, on a national average, of disposing of cases without the filing of a petition, and hence without a hearing before the court and without an official juvenile court disposition being recorded. The power has been derived, as a legal matter, from the authority given to almost all juvenile courts to make an inquiry prior to the preparation of a petition, to determine (in the language of the Standard Juvenile Court Act) "whether the interests of the public or of the child require that further action be taken." Thereupon "the court may make whatever informal adjustment is practicable without a petition," or may authorize a petition to be filed.

As a method of treatment, the "unofficial" procedure reflects a desire to achieve a voluntary atmosphere. The responsibility of the court is to see to it that the informal procedure does not become a cloak for actions which would be improper or which would not be taken if the case were before the court on a petition. Probably the first caution for the court is to be fully cognizant of the fact that there exists a clear legal limitation upon the use of unofficial casework. It must be remembered that an unofficial case, like an official case, is authorized *only when the child is in fact within the jurisdictional purview of the juvenile court act.*

Referring back to the statutory source of unofficial casework, we note that the preliminary inquiry and the unofficial adjustment may follow only when the court is informed that a child is within the purview of the act. In other words, unofficial casework is legal only if the information presented to the court is such that if verified, the filing of a petition could follow. The juvenile court is not given *carte blanche* to delve into any problem affecting children and families which comes to its attention. In its unofficial casework, as in its cases brought to petition, the court must find its authority in the jurisdiction section of the juvenile court law.

Since the unofficial casework is voluntary, the investigation must be made without coercion. Without a petition there is no authority to require the appearance of any individual. Perhaps more difficult is the problem of developing casework standards in unofficial proceedings. What are sound criteria for unofficial cases; what precautions are necessary to guard against coercion in the voluntary relationship? Some courts have produced written criteria for unofficial cases, but a greater elaboration and justification of the practices in use seems called for.

The Standard Act proposes statutory limitations. The court is authorized to make informal adjustments without a petition "provided that the facts appear to establish prima facie jurisdiction and are admitted, and provided that consent is obtained from the parents and also from the child if he is of sufficient age and understanding." Furthermore, "efforts to effect informal adjustment may be continued not longer than three months without review by the judge or the director."

In some courts it is the practice to consider that the legal authority for unofficial casework is at the same time legal authority for detention pending efforts at informal dispositions without petition. This is a highly dubious procedure. Of course detention conflicts with the voluntary setting of unofficial work. But "unofficial" detention is dubious from a legal point of view. Detention is derived not from the section authorizing unofficial procedures, but from the section on detention. It is clear from a reading of the detention provisions of the juvenile court laws, and it must be so in any event, that detention of juveniles, whether in the custody of an officer or of a detention home, is an exercise of legal authority which must be reviewed by the court promptly and which can be continued for only a minimum period of time without the filing of a petition. Unofficial casework seems clearly to be excluded where a child is in custody.

Informality characterizes the procedure of the "official" juvenile court cases (those in which a petition is filed) as well as the unofficial cases. The probation officer is permitted to study the child and his backgound before the child has been adjudicated (whereas in a criminal case, in the trial of an adult, such a study can be made only after a finding of guilt). Attorneys in court (the exception rather than the rule) cannot put up as aggressive a defense as in a criminal case. Of course the legal justification for this is that the consequences of adjudication are noncriminal, and there is no accusation of the child.

On the other hand the consequences of adjudication are serious, and basic rules of evidence are applicable in juvenile court cases as safeguards to reliability of information. If a finding may be based on a less rigid requirement than proof beyond a reasonable doubt, the test in a criminal case, there must still be a preponderance of the evidence, as in a civil case; while the probation officer may make a social investigation to guide the court in disposition, findings of fact for adjudication must still be based on direct evidence and not on hearsay.[20]

Treatment

We have observed that the constitutional basis for upholding the juvenile court laws is that they are *noncriminal;* adjudication in a juvenile court is not, legally, a conviction for crime. Of course it is recognized that the practical application of a criminal conviction comes in the form of communtiy rejection—denial of employment, denial of the right to serve in the armed forces, and social rejection in various forms. In these respects the juvenile delinquent is, in fact, often treated as a criminal, just as a "record" of juvenile delinquency is included in a presentence investigation for crime, although it is not considered a "conviction" in relation to increased penalties for repeated offenders. The "noncriminal" nature of the juvenile court adjudication is, then, a reality in some respects, and in others it is quite similar to a criminal conviction.

The federal government is among the offenders. The Job Corps, established precisely for the assistance and retraining of underprivileged children, established the policy of not admitting a person until it has examined his juvenile court record. If access to the record is denied, the application will be denied.

The National Council on Crime and Delinquency in 1966 made strenuous representations to the Job Corps to revise its policy so that it would not violate the requirements of the juvenile court laws. It said that in exceptional cases, if the youth would otherwise be rejected on the basis of the usual criteria, excluding the question of adjudication, and where the court's record might shed some light, application for information could be made to the court. Courts would cooperate in such circumstances. But this was not acceptable and nothing was changed.

Elsewhere the federal government has done better. An applicant for a civil service job is asked, almost everywhere, about his juvenile court record. Is this a practical necessity? No. The United States Civil Service Commission, in quite a radical breakthrough, revised its regulation in August, 1966, to benefit not only applicants with an arrest record as adults, but also those with juvenile court records. Previously, applicants were questioned about arrests as well as convictions. They were not, however, required to answer questions as to events that occurred prior to the age of 16. Now an applicant may not be asked about arrests, but only convictions; and as to juvenile court records, one may omit "any offense committed before the 21st birthday which was finally adjudicated in a juvenile court law or under a youthful offender law."

The destructive attitudes of the community here indicated are a problem which the juvenile court has in common with the entire correctional field, and its personnel join in efforts at community education to overcome these limitations on readjustment of offenders. Are there also legal attributes in the treatment of juveniles which require separate consideration?

What of the form of commitment? The child committed by a juvenile court is, in almost every jurisdiction, committed for the duration of his minority. Potentially, this means that the *younger* the offender, the longer the possible term of his commitment! The committed seven year old could theoretically be committed for 14 years; the committed seventeen year old, close to his eighteenth birthday, cannot becommitted for over three years. That the suggested logical absurdity is seldom encountered in fact is not a reason for the existence of this situation; it is a reason for changing it.

But the indeterminate juvenile commitments do have their effects, not only in children held unduly long in institutions, but held too long on probation. Why should not, then, three years be the maximum term of commitment for adjudicated juvenile delinquents as in the English juvenile court system?[21] Children in United States institutions for delinquents who remain for three years or more probably run to five per cent of all commitments. In terms of psychological development, in terms of relative punishment, is not a year of a child's commitment more severe than a year in the commitment of an adult?

The universal commitment-for-minority has another effect. Frequently children remain under the jurisdiction of the training schools until they attain their majority, no matter what their age when released. Consequently the length of time on parole depends upon the age at which they were placed on parole. The combined commitment and parole time of the older adolescent may be three or four years; for the younger delinquent, it is longer, often much longer. Such an outcome is not merely inconsistent; it is burdensome on the treatment facilities for children, and may be detrimental to treatment.

A recent study by Robert E. Coulsen led him to the following: "In discussing the training schools with the children from our county who have been committed to them, a few general reactions have been developed. For one, they are not outraged or made vengeful by moderate physical chastisement. . . . Without exception the graduates said that they preferred taking a beating to losing a privilege. *Their greatest complaints of injustice or mistreatment relate to the fixing of times for discharge.* This attitude also is widespread among the adults who have spent time in penitentiaries or reformatories."[22]

This appeared to the Standard Act committee to be an unsatisfactory situation. The 1959 Act accordingly provides that a transfer of legal custody shall not be for more than three years, although an order of renewal may be made (but not beyond a child's minority) .

But even this is not satisfactory. Three years may be much longer than the punishment of an adult. Misdemeanors, for which juveniles are often committed, are not punishable by over one year. The law should be changed so that punishment of a juvenile may not exceed that of an adult for the same offense.

In one situation the "non-criminality" of the juvenile court disposition becomes more fiction than fact. In a number of jurisdictions it is possible for a child committed to a training school by a juvenile court, to be thereafter *transferred to a penal institution* without further court order. This means simply that a child can land in a penal institution without an arraignment or trial.

The Ohio juvenile court law provides that a child 16 years of age or over may be committed to the reformatory if the basis of delinquency is an act which would be a felony if committed by an adult. In an early case, [23] a boy committed under this provision sought release from the reformatory. The court held that although the reformatory was a prison for adults, it was only a place of reformation for children. What this does is take the "noncriminal" phrase of the juvenile court law, the phrase which declares it to be the policy that the juvenile court law *shall* be noncriminal, as establishing that no matter what is done to the child is noncriminal, no matter how apparent the clash with reality.[24] As legal reasoning, it is dubious. A more recent case, forbidding such a transfer, seems more logical and sounder.[25]

A similar outcome is possible, as to younger children as well, under the laws of other states, and even where the act was not a violation of a penal law. The proper concept would seem to be in the passage quoted in a leading case on the constitutionality of juvenile court law: "The basic conceptions which distinguish juvenile courts from other courts can be briefly summarized. Children are to be dealt with separately from adults. Their cases are to be heard at a different time, and preferably in a different place; they are to be detained in separate buildings, and *if institutional guidance is necessary, they are to be committed to institutions for children.*"[26]

Balancing the Law

In plain sharp terms which well warrant repetition, Alan Keith-Lucas declared to the Midcentury White House Conference on Children and Youth: "We are much more aware of the needs of children than we used to be and much more concerned about them. But, although some of us feel that we have some answers, actually there is far less agreement than there was fifty years ago. . . . When, for instance, we advocated juvenile courts around 1900, I think we were not concerned that the personal opinion of a single official, however well-informed and speaking with authority but with little or no well-tried legal procedures to keep him within bounds, was a somewhat dubious way of deciding whether a family should continue to exist. We were concerned perhaps if the judge wasn't social-minded and didn't see things as we did, but the idea that he might be taking away the parents' rights to their child, or his rights to them, without any semblance of 'due process,' didn't occur to us too often. We were too sure we knew what was right."[27]

The concept of the juvenile court is a noble one—that the child should not be punished for his acts or condition, but should be helped and protected. The law has been creative enough to have established this special court with its purpose humanitarian rather than punitive. Fulfillment of this purpose has not yet been fully achieved. The juvenile court, like all other social institutions, is in evolution. Creative law can still make a contribution to means of protecting the child in trouble, not only by taking him into court, but by protecting him in the court. It appears that important reorientations in jurisdiction may support the protective role of the court. Existing legal provisions relating to detention, procedure and disposition have given unusual powers to the court. Are they in balance with provisions to protect the child and parental rights? Improvement may well come from additional protective provisions, even if—perhaps because—they limit the power of the court more than at present.

Notes

[1] For example, *Federal Probation,* September, 1949, "A Special Issue Commemorating the Fiftieth Anniversary of the Juvenile Court."

[2] Ibid. And also Lowell Juilliard Carr, *Delinquency Control* (Harper & Brothers, 1950), pp. 234-240.

[3] *A Standard Juvenile Court Act,* six editions, 1925 to 1959. Published by the National Council on Crime and Delinquency.

[4] Some state courts had led the way.

[5] *The Standard Juvenile Court Act,* section 12, provides, "The Petition and all subsequent court documents shall be entitled 'In the interest of ...., a child under eighteen years of age'."

[6] Roscoe Pound, foreword to *Social Treatment in Probation and Delinquency,* by Pauline V. Young (McGraw-Hill Book Co., Inc., 1952). Our emphasis.

[7] Such proceedings have their own difficulties, particularly that the criminal proceedings would be a duplication of the neglect proceeding; there are other difficulties. The merit of the proceeding itself is doubtful; see above, chapter 2.

[8] *Standard Juvenile Court Act,* section 11.

[9] Section 24 (8). The 1951 Georgia juvenile court act and the 1952 Kentucky act adopted this provision. The New York City Domestic Relations Court Act has such a provision applicable in neglect cases. The provision has been criticized, among others, by the Association of the Bar of the City of New York, as being subject to the same criticism as the "contribution to delinquency and neglect" statutes.

[10] See, for an illustration, *Simple Arithmetic About Complex Children: A Study of Temporary Shelter for Dependent and Neglected Children in New York City,* by Bertram M. Beck, (Community Service Society of New York, 1952). ii. "Only a minority of the children for whom shelter is sought are placed in shelter on the day for which it is sought. . . . Others must wait from one day to more than two weeks before being admitted to shelter. . . . The delay means that they must stay in situations to which they may be accustomed but which are less than desirable. For still others the delay means that they must stay in homes in which they receive inadequate physical care or in which they are in grave moral danger. . . . And for some children a placement cannot be found at all." 61. "The court workers point to an unknown number of cases in which shelter is not requested, although it is needed, simply because the justices and the probation workers have had experience during that given day indicating that shelter will not be available." One of the unique features of the shelter program in New York City is that a large part of the bed capacity is provided by private agencies over which public officials have only limited control.

[11] Dorothy Hutchinson, "The Parent-Child Relationship as a Factor in Child Placement," *The Family,* April, 1946.

[12] Martha Branscombe, "Basic Policies and Principles of Public Child Care Services—An Underlying Philosophy," *Child Welfare,* February, 1952. Similar comment is made by George B. Mangold in *Problems of Child Welfare* (The Macmillan Co., 1936; p. 49)—"since the treatment of neglect and cruelty is largely a casework problem, it may be desirable, if possible, to reverse the present tendencies and to invest in other public departments, such as county

boards of public or child welfare, the duty of child protection. Gradually states are granting wide powers to such local units, and since they are administrative and executive rather than judicial, they are theoretically the most logical agencies for this form of service. The White House conference suggests that the juvenile court relinquish the care and protection of neglected children and that public units, such as boards of children's guardians on a city-wide or county-wide basis, absorb this function.

[13] Truancy as juvenile court jurisdiction is better defined as neglect than delinquency. *The Standard Juvenile Court Act* gives truancy jurisdiction in the following words—it gives jurisdiction over any child "who is neglected as to proper or necessary support, or education as required by law. . . ."

[14] Herbert A. Landry, "The Prosection of School Non-Attendants;" quoted in *Children Absent From School* (Citizen's Committee on Children of New York City, Inc., 1949), p. 68. Dr. Landry's study is described as the "first compilation of objective data as to the effect of the court process on attendance rates, school adjustment and social adjustment."

[15] Mark Roser, "The Role of the Schools in Heading Off Delinquency," *Yearbook,* National Council on Crime and Delinquency, 1951.

[16] Court jurisdiction over neglected children is by no means an innovation of juvenile court laws. For many years, for much of our national history, in fact, courts have had such jurisdiction. See *The Care of Destitute, Neglected and Delinquent Children,* by Homer Folks (The Macmillan Co., 1902), particularly chapters VIII—"The Boarding-out and Placing-out System," and IX—"Laws and Societies for the Rescue of Neglected Children." This jurisdiction was a concomitant of inadequate care by the community. It is a mark of growth, of maturity in caring for children, when neglected children can be taken care of without court authority, except where a change in custody is necessary. In the same way, jurisdiction over handicapped children is now almost entirely removed from juvenile court jurisdiction.

[17] Quoted in Knight v. Superior Court of Tehama County, 102 Cal. App. 211, 1951; italics added.

[18] *The Detention of Children in Michigan,"* by Sherwood Norman (National Council on Crime and Delinquency, 1952), page 17.

[19] See above, page 52.

[20] In the Matter of Arthur Lewis, 260 N.Y. 171.

[21] The English juvenile courts may commit a child to an approved school for a period of three years or if under twelve until the age of fifteen. See "Children's Court in England," Basil L. Henrique (*Journal of Criminal Law, Criminology, and Police Science,* November-December, 1946).

[22] Robert E. Coulsen, "Evaluation of Institutional Experience," *American Prison Association Proceedings,* 1948. Italics added. And the comment of Richard A. Chappell, regarding the federal juvenile delinquency law: "Some of the courts which follow the practice of committing an offender for the period of his minority have been disappointed to learn that the juvenile frequently serves a long sentence, before being granted parole. As a rule the parole board is more likely to grant parole to a juvenile than to an adult, but if a long sentence is imposed originally and parole is violated, the juvenile may have to serve as much as five to six years for an offense for which an adult may have been sentenced to 18 months to two years. Therefore, in cases of juveniles who cannot be placed on probation, the courts may wish to consider sentences for a definite period rather than for the minority of the juvenile. If the welfare of the juvenile is the primary consideration it would appear that a sentence of about 2½ or three years is best, as this will provide for a year and a half in an institution and a similar additional period for parole supervision following institutional treatment." ("The Federal Probation Service," *Federal Probation,'* December, 1947.)

[23] Leonard v. Licker, (1914) 23 Ohio Cir. Ct. (N.S.) 442.

[24] The decision is criticized as going too far in upholding juvenile court legislation by Bernard Flexner and Reuben Oppenheimer, *The Legal Aspect of the Juvenile Court* (U.S. Children's Bureau Publication No. 99, 1922, p. 9).

[25] White v. Reid, 126 F. Supp. 867.

[26] Cinque v. Boyd, 99 Conn. 80, quoting Flexner and Oppenheimer, op. cit. Italics added.

[27] *Proceedings*; Health Publications Institute, Inc., Raleigh, N. C., p. 127.

References

See the material published by the Child Welfare League of America (New York City), for example "Caseworker and Judge in Neglect Cases," articles by Robert M. Mulford, Judge Victor B. Wylegala, Judge Elwood F. Melson (1956), and its magazine *Child Welfare*; and by the Citizen's Committee for Children of New Yorfk City, Inc. The American Humane Association (Denver) has published a survey of services by child protective agencies, *Child Protective Services in the United States,* by Vincent De Francis (1956). Several articles on "Detention and Shelter Care" are brought together in a pamphlet of that title, published by The National Council on Crime and Delinquency. in 1953.

This chapter is based on an article which originally appeared in *The Journal of Criminal Law, Criminology, and Police Science* for November-December, 1952.

Chapter 5

What Court for Children and Families?

It used to be said, particularly by juvenile court judges, that the juvenile court is not a court in the ordinary sense, but is more like a hospital or a clinic. The analogy may be carried through the entire course of a sickness—diagnosis, hospitalization, treatment and discharge.[1] But even before the recent Supreme Court decisions, others disputed this view. A child welfare consultant wrote, "The juvenile court," she says, "is first and foremost a court. Its legal responsibility with respect to children, and to adults who have obligations toward them, is established specifically by law in terms of the behavior or conditions which bring individual adults and children within the jurisdiction of the court."[2] Its procedures, although informal, are still court procedures. Contrasted with the court, in her article, is the public welfare agency, with broad responsibilities to administer child welfare activities, but without power to impose obligations on individuals or to enforce orders.

Thus the juvenile court is pulled or pushed in two directions. Although both the judge and the child welfare specialist stress the importance of nonjudicial, administrative processes in providing social services to children, they disagree about the nature and functions of the juvenile court.

Juvenile court structure and procedure receives a periodic going-over through the Standard Juvenile Court Acts of the National Council on Crime and Delinquency. We have already mentioned the most recent editions. The first edition of the Standard Act was published in 1925, by the NCCD, then the National Probation Association. Revised editions were published in 1927, 1933, 1949, and the sixth edition in 1959. All editions have had the endorsement of the U.S. Children's Bureau, and the 1959 edition was drafted in cooperation with the Bureau and the National Council of Juvenile Court Judges, a membership association of juvenile court judges.

Is it surprising that the juvenile court idea should be so malleable? It was an experiment sixty years ago and the basic idea survives—that of removing children accused of crime from the criminal courts to a specialized court geared to their needs. Conflicting views—revised views of court structure and function—are welcome signs of experimentation and growth. Our concept of the juvenile court has become, not more confused through all this history, but clearer.

Many of the standards first considered desirable have been continued. Reviewing them very briefly, we note that they are: 1) exclusive jurisdiction over children, and jurisdiction over adults in children's cases; 2) private, friendly court hearings and informal, noncriminal procedure; 3) a sufficient staff of professionally trained probation officers; 4) facilities for physical examinations and for psychiatric study of problem children; 5) a well-equipped detention home or selected boarding homes for temporary care of children; 6) an efficient record and statistical system; 7) cooperation with other agencies and community support through interpretation to the public.

Specially Qualified Judges

And there is one more requirement—a full time judge qualified for juvenile court work. The 1949 edition of the Standard Act was the first Standard Act to contain provision for a separate statewide court established on a district basis. The most important immediate purpose of the provision was to assure special court judges for an entire state, as in Connecticut, Rhode Island (later a statewide family court), and Utah. In each of these states there is a state juvenile court and a small number of full time, specially selected judges. No other judges sit in the juvenile courts in those states. But in the other states, with over three thousand counties, there are at most eighty counties with special judges, and only half of these serve full time in the juvenile court. In the other counties the judge sits part time in juvenile court by virtue of being judge of some other court. In not more than twenty counties do the ex-officio judges serve full time in the juvenile court. That is, except for the statewide courts, only two per cent of the counties in the country have full time judges, and one-third of these are not specially selected to serve in the juvenile court.

How well can an ex-officio judge perform in a juvenile court? Let us consider first the judge of a court with equity jurisdiction. We say that juvenile court law is rooted in equity jurisdiction. This means that the court draws on the equity principle that the child is a ward of the state, entitled to its protection, and the state assumes toward the child the position of *parens patriae*—guardian of persons who are not of full age or ability. But it is a far cry from the jurisprudence of a court of equity to that of a juvenile court. An equity court, like a court of law, is bound by many formalities, including rules of evidence. A juvenile court is informal in procedure and bound by very few rules of evidence. An equity court is concerned primarily with money and property affairs. When problems of human relationship come up in it, they are frequently solved by analogy to contractual rights.

On the other hand, the juvenile court is mainly concerned with the personality and behavior of individuals; there the "remedy"—if we call it that for purposes of comparison—is not a judgment between contesting parties, but an effort to find a mode of treatment, perhaps to be continued for a lengthy period of time, to improve a personal or family or social condition. A juvenile court is *not* an equity court, although it is based on equitable principles. It is a special, new type of court. An equity judge therefore has no special experience that qualifies him as a juvenile court judge. The same is true for a court of law.

Non-criminal Proceeding

Analogy is sometimes drawn between a juvenile court proceeding and a civil proceeding. It would be more accurate to say that the juvenile court proceeding is non-criminal rather than civil. It is a special proceeding of a new kind not found in civil law. A civil proceeding in law or equity is an adversary proceeding in which a preponderance of proof decides the outcome, and the precedents guiding the court to award of damages or grant of equitable relief are well established and are reviewable by an appellate court as to the evidence and the remedy. But in the great majority of juvenile court proceedings the facts are not disputed and the "remedy," which we prefer to call the mode of treatment, is in the discretion of the judge, whose chief precedents are social casework practices.

Is the criminal court judge closer to juvenile work, better equipped to sit as judge in children's cases? Our laws go to great lengths to make clear that the juvenile proceeding is non-criminal, that an adjudication shall not be considered to have the effect of a conviction of crime. Detention homes take the place of jails, and detention principles eliminate the right to bail. There are no juries. The philosophy of our criminal courts is based on a finding of guilt in an individual; not so in the juvenile court. The juvenile court has marked a great advance in dealing with juvenile offenses precisely because it is an attempt to break away from penal philosophy.

We could, but need not, show that a probate judge, or any other ex-officio judge, does not by virtue of his other judgeship acquire experience markedly applicable to a juvenile court. Nor should it be necessary to enlarge on the proposition that ideally a juvenile court judge should devote his full time to the office. His hearings take little time. On the other hand, the problems of children and of families in trouble involves study that can not be carried out "among other things"; it calls for much research and a good deal of creative work.

It must be recognized, however, that there are, fortunately, some outstanding judges who were assigned from general courts and who serve full time in the juvenile division. This happens in jurisdictions where the bench of a particular court is made up of a number of judges and where rotation of the juvenile judgeship is kept to a minimum. By the same token, however, not only are such judges exceptional but there is usually no possibility of extending these exceptional judgeships outside the larger urban centers. Credit is due to those ex-officio judges who, although they serve part time in the juvenile court, are devoted to their responsibilities, are capable and conscientious, spend substantial time outside court hours on children's cases, and are careful in selecting probation officers. Yet their energies are divided. It is in fact some of these men who are the likeliest candidates for full time judgeships, as in a state juvenile court.

Statewide Courts

Under the 1949 Standard Act the state would be divided into several districts according to population, area and other factors, one judge appointed for each district, which he would cover on a circuit basis. By this plan we can obtain full time, specially qualified judges for an entire state. In Connecticut, in place of 169 town and city judges who heard children's cases (only two of whom were juvenile court judges), there are now three special judges and no ex-officio judges. In Rhode Island there were formerly twelve district court judges functioning ex-officio in the juvenile court. With the establishment of a statewide court in 1944, the work was taken over by two special judges. Utah had twenty-six ex-officio juvenile court judges. The state court there now has five special full time judges.

The 1959 Standard Act continues to endorse the separate state juvenile court as one of two alternative forms. It no longer endorses a purely "local" court of ex-officio or even specially appointed judges; the second alternative is discussed below. It too, like the separate state court, provides for statewide organization.

A separate state system requires that the judge be specially selected but it does not automatically ensure his qualifications for the work. The 1959 Standard Act calls for appointments by the governor from an approved list of candidates nominated by a panel of representatives of the courts, the bar, and the departments of public welfare and mental health. In Utah the judges are appointed by the governor; in Connecticut by the general assembly on nomination of the governor; in Rhode Island by the governor with the advice and consent of the senate. It is noteworthy also that in each of these states the judges' terms are longer than the governor's; in Utah and Connecticut the term is six years; in Rhode Island it is ten years.

The salary paid these judges must be sufficient to attract persons of high calibre. Outside of the largest centers of population, a special judgeship may be prohibited by the cost, which generally must be borne by the local community. A local judgeship is likely to carry a very small salary or to be limited to part time service. The state can pay better salaries to the special judges than can most municipal governments.

Does the state plan create a difficulty because of the judge's absence in another part of the circut? Is there an advantage in the availability of an ex-officio judge? A characteristic of the juvenile court is that it has brought to the fore the probation officer as a most important part of the court. In the criminal court the probation officer is called in after conviction; in the juvenile court he is working with the problem from the beginning; before the judge knows about the case, and in fact before the proceeding is officially commenced by the filing of a petition. Only the judges in a state system travel in the circuit; the probation staff remains, for the most part, in each county or other district subdivision. In addition, the referee system may be expanded so that in certain cases the presence of the judge is not necessary to a hearing.

Courts in Rural Areas

To what type of state, from the point of view of population distribution, is a state court well suited? At the 1948 NCCD conference a resolution was adopted recommending state or district juvenile courts like those in Connecticut, Rhode Island and Utah. Observing that large areas of most states are still without effective juvenile courts, even where the need for an adequate separate court may be recognized, the resolution notes that "it is impractical to set up such courts in rural or less densely populated areas on a county basis because there is not sufficient population or sufficient volume of work to justify a full time qualified judge, a probation staff, clerical employees and detention facilities, with the attendant financial cost." To solve this problem the conference recommended the adoption of the state plan. The plan therefore is not limited to small states with relatively dense populations. This has already been proved in Utah.

The experience in the three states which have adopted the state system strongly supports the reasoning of this resolution. In each the adoption of the plan led to improvement not only in the special judgeships but also in the probation staffs, detention systems, and even in the use of psychiatric and other facilities.

Establishment of a state court unifies the juvenile probation service. It permits a planned distribution of probation service throughout the state on the basis of need rather than according to each community's interest and ability to afford it. In Connecticut there are scattered throughout each district area offices staffed by resident full time probation officers and office personnel. This staff is state appointed and state supported. Utah for a time had local probation service. In 1944 all local participation was discontinued, and now all personnel, except the judges, are selected under a statewide merit system and all are paid entirely by the state. In Rhode Island also the probation staff is part of the state probation system, entirely state paid and state selected by an excellent merit system.

By contrast, in juvenile courts whose staffs depend on local maintenance, few officers are appointed under a merit system, few have civil service tenure, and many are appointed locally. With the three exceptions, few states have state probation service for the juvenile courts. In short, introduction of the state system has meant improved standards of probation service, and it may be added, higher salaries.

What effect does a state system have on detention? Under the state system, detention becomes a part of statewide planning. Connecticut has a statewide detention system under the control of the juvenile court. In the largest city in each of the three districts there is a receiving or detention home, supplemented by foster homes for emergency detention, particularly in out-of-city cases. The result is that Connecticut is one of the very few states which have eliminated detention in jails and police lockups.

Utah has local detention, some of it good, much of it poor. Several years ago the state tried subsidizing local detention and some improvement resulted, but not enough. The state officials recognize that the detention problem can be solved only on a statewide basis. Several years ago a bill to establish a statewide detention system was enacted. Detention in Rhode Island is exclusively a state function. The state training schools are used for delinquents; the state home and school for shelter care of dependent and neglected children. Some private facilities are also used by the court. It is recognized there too that statewide planning goes hand in hand with the state juvenile court.

There is similarly a greater use of other community facilities where the state court is established. In Rhode Island the state psychological facilities, the state psychiatrist, and the state hospitals are available. A prevention coordinator has been added to staff to utilize all the resources of the community, assisting individuals and groups in initiating negihborhood projects. He is concerned also with public education in juvenile court work.

In Utah all children's services except in the health field were coordinated in one administrative unit in 1944. It includes not only probation service but also foster care, psychiatric and other services. The Connecticut court works closely with the Division of Child Welfare of the State Welfare Department, particularly in relation to neglected children. A uniform, well established procedure for cooperation with the schools has been developed. The State Department of Health provides psychiatric service. It is clear that such facilities are naturally and easily available for a state court, but difficult or impossible to obtain for most local courts.

The establishment of a state juvenile court does not solve all juvenile court problems. Improvement is not automatic. But it does provide a framework for the attainment of high standards in all phases of juvenile court work.

State Juvenile Court Division

The 1949 Standard Act stressed the state juvenile court plan. Yet, since then no additional states have adopted the plan. There is a steady growth in state support for probation service, or probation service provided by the state, but there is little favor for new separate state juvenile courts.

Probably the main reason for the lack of legislation on the judicial structure of the juvenile courts is that any judicial reorganization is very slow and difficult, not because the existing systems are not archaic—many are—and not because sound reorganizational measures are difficult to contrive—they are not—but because vested political interests fight any change under which their special properties would diminish in value or influence.

Yet there is some movement, and improved juvenile court organization can be expected as judicial reorganization gains momentum. But instead of the plan for separate state juvenile courts, probably a more readily achievable plan—and perhaps a better one—is the second of the alternative plans proposed in the 1959 Standard Act. Under this plan the juvenile court in each county or other jurisdictional district would be a division of the highest court of general trial jurisdiction. In a district with one judge, he would serve as juvenile court judge; in a district with more than one judge in the general trial court, one judge would be selected as juvenile court judge.

The plan more readily meets any court reorganization movement arising in a state. And it supports specialized judges within the general court: the Act provides that where in a jurisdiction judges are elected, the juvenile court judges should be designated as such on the ballot, and if appointed, should be appointed as juvenile court judges.

Under the 1959 Act both plans of court organization provide for the judges to constitute a board of juvenile court judges with considerable power of supervision of court services. More strongly than ever the Act recognizes the need for state organization not only for uniformity but for the strengthening of services. Thus for the first time the Act also provides statutory models for statewide detention services.

Family Court

Still another court plan for children's cases is available. It may in time become the dominant form, for it has advantages over the several court plans already discussed. For many years family courts have been talked about, courts or divisions of courts in which all or most cases involving family relations including juvenile cases would be handled by judges specially assigned, and by professionally trained case workers. There are few such courts in the country, and until 1961 there were no statewide family courts. It may well be that the achievement of true statewide special courts for juvenile cases will come through the establishment of family courts. There is considerable interest in many communities in such courts, and in response to that interest a Standard Family Court Act was published in 1959 by the NCCD. Like the Standard Juvenile Court Act, it was drafted with and has the endorsement of the U.S. Children's Bureau and the National Council of Juvenile Court Judges.

Under the plan of the Standard Family Court Act, the court would be a separate, autonomous division within the court structure at the level of and a part of the highest court of general trial jurisdiction. Its jurisdiction would include the usual juvenile court jurisdiction, and such family cases as the matrimonial actions (divorce, annulment, separation), desertion and abandonment, custody and guardianship. It thus provides a statewide system, with specialist judges, for juvenile and family cases.

The division would be authorized to establish a marriage counseling service, although where a community has such a service outside of the court, it may not be necessary to establish it within the court framework. The court would be in a position to set up an intake service so that prior to acceptance of a petition or complaint, counseling staff could interview the potential litigants and offer any help from its own resources, and any appropriate referral to other services. The court would be authorized to make its own investigation after filing of a petition or complaint, again for preventive purposes and for the guidance of the court.

The only acceptable form of family court under the Standard Act is one that is statewide, and at a high judicial level. It is unfortunately true that the lower courts, both criminal and civil, generally suffer from inferior judicial work and neglected auxiliary services. But the demands of juvenile cases are exacting, especially because some constitutional safeguards of a criminal trial are not applicable, the procedure is informal, and there are other attributes that put great responsibility on the judge. His judicial work must indeed be of a high order to carry out these tasks with justice and wisdom. As for family cases, in most jurisdictions family cases—divorce notoriously—are handled with routine and indifference.

Necessary court services, particularly probation service, are much more likely to be adequate if the court is a division of the court of general jurisdiction of a state, rather than a lower court. And as we see, services must remain spotty and often highly inadequate so long as each local community determines for itself what the services shall be, and relies on its own resources for developing them.

The committee that drafted the Standard Family Court Act wrote, "We believe that all jurisdictions will ultimately find that a family court will best serve the legal-social problems of children and families, and that for many jurisdictions the immediate creation of such a court is desirable and sound."

Although there has been no great rush of legislation establishing family courts, the events since then support the committee's view. Three states followed the model of the Standard Act in passing statewide family court legislation—Rhode Island 1961, New York 1962, and Hawaii 1965.

More Than a Name Needed

If the juvenile court is not to be equipped with special personnel and services, it is unconvincing to talk of juvenile courts as being important improvements in the handling of children in court. It is generally accepted that the first juvenile court was the Chicago court, established in 1899, but before then courts were dealing with children on a basis not too different from juvenile courts of today, at least those in which the courts are not provided with special courtrooms, specially qualified judges, probation staff and other casework and clinical resources, and where children are still detained in jails.

For example, consider the following description from a court decision in 1876, passing on a police judge's commitment of a boy of 16, charged with leading "an idle and dissolute life," to an industrial school, in accordance with an act passed in 1858. The issue—still raised today—was that the proceeding was without a jury, and hence in disregard of due process of law. The court said: "The action of the police judge here in question did not amount to a criminal prosecution, nor to proceedings against the minor according to the course of the common law, in which the right of trial by jury is guaranteed. The purpose in view is not punishment for offenses done, but reformation and training of the child to the habits of industry, with a view to his future usefulness when he shall have been reclaimed to society, or shall have attained his majority. Having been abandoned by his parents, the state, as *parens patriae,*[4] has succeeded to his control, and stands *in loco parentis*[5] to him. The restraint imposed upon him by public authority is in its nature and purpose the same which, under other conditions, is habitually imposed by parents, guardians of the person, and others exercising supervision and control over the conduct of those who are by reason of infancy, lunacy, or otherwise, incapable of properly controlling themselves."[6]

Here—100 years ago—was a special proceeding, without a jury, a non-criminal proceeding, the court speaking of "reformation and training" rather than punishment, and committing the child to a training school, familiar words in juvenile court experience today. But the court was held by a police judge, without the help of probation officers or child guidance clinic, and no detention facility but the jail. Today, 100 years later, there are many so-called juvenile courts that are no more modern.

Notes

[1] "Of Juvenile Court Justice and Judges," Judge Paul W. Alexander, in NCCD *Yearbook,* 1947.

[2] "The Responsibility of the Juvenile Court and the Public Welfare Agency in the Child Welfare Program," Alice Scott Nutt, United States Children's Bureau, ibid.

[3] See "The Standard Juvile Court Act, 1949," by Judge Justine Wise Polier, NCCD *Yearbook,* 1950; "Evolution of the Standard Juvenile Court Act," by Judge Monroe J. Paxman, *NPPA Journal,* October, 1959.

[4] "Parens patriae"—parent of the country, the sovereign power of guardian ship over persons under disability.

[5] "In loco parentis"—in the place of a parent.

[6] Ex parte Ah Peen, 51 Cal. 280.

References

For an intensive study of a juvenile court (the Children's Court of New York City) see *A Court for Children* by Alfred J. Kahn (Columbia University Press, 1953); or the many surveys of juvenile courts made by the National Council on Crime and Delinquency in every part of the country. The concept of a family court is stated in "The Family Court of the Future," by Judge Paul W. Alexander, in the 1951 NCCD *Yearbook.* A plan for a specific state is developed in a survey report, "A System of Family Courts for North Carolina" (NCCD, 1957). The family court is also discussed in "Divorce—A Reexamination of Basic Concepts" (in *Law and Contemporary Problems,* Duke University, Winter, 1953). The problems of family and children's jurisdiction in New York is the subject of Walter Gelhorn's, *Children and Families in the Courts of New York City* (Dodd, Mead, 1954).

That part of the chapter dealing with juvenile courts originally appeared in an article in *Focus,* in July, 1951.

Part III

YOUTHFUL CRIME AND TREATMENT

Chapter 6

Sentencing Youthful Offenders

It would seem to be evident that the young offender, being not fully developed, not fully matured, being at a stage of life where changes are inevitable and come quite swiftly, would be a rather fit person for correctional treatment aimed at rehabilitation rather than punishment. When one turns to the actual administration of criminal justice, however, there is evidence that the young offender receives harsh treatment that is a repudiation of rehabilitation. The result of superficial thinking about youthful crime, carried into administrative criminal justice, becomes harmful and wrong.

It seems comparable to the behavior of certain kinds of parents, who confront their children with a chronic contradiction of reactions. They exhibit extreme patience, on the one hand, but when their patience is pushed they become irate and punitive. We must surmise that these parents are operating from sentiment rather than understanding. When sentiment fails, they lack understanding of what exasperated them, and they give way to frustration and retaliation. This may be the explanation for the punishment of youthful offenders.

Will C. Turnbladh wrote as follows: "Authorities on human behavior agree that the years between sixteen and twenty-five in an individual's life are crucial for both him and society. This is the time when he comes to grips with the strong forces of society and with the realization of his responsibilities as a mature person. Out of this must inevitably come turbulence. How we accept, understand, and deal with it is a measure of our poise and maturity as parents, educators, pastors, judges, lawyers, social workers, and, yes, as legislators and city fathers. . . .

"Over 50 per cent of arrests are of persons under twenty-five. Some of our newspapers have whipped up fear if not active hostility, toward youth in general with lurid accounts of teen-age and youthful crime. As might be expected, the crimes of youth are crimes of strength, violence, and the struggle to achieve adult status in one way or another. . . . [But] people who work from day to day with youthful offenders through probation, in detention, or in long-term institutions, find that they are at least as responsive to correctional treatment as are young adolescents. Many respond more successfully. . . . Their record on probation is at least as good as the probation record for the younger group. Yet even where the older adolescent is a first offender, courts are not as favorable to probation treatment for them as they are for the younger offenders. . . .

"We . . . follow a policy that amounts to revenge against the very youth who can be a part of the strengthening, not the weakening, of America. Francis Bacon put it this way nearly four hundred years ago: 'Revenge is a kind of wild justice, which the more man's nature runs to, the more law ought to weed it out.' "[1]

The sentencing of youthful offenders in America exhibits a characteristic contradiction: On the one hand it uses measures which seek to understand and deal carefully with youth. On the which seek to understand and deal carefully with youth. On the other hand, in actual practice, it is generally punitive and rejecting, sometimes to a violent extreme.

1. IN JUVENILE AND CRIMINAL COURTS

Under the common law and, in fact, until the establishment of juvenile courts, children and youths were sentenced for their offenses in the same way as adults for the corresponding acts. To the extent that discretion was available, no doubt the youth of an offender was taken into account, but this discretion was *not* always exercised in the direction of greater leniency. The common law developed two presumptions—one absolute, the other rebuttable—which served as some protection to youth, but these protections were in terms of responsibility rather than punishment. The absolute presumption was that a child under seven was incapable of committing a crime; in effect, that he could not legally be prosecuted for crime. The rebuttable presumption was that a child between seven and fourteen was incapable of understanding the nature of his act; if the presumption was rebutted, he was triable and punishable as an adult.

The development of the juvenile court concept and the extension of juvenile court statutes created a substantial area of special consideration for youthful offenders. In some states the juvenile court jurisdiction was not exclusive and many juveniles continued to be tried in the criminal courts. But in other states juvenile court jurisdiction was exclusive, subject to transfer of older youths to criminal court. In the latter states, this meant almost complete removal of juveniles from criminal courts, a great humanitarian advance in criminal justice. Probably two-thirds of children committed by juvenile courts spend less than a year in institutions under the commitments, and perhaps only one out of five spends more than two years, as compared with typically severe criminal court commitments. Despite the poor quality of many training schools, it is still true that juvenile court commitments have been at least as successful as criminal court commitments. As we go on to speak of commitments by criminal courts, we have this as a standard of comparison.

On the other hand it should not be forgotten that some children who are brought into juvenile court and committed would not be dealt with at all under the criminal laws if the juvenile court did not exist. The reason is that the juvenile court laws define as delinquency many acts which are not criminal, as we saw in chapter 3. And as we saw in chapter 4, in many situations a juvenile court disposition may be more punitive than a criminal court sentence for the same act.

It is regrettable that substantial information on such experience and a comparison of juvenile and criminal court dispositions (for equivalent offenses) are not available. It is a lack that should be remedied, especially since we are not at all sure at present how much the spirit of the juvenile court is maintained in disposition, compared with criminal court dispositions.

Retaliation: Sentencing Youths in Criminal Court

Although large numbers of youths are dealt with as juveniles in the juvenile court, the bulk of youthful offenders are dealt with in criminal courts and are disposed of as adults. The ordinary criminal courts are our principal "youth courts." If judges, correctional administrators, legislators and others are to understand youth sentencing, they must have a breakdown of sentences by age, offense, and length of commitments as well as of the relative use of the forms of community treatment (probation, suspended sentence, and fines). Although the National Prisoner Statistics provides much indispensable information, it omits a number of important items, and few states have reporting systems which are more comprehensive. On the immediate question—dispositions by age and offense—the information does not seem to be available.

A great deal of our thinking, therefore, has to be based on surmise and common-sense observation. Though these are admittedly unsatisfactory methods for analysis, at least they emphasize the necessity of adequate statistics. But the data we do have indicate that the youths in our criminal courts are not getting the greater consideration which they need and which is warranted; and may actually be receiving *greater punishment* than older offenders, perhaps for the same crimes. A table in a New York State Department of Correction report for 1944 established clearly the greater severity of sentences for youths generally, as compared with older criminals. It showed that the median of the *minimum* prison sentence for youths sixteen to eighteen years of age was 5 years 3 months; for those nineteen years of age, it was 6 years 3 months. For all other higher ages, the median of the minimum terms was *under 5 years*. But even among these, young adults under twenty-five had higher terms than the older offenders. The median of the *maximum* terms imposed was 11 years 1 month for those sixteen to eighteen years of age, and 11 years 4 months for the nineteen-year-olds. *For all other higher ages,* the median of the maximum term was in all cases *under 10 years,* and in most cases under 9 years. Again, those under twenty-five had relatively high maximum terms. (The reader should not lose sight of the fact that we are dealing with a *median* of both the minimum and maximum terms. This means that *half* of the youths were committed for terms *longer* than the figure cited.)

Unfortunately, more recent information does not appear to be available. For previous years, the situation was as in 1944. Has the situation been changed in New York by the Youthful Offender

Law, which has since come into use? It is not likely, although we are not certain. In its *Proposal for Dealing with Youth in the Courts,* the New York Temporary Commission on the Courts has this to say:

> One of the serious weaknesses of the Youthful Offender Law is that it has been too cautiously applied with the result that many youths having good prospects for reformation have been stigmatized by a criminal record. Apparently, youth who require institutional commitment are less likely to receive Youth Offender procedure, as evidenced by the fact that in 1953 only 14.6 per cent of adjudged Youthful Offenders were committed to an institution, while 78.9 per cent of convicted felons were institutionalized. In New York County, where the Court of General Sessions keeps excellent statistical records, we found that only 40 per cent of all youth qualified under the statute were approved for Youthful Offender treatment, and 20 per cent were rejected without investigation. Our information indicates that the number of these summary rejections in other counties is much higher.

Youths are also affected by special reformatory or indefinite sentences. Are these sentences less or more punitive than the ordinary criminal commitments? We must measure this in terms of *time actually served,* as well as time on parole. Are reformatory commitments possibly being used in place of probation? There is evidence that all this may well be happening in the youth authority movements (as we note below: see page 104), and there is some evidence that it is happening more generally, under laws providing for reformatory sentences.[2] Furthermore, in view of reformatory sentences for the younger effender, it is not enough to consider only state institution sentences. It may well be that a larger percentage of older offenders are committed to local institutions, as compared with the younger offender (commitments to local institutions being for short terms).

Wasting Our Young People

The indicated research is complex perhaps, but vital. Much of it can come from institution statistics; but it would be quite incomplete without comprehensive data on court dispositions, especially on the relative use of probation. Youth should be a factor favoring probation. Is it, in practice? Is it possible that the special institutions for youths and the few "probation camps" (which are institutions, not probation) result in commitments for youths, where in comparable situations an older offender would receive probation? The data required for answering these questions do not seem to be available.

Some years ago, in an article on "Injustice in the Courtroom," former United States Attorney General Francis Biddle described two incidents. The first involved Joseph Smith, a taxi driver who stole some letters containing $1,000 in checks from an apartment-house mailbox. He was caught by postal inspectors and pleaded guilty. An older accomplice was tried with him and sentenced to five years. Smith, a first offender, was sentenced to fifteen years. Stunned, he exclaimed to the judge, "I hope you're here when I get out." The judge called him back and raised the sentence to twenty years.

The second incident: "Three youths of seventeen hired a taxi, robbed the driver of about $8 after placing a soda-pop bottle against his back. They then tied him up, crossed a state line, and after spending the night in the woods with the driver, returned his cab and some of the money to him. Arrested later, they were sentenced to thirty years in the El Reno (Oklahoma) reformatory, for technical violation of the Lindberg kidnapping law. The sentence was later reduced to fifteen years. I have recommended that a further reduction be made. In contrast, Bill ————, a repeater who had already served a sentence for automobile theft, kidnapped a taxi drive, robbed him, and left him bound and gagged on the bank of a canal. He was given only eight years—by a different court."

Although we do not know (but should) how often such things happen, we frequently read accounts in the press of a youth who has committed an admittedly grievous crime—perhaps in the course of a gang war in a city slum—and is sentenced by an indignant judge to twenty years or more, possibly a life term or even the death penalty. These sentences can only be described as scandalous, from the point of view of correction. Often the act is not intrinsically different from the many other acts which take place among and between adolescents. Yet the life is discarded—to say nothing of the damage this does to the correctional system, which must keep the individual in custody practically for life and which has the problem of maintaining discipline and morale. Treatment is excluded. All of this is needless.

And what shall we say of the expense involved? It costs the community perhaps $50,000 to maintain a youth in prison under such a sentence. Does the sentencing judge feel that better use cannot be made of this money and this life?

This is not the place to discuss the development process of child and man. But the essential psychological background of youth crime is well known. We have to bear in mind not only the aggressive psychology common to many youths, evidenced among some in the physical behavior taking the form of burglary, robbery, or rape, but also the basic proposition that, with respect to most crime, individuals mature: those who commit a particular kind of offense in adolescence usually grow out of that behavior in a fairly short time. "Most persons are punished for offense against the criminal law only once in a lifetime," says Thorsten Sellin in "The Criminality of Youth." Theft by juveniles, for example, is so common as to be almost universal. As we have seen, the delinquency laws are so broad that almost every child could conceivably be processed as a delinquent. But for most of these children nothing is done and the delinquency matures not into youthful or adult crime but rather into generally law-abiding behavior. This is true even of the youthful burglars and rapists, many of whom are never caught and almost all of whom mature into average law-abiding citizens.

Capital Punishment and Youth

It is in the criminal courts that sentences of death are imposed. Here we *do* have data, presumably complete. The Federal Bureau of Prisons gives the following information on executions for the years 1947 to 1967:

Age		*White*	*Negro*	*Total*
Total	1298	561	728	9
15-19 years	63	10	53	—
20-24 years	300	91	207	2
25-29 years	301	133	164	4
30-34 years	226	102	124	—
35-44 years	251	137	114	—
45-54 years	118	63	52	3
55 and over	39	25	14	—

Whatever our feelings about capital punishment and its abolition, it is evident that we do not spare our youths from the death penalty. It will not be many years before students will read of a period in our history when the capital penalty was used, and especially for youth, and this will be thought of—as we can see if we project our thinking only slightly into the future—as a dark period. There was a period in the United States, for example, when the age bracket with as high a number of executions as any was the 20-24 year group—300 young people executed. But even children under 20 were executed—63 of them.

It is evident, too, that executions of Negroes, particularly of young Negroes, comprise a greatly disproportionate part of the total. Whereas 20 per cent of the executed whites were under twenty-five, the percentage of executed Negroes under twenty-five was almost twice as much, 36 per cent. Let us refer to one other figure: In the 1947-1952 period, *no* white person under twenty-five was executed for rape, as against 38 Negroes under twenty-five who were. This is not in the slightest degree a reflection of relative criminal behavior. It is *entirely* a matter of differential sentencing, especially for young Negroes.

2. SENTENCING UNDER THE "MODEL PENAL CODE"

The American Law Institute, an important scholarly organization of lawyers, law professors and judges, after years of work published a draft "Model Penal Code" in 1962. The penal codes in existence are notoriously the product of particles of social policy and group interests and emotions incorporated in the law from time to time, some of them derived from the most ancient eras. It is eminently proper that periodically a grand overview be taken of this body of definitions and sanctions to integrate the particles and to have them reflect a common philosophy deemed at the moment to represent the best wisdom available. But not every such attempt is inevitably a success, even in the drafting stage and before the document braves the public and the legislatures. Seeking the best wisdom is not always easy and the result is not always certain. There is a choice of wisdoms.

It may seem hackneyed, but the basic choice in dealing with criminals is, by and large, punishment or community treatment. But the ALI proposals relating to youthful offenders in the present draft,[3] is set on behalf of a drastically punitive policy, one which relies on imprisonment to a threatening and destructive extent.

No discussion is required for the assertion that the system of imprisonment in the United States is suffering from many ills. One thing wrong is that many individuals are imprisoned who should be treated in the community. Another is that most individuals committed to prison serve sentences which are far too long for the needs of treatment. Only if these two facts are recognized, acted upon, and remedied can our prison populations become small enough for treatment programs to be operated. We must look, therefore, for increased community treatment. This is why the position has been taken in the Standard Probation and Parole Act that "this act shall be liberally construed to the end that . . . persons convicted of crime . . . shall be dealt with by a uniformly organized system of constructive rehabilitation, under probation supervision instead of in correctional institutions, or under parole supervision when a period of institutional treatment has been deemed essential, whenever it appears desirable in the light of the needs of public safety and their own welfare."

Under the ALI plan as drafted at present, the penalties applicable to adult criminals may be utilized for youthful offenders. The proposed penalties for adult criminals in this new, supposedly reformist code are very severe, more severe than in most existent codes in the United States. By endorsing the extremely lengthy terms which characterize American penology in contrast to, for example, penology in Britain and Scandinavia, the Institute destroys what good might otherwise be accomplished.

In "The Treatment of Offenders in Sweden," Thorsten Sellen made this statement:

> In 1943 . . . there were about 179,000 sentences imposed by the courts of first instance. As Sweden abolished the death penalty in 1921, these sentences were either to fines or to some form of imprisonment. All but 9,500 were sentences to fines; 8,500 sentences to imprisonment were for one year or less (most of them for six months or less). Only seven sentences were for six years or longer and only two for life, while 65 persons were given indefinite sentences as recidivists or defective delinquents, 314 were sent to a reformatory for youthful offenders, and 224 were sent to a correctional school. . . . To a country which places a statutory

> limit of ten years on prison terms (except life sentences, sentences to preventive detention of defective delinquents, or sentences to internment of recidivists), some of our criminal laws and judicial practices would, therefore, appear almost barbarous.[4]

After his return from the first U. N. Conference on the Prevention of Crime and the Treatment of Offenders, where he served as chairman of the U. S. Delegation, Deputy Attorney General William P. Rogers wrote:

> I was surprised also to note the wide difference in sentencing methods. Usually sentences are much longer in the United States than in most of the other countries represented at the United Nations conference. . . . Sentences abroad average considerably less than in this country for the same type of offenses. Few men are sent to prison for more than five years in any Western European country. Only in cases of murder or extreme violence do the courts pronounce a sentence of more than five years.

The ALI plan must be evaluated against such data. Under the present draft a judge sentencing a youthful offender could sentence to terms authorized for adult offenders. That is, for a felony of the first degree, the court would fix minimum and maximum terms, the minimum not less than one year or more than ten years, and the maximum up to life imprisonment in all cases. (The ALI has not taken a position on capital punishment.) For a felony in the second degree the maximum term would be fixed at ten years in all cases. In some situations a youthful offender could be sentenced for so-called "extended" terms of imprisonment which are even more severe. *In addition,* each term would be followed by an added "parole term." The fact that the judge may fix a lesser penalty for young adult first offenders saves little. Our most backward states even now permit the judge a similar discretion as to most serious *adult* offenders.

Further, sentencing governs parole flexibility. The proposed ALI minimum terms bar earlier release on parole. In support of this the ALI draft refers to the NCCD Standard Probation and Parole Act and states that it "proposes . . . that the courts set a minimum as well as a maximum." The Standard Probation and Parole Act does *not* propose that the judge set a minimum term. It does, however, authorize the judge to set a minimum term if he chooses, but in no case may the minimum term exceed one-third of the maximum term, and in no case may the minimum term exceed seven years, no matter what the offense, no matter how many prior offenses were committed by the inidividual, and no matter how great the length of the maximum term. In *any* case the minimum may not be over seven years. Under the Standard Probation and Parole Act, where the minimum term is not fixed, the parole board may release on parole at any time. It also provides that the court may reduce the minimum time on recommendation of the parole board. Certainly the Standard Act provision supports early release, preferably, as in the 1940 act also, at any time.

Furthermore, not only was the policy on minimum terms a source of conflict in the committee,[5] but since soon after publication of the Act, with its further experience and staff work in connection with sentencing, the NCCD has supported as the most desirable form of commitment one in which the judge fixes a maximum term, which may be a term less than the maximum authorized by statute, and in which no minimum term is or may be fixed. Since then, under the Model Sentencing Act published by NCCD in 1963, *no* minimum term of parole eligibility would be authorized.

It must also be remembered that the Standard Probation and Parole Act is a pattern for adult criminal court sentencing. Here we are dealing with a plan for youthful offenders. *All* the youth authority acts provide for parole release at any time,[6] and this is true also with respect to reformatory (i.e., principally youth) commitments in many non-youth authority states.

It may be added that, for youthful offenders, NCCD has endorsed the Youth Plan of the New York State Temporary Commission on the Courts, proposing indefinite terms of not over three years, and not over five years if the underlying act is a felony. Rare and exceptional cases may be transferred for regular criminal proceeding. By comparison, the sentences for youths as proposed by the ALI are barbarous and vindictive.

Classification of Offenses Under the Code

The sentencing of offenders is governed not only by provisions relating to forms of sentence, but also by penal code provisions which determine the kinds of penalties and the terms which may, or must, be imposed for particular crimes. The present draft of the Model Penal Code proposes a simplification of penalties, establishing three degrees of felony, as well as misdemeanor,

As good an illustration as any is the following statement, which appears in the comment to section 207.4, dealing with rape and related offenses (page 241): "Rape is most often committed by males between the ages of sixteen and thirty; and forcible rape is especially the crime of younger men."[7] This certainly is supported by such knowledge as we have, and the proposed classification of this offense in the total range of offenses is highly significant for the disposition of youths who commit it. The present draft proposes that certain categories of forcible rape shall be classified as first degree felonies, and other offenses within the definition of forcible rape shall be lesser felonies.

As already indicated, the drafters refer to and accent the maturation of offenders, a process even more operative for those who commit rape than for those who commit other typical crimes of youth.

Possibly we become more punitive toward the youthful offender who commits rape *because* we feel that he is normal and, therefore, in contrast to the older individual who is the typical person convicted of sodomy, more responsible. We know, however, that sexually and in other ways the adolescent is in a turmoil of directions, Kenneth Walker and Peter Fletcher write as follows about "conflict in the adolescent who is trying to orient himself to his social and personal environment by investigating experimentally, among other things, the meaning of his sexuality":

> The older child, frightened or shamed when he obeys the impulse to sexual experiment and exploration, represses both his sexuality and his desire for personal freedom. . . . The point we are most concerned to emphasize, however, is that the social pressures nowadays brought to bear upon young people by us, their elders, could hardly be more effective in canalizing into sexual channels all their latent resources of vitality and creativity if they were deliberately designed to that end. We are therefore to the largest extent responsible for precipitating the sexual tensions and dilemmas they must try to resolve.[8]

Elsewhere they write as follows, about the adolescent male and his responsibility:

"Sexual capacity and activity both reach a peak very shortly after there is any activity at all. Yet in our civilization there has been no recognition of this fact, nor is there any provision for a socially acceptable outlet for an activity which is at its peak in the middle and late teens." (M. L. Ernst and David Loth: *Sexual Behavior and the Kinsey Report,* The Falcon Press, 1949.) Now unless Nature herself is in this instance making a grave error, this can only mean that the emotional and spiritual development of our children is being *actively retarded from without,* that is to say, by conditioning influences brought to bear on them by the social environment. In other words, if the Kinsey report is to be trusted, something is alarmingly wrong with our methods of family training and formal education. In this event it is as cowardly as it is immoral to require our young people to assume responsibility for the consequences of our ineptitude, and unjust to blame them if the burden proves too heavy for them to bear.

What of the victim of the rapist? The largest number of victims of forcible rape in a New York City study was in the seventeen-year-old group, in contrast to the average of under fourteen years for all victims of sex offenses. This is additional evidence that rape is a result of normal, not perverted, drives, although the form of satisfaction is, of course, not normal. Just so, hunger is a normal drive, but stealing to satisfy hunger is criminal.

Consistency in a Penal Code

For sound classification of crimes and penalties, two tests must be applied. The first is consistency with sociological and psychological knowledge, which we have just discussed. The second is *consistency of penalties with each other.* Commitment for a first degree felony (which is the classification proposed in the ALI draft) carries mandatory life imprisonment. The code would call for this extremely severe maximum penalty for rape by force or violence, even without serious physical injury, if the victim is not a voluntary social companion of the actor and has not previously permitted him sexual liberties. *No other sexual offense carries so extreme a penalty.* Even the most violent form of sodomy is classified as a felony of the second degree. Incest is a felony of the third degree, and bigamy is classified only as a misdemeanor.

All sorts of violent emotions are aroused by the mere mention of rape, and no doubt these emotions are aroused by the approach taken in the discussion of rape above. But they should not becloud our view of the realities. We must adhere to sound treatment, having regard to necessary protection for the community.

There is still another point to remember. The model act will be applied in the real world and it must take account of unpleasant realities. One to be reckoned with is administration related to the offense of rape. We have seen the savagely discriminatory use of the capital penalty for rape, its exclusive use for Negro youths, and its almost exclusive use for Negroes of any age. Rape, like some other offenses, is peculiarly subject to discriminatory enforcement, exhibited not only in the dramatic capital punishment statistics, but in the more routine everyday enforcement.

This is not to suggest that rape is not a dastardly crime that should be suitably punished, or that the community should not be protected. But the ALI proposal is one which invites and encourages precisely this discriminatory enforcement. It is unnecessary to adopt such a proposal from the point of view of treatment or of the psychological, sociological, or penological realities of youthful behavior. In classifying this crime and in providing for the maximum penalty which may be imposed, we must consider realistically the question of treatment or punishment.

Whether in the prisons as we know them or in prisons with improved treatment staff, the maximum time which can be therapeutically used is not more than a few years. Keeping an individual in prison longer destroys his personality and makes him more useless or more dangerous. Our prisons are notoriously destructive of normal sexual behavior; they push individuals toward abnormal behavior, toward perversions, toward victimization. Finally, all our experience is that the proposed punishments will not deter other crimes one whit more than the same process of conviction and sentence, but where sentences are more moderate and more consistent with rehabilitative efforts.

A Rehabilitative Code for Youth

What has been said about rape in terms of its being a crime characteristic of youth is only the introduction to a great deal more than must be considered with respect to youth and our penal codes generally. Certain other property and aggressive offenses are characteristically offenses of youth, just as other property crimes and certain sexual offenses are characteristically offenses of the older adult.

What then should we try to achieve? Sentencing is the framework of treatment. As such it must be related to realistic treatment needs and facilities. That is, where a commitment is needed, it must be measured by what can be done from a therapeutic point of view. If we have a treatment program, we do our best (except in rare cases) in two years or less. Even in the unusual cases, requiring longer commitment, the duration must not become utterly punitive. Lengthy commitments—five, ten, even twenty years and more—are no more needed here than in other countries we have referred to, whose cultures are not too different from ours. Wide-open penal provisions, such as the ALI is considering, invite a *worsening* of youth sentencing. If it is to make a useful contribution, the ALI must proceed in a direction precisely opposite its present course. Most of the states face the same imperative challenge.

Notes

1 "Revenge Is a Kind of Wild Justice . . ." by Will C. Turnbladh, NPPA *Journal*, April 1956.

2 E.g., in New York the Penal Code provides for a maximum prison sentence for attempted grand larceny of 2½ years, but a youth sentenced to a "reformatory sentence" may validly be held for five years; failure to discharge after 2½ years upheld. People ex rel. Vivona v. Conboy, 7 App. Div. 2d 810, motion for leave to appeal denied, 6 N.Y. 2d 706 (1958). For a similar ruling under the California youth authority act, People v. Scherbing, 209 P. 2d 796, 93 Cal. App. 2d 736 (1949).

3 American Law Institute, Model Penal Code, Tentative Drafts No. 3 and 7; Proposed Official Draft (1962).

4 *Federal Probation,* June, 1948, p. 15.

5 *Standard Probation and Parole Act* (NCCD, 1955), section 12, comment.

6 In Wisconsin, court approval is required for a parole release within two years on a felony conviction.

7 American Law Institute, Model Penal Code, Tentative Draft No. 4.

8 *Sex and Society* (Penguin Books, 1955, p. 97).

References

The foregoing chapter is based on an article which appeared originally in the NPPA *Journal* for April, 1956. The issue was entirely devoted to the subject of the youthful offender, and the quoted material from Will C. Turnbladh is from his article, "'Revenge Is a Kind of Wild Justice . . .,'" which appeared in the issue. The other articles are "The Community's Attitude Toward Youth," by Stafford Derby; "Dynamics and Treatment Needs of Adolescence," by Joseph A. Shelly; "The Detention of Youth Awaiting Court Action," by Harry M. Shulman; "The Courts for Handling Youth," by Mary C.

Kohler; "Commitment of the Youthful Offender," by Lowell Juilliard Carr; and "Highfields—A New Slant in the Treatment of Youthful Offenders," by Albert Elias. *Youth and the Law,* by Frederick J. Ludwig (The Foundation Press, 1955), containing interesting legal material, deals mainly with New York laws.

Part of the theme of the chapter was broached thirty-five years ago in an almost forgotten report, which suggests that the contradictory treatment of youths exists not only in sentencing, but in many other phases of law enforcement. The report is by Harry M. Shulman, Professor of Criminology at the City College of New York, and former deputy commissioner of the New York City Department of Correction. The report is entitled, "Report of the Subcommittee on Causes and Effects of Crime: The Youthful Offenders, A Statistical Study of Crime Among the 16-20 Year Group in New York City," and is included in the 1931 Report of the New York Crime Commission.

Thoughtful writing on youth crime and correction is to be found in "The Correction of Youthful Offenders," the Autumn, 1942 issue of *Law and Contemporary Problems,* published by Duke University; and *The Criminality of Youth,* by Thorsten Sellin (American Law Institute, 1940). Sellin has also written an article, "How Sweden Handles Its Juvenile and Youth Offenders" (*Federal Probation,* March, 1956). He points out that although Sweden has a population of about 7 million, in 1953 (the most recent statistics available) only nine offenders in the 15- to 18-year-old group were sentenced to prison! A 1954 law forbids the courts to sentence offenders under 18 to an adult prison, except in very serious offenses. There is a separate "youth prison" system for 18- to 21-year-old offenders only.

Information on capital punishment, treated briefly in the chapter, and on the movement for abolition, may be obtained from the American League to Abolish Capital Punishment, Brookline, Massachusetts.

The author discusses the sentencing plan of the American Law Institute draft Model Penal Code in "Sentencing and Correctional Treatment Under the Law Institute's Model Penal Code," American Bar Association *Journal* (September, 1960).

Chapter 7

The "Youth Authority" Plan

Concern with the problem of youth crime and treatment led the American Law Institute to promulgate a "Model Youth Correction Act" which they urged for adoption by the legislatures as a mean of marshalling the resources of the communities at a state level. In the ten-year period after its promulgation in 1940, five states adopted laws patterned on the model act, and several more have in the years since.

The first five youth authority acts clearly showed a gradual departure from the model act developed by the American Law Institute and adopted by it in 1940. First it may be noted that none of the laws used the word "correction" in the name of the governing body. The California Act of 1941 (chapter 937; in the Welfare and Institutions Code, Division 2.5, chapter 1), the first such enactment, among other changes did not take away from the courts the power of releasing on probation, nor did it provide for completely indeterminate commitment or mandatory rather than permissive commitment of youths, as did the model act. In 1947 Minnesota established a Youth Conservation Commission (Laws of 1947, chapter 595), and Wisconsin a Youth Service Division in the Department of Public Welfare (Laws of 1947, chapters 546, 560, renamed Division of Child Welfare and Youth Service in 1949 by chapter 376), both states utilizing as models the American Law Inistitute draft and the California act. In 1948 the Massachusetts legislature established (Laws of 1948, chapter 310)) the Youth Service Board, incorporating many of the provisions of the other acts, but making an important departure by limiting commitments to the board to children within the juvenile court age, whereas the model draft provided primarly for commitments from the age group sixteen to twenty-one. In 1949 (by enactment of chapter 538) the Texas legislature established a Youth Development Council whose basic function was the administration of the state facilities for committed delinquent children.

In the model act the administrative head is a board of three full time members appointed by the governor for terms of nine years, the terms being staggered, as in laws now enacted. The California Authority was at first a board of three men appointed by the governor for four year terms. Two of the appointments were made from a list of persons recommended by an ex officio advisory panel of six, consisting of the presidents of quasi-public professional associations named in the law. One member of the authority is appointed director with full executive powers. The Minnesota Youth Conservation Commission consists of six members appointed by the governor for six year terms, three of them public officials serving ex officio (the director of the division of institutions, the chairman of the state board of parole, a juvenile court judge). The governor designates the chairman who serves as director of the commission and who is the only full time member. The Wisconsin Division of Child Welfare and Youth Service is one of several divisions in the Department of Public Welfare. The board of public welfare may establish, with the approval of the governor, advisory citizen committees. The Massachusetts Yout Service Board is composed of three full time members serving six year terms, appointed by the governor from a list submitted by an advisory committee on children and youth, composed of fifteen citizens appointed by the governor. In Texas the Youth Development Council is made up of fourteen members, six appointed by the governor, and eight state officers ex officio, who serve as a research and advisory body. Its executive committee (the director of the Department of Public Welfare and two others designated by the council) has the administrative responsibility, but the duties relating to placement and release may be delegated to the director of public welfare alone.

Commitment Provisions

Mandatory commitment to the youth correction authority as provided in the model act embraced persons under twenty-one at the time of apprehension, convicted of a crime punishable by imprisonment for less than life; children sixteen years of age and over might be committed by the juvenile court. The granting of probation was at the discretion of the authority and not the court. The California Youth Authority similarly receives all commitments of minors subject to the same imprisonment, but the decision as to probation remains with the courts. It receives commitments from the juvenile court without a lower age limit, whereas the act in Massachusetts covers only children of juvenile court age. The Minnesota Youth Conservation Commission may receive minors convicted of crime and sentenced to imprisonment for less than life, but children adjudged delinquent in the juvenile court, if not remaining at liberty in the community or committed to an agency other than the state training schools, must be committed to an agency other than the state training schools, must be committed to the commission, and the commission must receive such commitments, whereas in California the authority has the discretion to refuse such commitments.

The Wisconsin Department of Public Welfare receives minors sentenced to less than life imprisonment and juvenile delinquents not released or placed on probation by the juvenile court. As already indicated, the Massachusetts board receives only children adjudicated as wayward or delinquent by the juvenile courts, or children convicted of crime after waiver of juvenile court jurisdiction (i.e., generally under seventeen).

In California and Massachusetts the board is both an agency to manage the industrial schools, and a diagnostic service which may utilize other facilities for children. The Texas Council similarly manages state training school facilities, receiving children on commitment from the juvenile court. In Wisconsin management of treatment facilities may be given by the board to the Division of Child Welfare and Youth Service. In the American Law Institute draft the authority was to be primarily a diagnostic agency enabled to place minors in state and private institutions and agencies. However, it also provided that the authority could in the future acquire any type of facility.

The model act provides for discharge or release on parole by the authority at any time, and present statutes follow it in this respect, except that in Wisconsin the Department of Public Welfare may not discharge a person convicted of a felony within less than two years after commitment without approval of the committing court. The draft also provides for continuing control by the authority where an institution not governed by it releases an inmate. California and Massachusetts follow this provision. In Minnesota release on parole may be granted only by the Youth Conservation Commission. In Wisconsin an institution having custody of a person in the control of the Department of Public Welfare may grant release where it now has such power, upon giving prior notice to the department.

Release Provisions

What is specified regarding duration of confinement? The original draft provides that if not previously discharged, persons within the control of the authority shall be discharged before the age of twenty-five, children under eighteen committed by the juvenile courts, before reaching twenty-one, and children over eighteen committed by these courts, within three years of commitment. However, by order subject to approval of the court, the authority may continue control of persons committed to it where it considers that release would be dangerous to the public. By repeated orders control may continue until death. Thus there was proposed an absolutely indeterminate sentence not limited by penal provisions, a measure not yet adopted for adult criminals in any jurisdiction. Massachusetts with its jurisdiction limited to children of juvenile court age, and Wisconsin have adopted this provision.

The California act provides for discharge of a person convicted of a felony when he reaches twenty-five, a person convicted of a misdemeanor at twenty-three, or after two years, whichever occurs sooner, a person committed by the juvenile court at twenty-one or after two years. Orders continuing control may be made, but the period of control by the authority may not exceed the maximum penalty provided by law, although the commitment to twenty-five is not limited by a shorter legal maximum. The Minnesota act provides for discharge at twenty-five, or earlier where the maximum term for the offense would expire prior to the inmate's reaching that age; control of delinquent children ceases at twenty-one. If an inmate who would normally be released at twenty-five is considered dangerous, control may be continued to expiraton of the maximum term provided by law, but is transferred to the court, parole board or penal institution which would have had control if the intervening commitment had not been made to the Youth Conservation Commission.

Indeterminate Commitments

Whereas in the American Law Institute draft the commitment may be wholly indeterminate, in the California act it is indeterminate to twenty-five, subject to increase to the legal maximum; in the Minnesota statute the maximum provided by law controls commitment whether it falls before or after twenty-five; and in the Wisconsin act the definite sentence is introduced. The court may fix the term of commitment (which may not exceed the legal maximum sentence, nor be less than one year), or may make an indeterminate commitment limited by the maximum. By order issued by the department and approved by the court, control by the Department of Public Welfare may be continued indefinitely, but a jury trial on the question of danger to the public may be demanded. Juvenile court commitments terminate at twenty-one.

In Massachusetts and Texas the pattern is similar to provisions in many other states for control of children in training schools—children adjudicated in the juvenile courts may be held until they reach twenty-one. In Massachusetts a boy between fourteen and eighteen years of age convicted of an offense punishable by imprisonment may be committed to the board until he is twenty-three, or he may be punished as provided by law (that is, as an adult). As in the other youth correction authority acts there is in this state provision for extending control over persons whose release would be dangerous to the public. Whether control would ordinarily cease at twenty-one or twenty-three, the Youth Service Board may order continued control, subject to approval of the court, and such orders may be repeated indefinitely.

What Is a Youth Correction Authority?

In view of the changes which have been made in the acts modeled on the American Law Institute draft, what is a youth correction authority today? Are there elements or combinations of elements which distinguish it? This chapter is not concerned either with the vital arguments for or against removal of the sentencing power from the court (as the model act proposed, but no act adopted), with the sentencing features of the original act, or other controversial provisions. It attempts only to discover what a youth authority is—if it is a distinct concept.

Is the administrative setup of the youth authorities unique? It is neither unique, nor is the pattern consistent in the various enactments. The appointive procedure varies; even the three man board is not included in all the acts. Except for Minnesota all the acts draw in, at least in an advisory capacity, representatives of the community at large. This lay representation is of course not unique in administrative structure. No specific age jurisdiction of commitment is a cardinal element of a youth correction authortiy, since it started with the sixteen to twenty-one group, almost excluding the juvenile court age group, and has changed in Texas and Massachusetts to an authority concerned *only* with that group. In California committed adults of any age come within the scope of a parole and sentencing board called the Adult Authority.

Is the release procedure unique? No; parole in similar form was well established before the model act was published. Is the type of commitment an essential element? The original draft proposed in effect an absolutely indeterminate sentence (or commitment). The established authorities use all types of sentence—definite, indeterminate within the maximum fixed by law, absolutely indeterminate.

Is the authority essentially diagnostic, or is it an institutional management apparatus? It is both, and either. However, the youth correction authorities have one important feature in common. It is a feature of the English system of Borstals, but it also existed in the Unitel States prior to 1940. Where a commitment is decided upon by the court, the particular institution is not selected by the court but by the state institutional department.

Is the authority a combination of structural or procedural elements? It does not seem so, in view of the fact that all the acts differ in some respects among themselves, and all differ from the original draft. What then is it? To this reader of the youth correction authority laws it seems a *reorganizational movement, concerned with renovation of a state's apparatus for dealing with juvenile delinquents or youthful criminal offenders, through an autonomous agency, drawing on highly responsible community representatives.*

YOUTH AUTHORITY PROVISIONS

	MODEL ACT	CALIFORNIA	MINNESOTA	WISCONSIN	MASSACHUSETTS	TEXAS
Name	Youth Correction Authority	Youth Authority	Youth Conservation Commission	Div. of Ch. Welf. and Youth Service in DPW	Youth Service Board	Youth Devel. Council
Stat. Ref.	1940 Adopted American Law Institute	1941 ch. 937; Welf. & Insts. Code Div. 2.5, ch. 1	1947 ch. 595	1947 ch. 546, 560 (1949 ch. 376)	1948 ch. 310	1949 ch. 538
Admin. Org.	3 man full time bd. apptd. by gov., 9 yr. staggered terms, bd. selects chmn.	3 man full time bd. apptd. by gov.; 2 from list of advisory panel (6 pres. of quasi-public prof. assns.) 4 yr. staggered terms, gov. selects chmn.	6 apptd. by gov. (3 pub. officials ex-off.; dir. of div. of insts., chmn. of parole bd., juv. ct. judge). 6 yr. staggered terms, gov. selects chmn.	Div. of DPW. Bd. may appt. citizen committee with gov.'s appvl. to advise on programs and problems, DPW dir. selects div. head	3 man full time bd., apptd. by gov. from list of adv. committee on children & youth (15 apptd. by gov.) 6 yr. staggered terms, gov. selects chmn.	6 apptd. by gov. and 8 state officers ex-off.; DPW dir. is chmn.
Age Juris.	16-21 from crim. or juv. ct.	Discretionary, 16-21 from crim. or juv. ct.	Minors convicted of crime, sentenced to less than life. Juv. ct. commitments to tr. schools	Minors sentenced to less than life, juvs. not released on probation	Juv. ct.; children convicted of crime after juv. ct. waiver (under 18)	Juv. ct.
Type Commitment	Indeterminate	Indeterminate to 25, subject to max.	Indeterminate to max.	Definite (fixed by ct.), 1 yr. min.; or indeterminate to max.	Indeterminate to 21	Indeterminate to 21
Prob.	Granted by auth.	By ct.	By ct.	By ct.	By ct.	By ct.
Admin. of Facilities	Auth. is mainly diagnostic; permitted to admin. facilities	Manages insts.	Manages state schools	May be given management of treatment facilities	Manages insts. may use other facilities	Manages insts.
Duration of Control	To 25. Juv. ct. commitments to 21; if over 18, 3 yrs. Unlimited control on appvl. of ct. may continue where release is dangerous.	To 25 for felons; 23 for misdems. Control may continue by ct. order but only to max. for offense. Juv. ct. commitments to 21	To 25, or max. for offense, if shorter. To 21 for delinquents. Control may be trans. to another agency after 25 where release is dangerous	Unlimited, with appvl. of ct. Jury trial on dangerousness may be demanded. Juv. ct. commitments to 21	To 21; unlimited with appvl. of ct. Boy 14-18 convicted of crime may be committed to bd. to 23, or punished as adult	To 21
Disch. Parole	At any time	At any time	At any time	2 yr. min. for felons, except with appvl. of ct.	At any time	At any time

To this extent it is a movement of considerable value, despite the lack of a unique pattern. A vital element in the success of the youth authority programs is the autonomous character of the agencies for youth treatment. It has been important in focusing public and legislative attention on the authorities, with impressive results in sufficiency of budgetary appropriations, and in public interpretation. Probably the most important organizational lesson in the applications of the Model Act is that a department of correction should have a separate youth division, if the jurisdiction does not have a youth authority or its equivalent.

At the same time it should be clear that the greatest benefit can come from this movement if a state carefully examines its entire process of treatment of juvenile, youth and adult offenders. Do the institutions need to make operative changes? Are new facilities needed in them, different facilities? On the other hand, is probation underdeveloped? Should a state probation commission be established, or if one exists, should it be expanded in power or function? Is the state parole staff adequate? Are parole standards high or low? Is a statewide state administered juvenile or family court or division advisable? In these considerations the experience of the states which have adopted acts based on the draft, and the broad general experience of other states offer valuable suggestions. Laws and experience in England, Sweden and elsewhere are sources also. (The English Borstal system was studied by the proponents of the American Law Institute draft, but the law regulating the Borstals differs in important respects from the model act.)

But there are dangers also. Perhaps the greatest danger in the youth authority movement is the possibility of its increasing the use of institutional treatment, both in length of term and in an increase in the relative use of commitment as against probation and suspended sentence. Under the federal youth correction act (passed in 1950) for example, committed youthful offenders are being held for longer terms than under previous law.[1]

The federal authorities are concerned about the development and are seeking the answer to it. The answer, or answers, may be unhappy. The federal law offers the judge alternative forms of commitment, either the commitment for the offense, or a six-year commitment. The six-year commitment may be more than the maximum an adult could receive for the same offense. A judge who senses magic in the term "youth authority" may feel he is doing the right and liberal thing in preferring the youth act commitment. Another judge may use the old-style sentence, and sentence to one year.

Or the liberal judge may feel that the youth authority, being a superior treatment resource (because it is a "youth authority"), should be preferred to probation, in some cases in which he would formerly have used probation. Institutions have developed and expanded in California since the youth authority was established there, and the state subsidizes local institutional construction and care. But the probation service is local, not assisted by state subsidy, and in many places lagging.

Although no uniform pattern exists, it is made clear by the acts that our machinery for dealing with offenders is greatly in need of improvement, that public participation is an important adjunct, and that the *whole* process must be examined and improved. The administrative designs of the youth authorities, drawing in lay leaders and ex officio representatives of other departments, concentrate the concern of the state with the problems of delinquency and crime on the institutional program. Delinquency prevention, community organization to this end, general planning, should perhaps rather be oriented to the community as a whole, therefore attached administratively to state agencies such as probation commissions, juvenile or family courts, or comprehensive state welfare or state correction departments.

Defining the correction authority as a movement rather than as an administrative pattern, points up the requirement that success depends on the extent to which state official bodies and public organizations concerned with social welfare and offenders against the laws, participate seriously and unselfishly. Once new administrative setups are achieved, that is not the *end* of the movement, but the beginning.

An agency which is satisfied that its critical work is done when a smoothly operating department is in existence, will no longer be a youth authority defined as a movement. It will probably be destined to fall behind the needs of the individuals whose total care it is charged with.

Notes

[1] We have seen the same result occurring in the older reformatory movement (above, page 85).

References

The article on which this chapter is based, published in *Focus* in 1950, contained an analysis of the statutes of the five states that had enacted youth authority acts to that date. Some changes have since been made by statute in the administrative structure of several of the youth authorities listed. There is no need to note them; the changes serve to emphasize what was said about the pattern in the authorities. Since then a youth authority plan has been adopted also in the federal system (1950), Arizona (1951), Kentucky (1952), Illinois (1953), and Idaho (1955). The suggested analysis, together with the debate which continues in the field, are discussed in an article which appeared a little later (also in *Focus,* January, 1951), under the title "More About Youth Authority Concepts," by Will C. Turnbladh. The American Law Institute has made a follow-up study—*Five States: A Study of the Youth Authority Program as Promulgated by the American Law Institute,* by Bertram M. Beck (1952). For a descriptive review, and a more optimistic one, see John R. Ellingston, *Protecting Our Children From Criminal Careers* (Prentice-Hall, 1948).

The American Correctional Association and the National Council on Crime and Delinquency published in 1965 a model for a state department of correction, including services for youthful offenders ("A Standard Act for State Correctional Services, NCCD, 1965).

Part IV

SENTENCING ADULT CRIMINALS

Chapter 8

Prison Sentences

The decade of the 1950's witnessed a veritable epidemic of prison "riots," as they are usually called. They occurred in institutions in almost half of the states. Perhaps a more accurate term than "riot"would be "demonstration." An only slightly diminished number of demonstrations or riots occurred in the 1960's. Practically all of the events we refer to did not involve either an attempt to break out of the prison, or an attempt to usurp authority of the prison administrators, except momentarily. They were plainly disturbances which had as their goal calling the attention of the press and public to what the prisoners considered were serious grievances.

Correctional authorities agreed with them. Under the auspices of the American Correctional Association, the national agency in the field of adult correctional institutions, a Committee on Riots was appointed with a membership of the heads of important state correctional systems, the director of the United States Bureau of Prisons, James V. Bennett, and other acknowledged experts.

After making their study, the riots, they said, "are almost always the direct result of the shortsighted neglect of our penal and correctional institutions, amounting to almost criminal negligence in view of the costly results, by many governors, legislators, governing boards, directors, wardens, and others basically responsible for the administration and management of these institutions. Prison riots," they declared, "should be looked upon as costly and dramatic symptoms of faulty prison administration."

The faults they listed were these: a) inadequate financial support, and official and public indifference; b) substandard personnel; c) enforced idleness; d) lack of professional leadership and professional programs; e) excessive size and overcrowding of institutions; f) political domination and motivation of management; g) unwise sentencing and parole practices.

Among all of these, probably the most serious and urgent is the factor of unwise sentencing. We suggest that the greatest fault of all is the American phenomenon of long prison sentences, joined with the overuse of prisons generally. Even if nothing else were done (but of course a great deal more should be done), if the problem of long prison terms were to be dealt with constructively, it would accomplish an enormous improvement in our correctional treatment systems, and very likely would reduce the incidence of prison demonstrations.

A paragraph from the committee report is descriptive enough: "The violent, and often hysterical and irrational, behavior of people confined in penal institutions results from the development of emotional tensions. These tensions are always present in some degree. The potentialities for an outburst of pent-up emotional energy, resulting in riotous incidents, are inherent in the very nature of imprisonment. They feed upon monotony and boredom, a sense of injustice and frustration, hopelessness for the future, sexual privations, anxiety about family and friends, and similar factors. These everpresent tensions burst into open rebellion under the stimulus of such immediate factors as bad food, brutality, unfair or capricious treatment, race conflicts, staff disharmony, inept and vacillating management, or other similar basic conditions which serve to stir man's elemental emotions."

Long Prison Terms

Yet as bad as the conditions in the prisons are, it is only when an individual is subjected to them over a prolonged period that riots occur, and, worse, that the prisoners gradually deteriorate as men and women. Simon E. Sobeloff (then United States Solicitor General, later judge of the United States Court of Appeals) wrote that "we have two and a half times the number of prisoners [England has] per 100,000 population, and our sentences are longer. In all England in a recent year not more than 588 men received terms of five years or more and in the United States in the same year 18,000 offenders were committed for maximum terms of five years or more."[1] As we have noted in an earlier chapter, William P. Rogers made similar observations as to sentences in most European countries, compared with those in the United States. There is no doubt that the statements refer to both cause and effect. One of the reasons for our greater prison population is the longer commitments.

Such facts point to a truly critical problem in American correction and a key to many of its ills. One effect of our pattern of lengthy terms is to increase the size of the prison population, hence the size of our prisons, making it well nigh impossible to operate prisons as centers of treatment. The prisons in the United States have always been plagued by periodic riots; they can break out almost anywhere. The riots, or demonstrations, certainly are a protest against the mass custody methods. Certainly also they are a protest against terms so lengthy as to engender extreme desperation and hopelessness.

What happens to the prisoner over a period of time? For not more than a year or two, constructive work can be done with him. Thereafter he receives little more than custody, and mere custody without treatment is a predominantly destructive experience. With very few isolated exceptions, the individual who stays longer is a poorer risk for successful living after release. Robert M. Lindner has referred to "the regressive effect of detention, the peculiar liability of imprisonment to move back the clock and to foster a slow but progressive return to the psychic stages of childhood and infancy. Inexorably, touched off by the total dependency of the confined individual, there comes about a gradual decay of those elements in the personality which have won through to maturity, and most detained persons tend to move back psychologically upon their own timelines, abandoning one by one whatever independent qualities and characteristics accompanied them through the prison gates. Like some vampirous creature, prison literally drains its wards of all that makes for maturity. Fed, clothed, housed, robbed of all independence of thought and action, told what to do and where to go, all vestiges of adultism in the individual, in most cases, succumb to the disintegrating process."[2]

The negative effects are emphasized when the prisoner is facing a long term and an uncertain release date. The literature on prisons amply confirms these results of "prisonization" (the term suggested by Donald Clemmer).

Of course for certain seriously disturbed dangerous offenders, sentences of commitment must be for substantial terms. But if we have our eye on the goal of treatment, the long term should be the exception rather than the rule, or at least the long term (five years or more) should be a definite minority of sentences.

Is public security endangered by a pattern of shorter terms? The answer is clearly No, and it is a matter not of speculation but of current fact. There is the European experience. In this country in almost half the states the definite sentence is used predominantly, and in these states two-thirds of the prisoners are committed for terms of under five years. In the indeterminate sentence states two-thirds of the prisoners are committed for terms of five years and over. As late as 1951 fully 96 per cent of federal commitments (which are in the definite form) were for five years or less. There is no evidence whatsoever that the public is less secure in the definite sentence jurisdictions than in the indeterminate.

The unwholesome situation in sentencing is not new either as a problem or as discovery. The following was written thirty-five years ago:

> It is a matter of common knowledge that courts are imposing longer sentences than formerly. Where state laws have not required this, judges have exercised their own discretion or have been influenced by public opinion. In consequence, many prisoners are willing to take long chances to escape. Most significant is the remark of M. Liepman, professor of criminology at the University of Hamburg, who four years ago, on a tour of America, said: "Offenses that in England or Germany would have been punished by a maximum sentence of from one to five years in America resulted in terms of from thirty to forty years. In the prisons, men sentenced to long terms under these new conditions sit side by side with men who committed the same crimes, but whose sentences were many years shorter and the result is bitter discontent."[3]

A little over 100 years ago the Prison Association of New York conducted a national survey of sentences and reported as follows:

> Observation has convinced us that the discretionary power now confided to the judiciary is so exercised as to

> occasion great disparity of punishment for the same offense, and that convicts from one part of the state pay a greater penalty for their crimes than those from another. . . . But this inequality in the length of sentence is not perhaps so great an evil as the length of sentences themselves. This is a matter of vast importance both in its relation to the ends of justice and reformation of the convict. To those most familiar with prison discipline, it is apparent that in many prisons, and for many crimes, the period of confinement is too protracted.[4]

When we examine the facts of sentencing in the United States, the necessity for change becomes clear.

A Drastic Proposal

We are badly in need of a fundamental reversal in our sentencing practices, a reversal such as has occurred in other countries but not in this, a reversal which would turn principally on the length of terms, reducing those of over five years to a very small number.

The experience in the definite sentence states shows that the number of terms of more than five years can generally be reduced to a fraction of the number being committed for such terms in the other states. The testimony of wardens and directors of correction is that sentences are too long.

There is additional evidence. From time to time large groups of long-term prisoners are suddenly released years before the correctional authorities planned, sometimes as the result of court decisions. These releases have not caused unusual hurt to the community! The same is true of cases in which scandalously large numbers of prisoners received pardons through political favor or graft. No crime wave resulted! During World War II prisoners who would otherwise have been held for long terms were released for enlistment or war work, and their record was quite favorable.

On this and other evidence, I feel that the lessening of long terms, to the extent I have suggested, should be our goal. If we agree on it, suitable devices would not be at all hard to find. The one that I first proposed, in an article in 1956 and in the first edition of this book, was that terms be limited to five years, within which the judge could fix a lesser maximum term, but could not exceed it without his applying to an appellate court. The appellate court could increase the penalty to some term within the statutory limit for the offense. Parole provisions would be applicable to the sentences as they are now.

Since then, through the work of the Council of Judges of NCCD, great conceptual advances have been made in its Model Sentencing Act, published in 1963.

First: as indicated above, although I had suggested that only the appellate court could impose a sentence of over five years, I had suggested no criteria to guide it. The committee draft supplies these criteria. With marked precision, it defines a category of individuals suffering from severe personality disorder, guilty of a crime which inflicted or attempted to inflict serious bodily harm. Such an individual may be sentenced to a lengthy term. The act also defines racketeers as individuals subject to lengthy terms as dangerous offenders. If a defendant does not come within these criteria of dangerousness, the sentencing judge may impose at most a five-year term (if he does not use probation, suspended sentence, etc.).

Second: I had not suggested a procedure to guide either the sentencing judge or the appellate court, counting on the resources usually available, principally presentence investigations by probation staff. The Model Sentencing Act, where personality disorder is a necessary finding, provides for remand to a diagnostic facility for study and report, together with a mandatory presentence investigation. Upon these the sentencing judge may commit the defendant to a long term if he makes the necessary findings.

Let us look at the plan's procedure of having a defendant face alternative dispositions depending on findings related to seriousness of the charge and the defendant's personality. A precedent is found in the juvenile courts. There the common jurisdictional level is to under eighteen years of age, but the usual provision (and it is so in the Standard Juvenile Court Act) is that courts may transfer children sixteen years of age or older for a criminal proceeding, and in some jurisdictions may so transfer even younger children. The provision enables imposition of a penalty greater than is available in the juvenile courts, where the commitments must terminate at the age of twenty-one.

Another precedent is found in the New York Youthful Offender Law. Under it a youth charged with an offense (other than an offense punishable by death or life imprisonment) must be considered for youthful offender procedure, and upon adjudication as a youthful offender may be committed (if probation or some other disposition is not used) for an indefinite term not to exceed three years. This is applicable to *all* offenses except capital or life imprisonment cases, and the limitation of three years applies to all youthful offenders. The law provides, however, that the judge may transfer for criminal proceeding if the greater penalties applicable under the penal law generally are indicated for the particular defendant. Some of the youth authority acts are similar.

For adult offenders the MSA sets the ordinary limit of sentences at five years. Within this term parole would operate without any minimum. To put the ordinary limits at, say, five or ten years would be an improvement over what we have, and yet it would encourage the notion that ten years is a term which accords with a correctional program of rehabilitation. It does not. The purpose of the proposal is to make it a strongly evident policy that a sentence in excess of the proposed ordinary limit would be appropriate only for extraordinary cases.

Out of these technical precedents, when applied to sentencing of adult offenders, a change of great significance emerges: for the first time (so far as their writer knows) a plan is available that provides for determination of sentence on the basis of (1) the defendant's make up, his likely threat in the future, (2) but varying not merely according to the offense, but whether the crime was one of grave harm to the person of a victim.

Could not judges achieve this reform voluntarily? No doubt some judges now impose few sentences of over five years. Others would accept such a policy and welcome it. There are others who, having great faith in long sentences, would resist the new policy. They—and other judges in cases they consider appropriate—could apply the test of the statute whenever they thought a long term warranted. But the plan proposed would allow long terms only after more consideration than they receive today, keeping them to as few as necessary, consistent with the needs of public protection and within an underlying policy of community treatment of offenders. The plan adds a check and balance on long terms, through a procedure relying on the judge's judgment supported by the information without which he should not sentence.

The plan would indeed be a radical change in American correction. But it offers a simple and, I believe, a sound way of transforming our penology, which now relies so heavily on prisons that we are saddled with expensive institutions for whose hordes of prisoners no true treatment programs can be undertaken. There are very few prisons in America to which this statement does not apply.

Is It Practicable?

What objections can there be to such a plan? Probably the principal objection would be that the public would not be safe. The second might be that the deterrent value of imprisonment would be lost, with a consequent increase in crime.

The first objection: lessening of public safety. That long terms are a protection to the public is a dangerous illusion. Most long terms today are imposed without sufficient consideration, through mechanical application or because of mandatory laws. Most long term prisoners are not dangerous individuals. The real protection to society comes in *careful selection* of defendants to receive long terms. This does not exist today, by and large. It would be regular sentencing procedure under our proposal. The great majority of long-term prisoners were originally, or become so after service of a substantial part of their terms, relatively harmless. Oddly, many of them not only are a menace, but are pitiful individuals who must rot out their lives in the most expensive unrealistic way we can think of. M. R. King, Superintendent of the California Medical Facility at Terminal Island, spoke on the subject at the 1953 Congress of Correction. He pointed out that as of June 30, 1953, California correctional institutions held nearly 13,000 inmates, 1,438 of them forty-five to fifty-five years old and 726 fifty-five years of age and over. He stated that older inmates often find themselves out of place and "*unwanted*" in institutions whose programs are geared for younger prisoners and that the great majority are no longer security risks, some indeed being so slow and infirm that they have difficulty in keeping up with the lines. At times they must be fed in their cells or admitted to the hospital for special care.

In 1959 New York's prisons held 1,000 prisoners 65 years of age or over, housed mainly in maximum security facilities. The New York Prison Association in its 1959 report to the legislature stated: "This housing is costly and in some instances the physical layouts impose a hardship on the older prisoners because of conditions of health or various infirmities." It cited as examples Sing Sing and Clinton prisons, whose long passageways and stairways were a hardship on these prisoners.

The second objection: loss of deterrence. Most correctional people agree that the deterrence in our penal law lies not in the long terms that may be imposed, but in the *certainty* of arrest and punishment. If the history of penology teaches us anything, it is that the concept of harsh punishment is unsound. We have abandoned torture as punishment, and to a considerable extent given up capital punishment, not only because they are inhumane, but because they are ineffective. Can we really believe that a person will be encouraged to commit crime because his punishment will be "only" a five-year maximum term, and perhaps more? The thought is absurd.

Are the important racketeers *now* deterred by the threat of a long term? Of course not. They—and our citizens generally—have become cynical about the failure of law enforcement to control rackets. That failure has little, if anything, to do with long or short terms.

A pathetic illustration is the report of a Congressional committee on narcotics. Condemning the law which allowed first offenders under the narcotics laws to be placed on probation, the report recommended not only that terms be increased but that probation be barred, even for first offenders. Did the committee expect these penalties to deter the racketeers? Not at all! The report reads: "This possibility of suspension of probation for the first offender has resulted in the big time operators who have previous narcotic convictions remaining in the background. They operate through antisocially inclined persons who have never been convicted of a narcotic violation and who are willing to risk apprehension, particularly in those areas of the country where the judges are inclined to impose minimum or suspended sentences and where probation is easily obtained." Stiffer penalties, no probation—for the dupes.

The big lack in combating organized crime lies in the failure of law enforcement, not in sentencing. Probably new strength is needed in the definitions of racketeering crimes. However the Model Sentencing Act draft takes a big step forward in public protection, as far as it can be taken in sentencing, by including the racketeer as one category of dangerous offender, subject to a long term. This is possible because, as already noted, the long term may be imposed where existing codes authorize only limited penalties; length of term is not governed by the crime but by the dangerousness of the defendant, established by the presentence investigation and other data.

If I find no merit or obstacle in the objections to the proposal, what do I consider to be the special merit or advantage of the plan? Our typical huge state prisons have too many prisoners to be dealt with on anything but a mass basis, and they cannot possibly obtain sufficient professional staff to deal with such large numbers of inmates on a treatment basis. With the discharge of many long-term prisoners who now clutter up the institutions, prisons would markedly decrease in population, under the proposed plan, to the point where they could become truly correctional. We could then begin to realize the promising potential of short-term institutional treatment. Certainly the danger of prison riots would be greatly lessened. And the disturbed, dangerous offenders, sentenced to long terms, in number would be so much less than the numbers in the maximum security institutions of today that a truly therapeutic institution would be feasible.

I believe that the plan would increase the use of probation and bring about the kind of penology for which we have been hoping for a long time, a penology relying principally on treatment in the community. It should be a matter of deep concern that although probation has existed for 100 years and now is used in every state, it has *not* had the impact on our prison penology that we hoped for, and imprisonment is being used now more that cver. In 1846 the ratio of state prisoners to the general population was one in 2,436.[5] Today it is one in 1,000. In England the ratio has altered in exactly the opposite direction. The number of prisoners in custody in England in 1930 was less than half the number in 1857, although the population of England was twice as large.[6]

The United States experienced a significant (although temporary) alteration in prison population during World War II. The great need for manpower forced parole boards, legislators, and judges to be more liberal and sentences were markedly reduced. During the early forties the prison populations dropped markedly; but the renewal of "normal" policies has steadily restocked them, and each year now we reach new high points in prison population.

With the general reduction of terms, sentencing judges would rely more on probation and suspended sentence without probation. Some of the money saved by the reduced cost of prisons could well be spent on probation personnel, more professional treatment personnel in the now smaller institutions, and additional clinical facilities, including the needed diagnostic centers for operation of the Model Sentencing Act plan. With all that, we would still be saving money, and the money spent would be used more constructively.

With this proposal in mind, let us examine the facts of sentencing in America, particularly as related to the problem of long terms.

We know that sentences vary considerably from one jurisdiction to another, even where the sentencing system is the same. Even within a single jurisdiction sentencing practices vary; and they differ sharply even within a single court where there is more than one judge. Sentencing policies vary according to the general community attitude, which differs in place and time, and according to the treatment resources available. But certain factors operate generally.

The Penal Code and Long Terms

Throughout our history the pattern of penal legislation has been dominated by a steady increase of penalties which may be imposed, and, along with it, penalties which are actually imposed. Exceptions to the upward line occasionally occur, but they are unusual and have not permanently altered the pattern.

The following was written a generation ago:

> In general the potential penalty authorized by the law is more severe now than it was thirty years ago. The penalties

> of 1,932 offenses listed in the penal codes of eight states [Connecticut, Georgia, Indiana, Michigan, Missouri, Nebraska, Nevada, and South Dakota] were different in 1930 than they had been in 1900. Of these alterations 68.9 per cent were increases in severity of the maximum or minimum or definite penalty and only 31.1 per cent were decreases. Of the changes in penalties for the more serious offenses alone, 74.7 per cent were increases in severity. The severity of penalties for serious offenses must therefore have increased more frequently than for minor offenses. In 1880 the maximum penalty for carrying concealed weapons in the median state in the United States was $110 fine and 6.8 months imprisonment; in 1930 it had increased to a fine of $367 and 14.4 months imprisonment. Twenty-seven states have special laws on armed robbery, of which sixteen were enacted before 1900, one in 1907, one in 1913, and nine from 1923 to 1929. The penalty in such laws enacted in the last decade is much more severe than in the earlier laws. If the new laws and amendments enacted prior to 1900 regarding armed robbery are compared with the new laws and amendments enacted in the period 1922-1929, it is found that only 12 per cent of the earlier laws had a minimum penalty as high as five years imprisonment, while 40 per cent in the later laws had this much as a minimum.[7]

Unfortunately this development did not characterize only the period discussed. Our legislatures today are following the same pattern of important increases in terms which may be imposed; reducing the term is extremely rare.

The "habitual offender" statutes, which took hold a generation ago, lend greatly—and unwisely—to the current pattern of long terms. The defects and ill results of these acts are too numerous to discuss here.

Results of "Indeterminate Sentence"

The introduction of the indeterminate sentence has also resulted in increased terms.

Neither "indeterminate" nor "definite" is particularly descriptive of the form of sentence to which it is applied. The indeterminate sentence has developed in two principal forms in the United States:

1. Under most indeterminate sentence statutes, the judge fixes a minimum sentence and a maximum term, both within the limits

specified in the statute for the particular crime. The minimum term governs parole eligibility.

2. In eight or nine states, the court has no discretion as to the maximum, being required to fix it at the maximum provided by law for the offense. In these states the minimum may be fixed by law, or it may be within the discretion of the court or (in Washington) a board, or there may be no minimum term.

Under a "definite sentence" the commitment is for a term fixed by the judge at some definite figure, which may not exceed the maximum term authorized under the statute. Parole eligibility under such a sentence occurs when a percentage of the term—for example, in the federal system, one-third—has been served.

In an article pubished in 1949[8] I made the point that the indeterminate sentence states long terms were predominant, whereas in the definite sentence jurisdictions the predominant terms were short. For the purposes of designation I described a commitment of five years or over as long and a commitment of under five years as short. The statistics used were the 1945 commitments reported in "Prisoners in State and Federal Prisons and Reformatories, 1945," published by the United States Census Bureau. In that year, sentences of under five years were imposed in 67 per cent of the definite sentence cases (for the whole country), and in only 24 per cent of the maximum-indeterminate sentences. Excluding death sentences, sentences of five years and over comprised 76 per cent of all the maximum-indefinite sentences, whereas definite sentences of five years and over were only 33 per cent of the total.

Later figures became available in 1955, in the National Prisoner Statistics, published by the Federal Bureau of Prisons, presenting data for 1951. The range of sentences imposed is similar to the range of the 1945 sentences, although there is a reduction in the ratio of long indeterminate terms in 1951. For 1951, sentences of under five years were imposed in 68 per cent of the definite sentence cases and in 33 per cent of the maximum-indeterminate sentences. Sentences of five years and over comprised 67 per cent of all the maximum-indeterminate sentences, whereas definite sentences of five years and over were only 32 per cent of the total.

COMMITMENTS TO STATE INSTITUTIONS, 1951, BY MAXIMUM TERMS

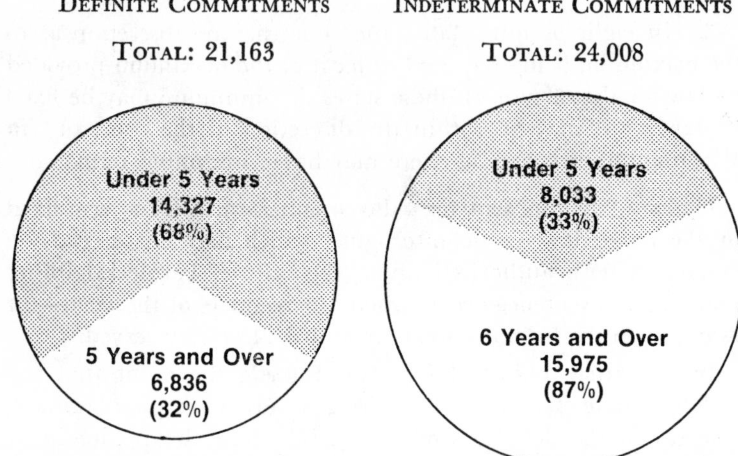

The substantial disparity in sentencing between the two systems is obvious. Approximately two-thirds of definite sentences are "short terms"—under five years—whereas two-thirds of the maximum-indeterminate sentences are "long terms"—five years and over.

But, to be valid, the comparison must be based on the *time actually served* under each form of sentence. We have classified the terms on the basis of their maximums and, of course, many prisoners—under both sentences—are released before the maximum. The 1945 statistics showed that the time served under a definite sentence of a particular length (say, seven years) coincided quite closely with the time served under indeterminate sentence, the maximum of which was the same (seven). This was true for sentences of up to ten years. On sentences of over ten years the individual sentenced to a so-called definite term actually served substantially more time than the one sentenced to a corresponding maximum under an indeterminate sentence. Although the 1951 data are more irregular (perhaps because the tables are set up somewhat differently), essentially the results are similar. That is, for most maximum sentences (definite and indeterminate), of two, four, five, etc., and up to ten years, about the same length of time is actually served under either form of commitment. When the maximum terms are over ten years, the

MEDIAN TIME SERVED BY FELONY PRISONERS BEFORE FIRST RELEASE FROM STATE INSTITUTIONS, BY TYPE AND LENGTH OF SENTENCE, 1951; AND NUMBERS OF COMMITMENTS, BY LENGTH OF MAXIMUM TERM. (Source: *National Prisoner Statistics*)

Length of Definite and of Maximum of Indeterminate Sentences	*Median Number of Months Served*		*Number of Commitments*	
	Definite	*Indeterminate*	*Definite*	*Indeterminate*
Months:				
6-11	5	5	707	111
12	9	9	2,884	658
13-23	13	12	1,158	693
Years:				
2	16	13	4,959	1,754
Over 2-under 3	20	22	327	274
3	24	19	2,750	3,420
Over 3-under 5	24	25	1,542	1,123
5	31	24	2,604	5,086
Over 5-under 7	36	36	714	627
7	54	28	323	1,268
Over 7-under 10	46	45	398	426
10	43	32	772	3,385
Over 10-under 15	56	36	439	586
15	65	24	258	1,484
Over 15-under 20	93	86	75	99
20	85	28	220	1,788
Over 20-under 25	90	45	102	146
25	101	48	92	384
Over 25-under 30	113	103	13	10
30	117	85	49	245
Over 30-under 50	144	140	71	140
50-less than life	161	96	70	96
life	128	124	636	205
Totals			21,163	24,008

indeterminate sentence prisoner serves substantially less time than the definite sentence prisoner under the same maximum term. Excluding life terms (which are inaccurately listed, as we shall show), 70 per cent of definite sentence prisoners actually served two years or less; 57 per cent of indeterminate sentence prisoners actually served two years or less.

In the "Number of Commitments" columns the number of life terms listed as definite sentences is surpisingly high as compared with numbers of other long definite terms or with the number of indeterminate life terms. The 1950 figures are quite different—768 definite life terms, 865 indeterminate life terms. But in any case many of the 636 life terms are in fact imposed in indeterminate sentence states! This is evident from the more detailed data in the 1950 report (in which see tables 29 and 30). The situation compares with the practice in the National Prisoner Statistics of listing executions as "definite sentences." "Definite" indeed, but in a different sense. The tables are of commitments in definite and indeterminate form; executions are not commitments. I suspect that many sentences in the definite sentence column which show long periods of time served are actually sentences in a state that has an indeterminate sentence system and are designated as "definite" because they carry no eligibility for parole. (What a confusion of terms!)

The table refers only to state commitments, not federal. If the federal sentences (which are in the "definite" form) were included, the emphasis on short terms would be even greater. In 1951 there were 11,254 commitments in federal courts. As we have already observed, *fully 96 per cent of the commitments were for five years or less.* Only eight life terms were imposed. Nevertheless, the Federal Bureau of Prisons is concerned with the increase in its long-term prisoners. A recent report contains the following statement:

> Another factor contributing to the growth of the prison population is the tendency towards the imposition of longer sentences for violation of federal statutes. In 1930, for example, only 735 prisoners were committed to federal institutions with sentences of five years or more. In 1949 the number of such commitments stood at 920, but since then the number has steadily increased—to 1,791 in 1955, or by 95 per cent. As the commitments of long-term prisoners continue to increase, such prisoners tend to accumulate in the institutional population. Thus, from 1952 to 1955, prisoners received in federal institutions with sentences of five years or more increased from 1,340 to 1,791, or by 451; but at the same time the accumulation of such long-sentence prisoners in the year-end population increased from 5,312 in 1952 to 6,703 in 1955, or by 1,391. This combination of more serious offenders, a larger proportion of younger men, longer sentences, and the overcrowding created by increasing population creates a portentous situation and aggravates the problems of administration.

It is clear that no matter what other factors govern sentence length, the inevitable result of the indeterminate sentence is that sentences of over five years will strongly predominate; and in a definite sentence state sentences of under five years will strongly predominate.

Why is this so? I suggest the following theory: First, the definite sentence is the common-law form (although parole has been added to it), and perhaps the judges sentencing in this fashion have been less affected by the continued trend to longer and longer sentences. Second, the usual form of the indeterminate sentence is for the judge to fix both a minimum and a maximum term. The awareness that the individual will be released between those two limits has encouraged judges to set the upper limit quite high. In other words, the judge is sentencing on the basis of his ordinary sentence, to which is added an additional term for parole. This has been observed in a number of studies. Courtlandt C. Van Vechten wrote:

> While parole was originally conceived of as a means of shortening the period of incarceration of deserving inmates who could be trusted with conditional freedom, it has become, in actual practice, a mechanism by which something is *added on* to prison sentences. The universal conclusion of studies of time served *in prison* under the indeterminate sentence laws and time served under the old definite sentence laws in the same jurisdictions has been that the indeterminate sentence laws in the same jurisdiction have very materially increased the time served within the walls.[9]

There is probably another reason. As I have said, the trend in America has been to lengthen terms. I suspect that often the indeterminate sentence has been adopted not only for the reasons advanced by the original theorists who advocated it, but precisely *because* it was known to the legislators that its effect was to increase terms of imprisonment.

Long Terms Under the Definite Sentence

As we have seen, on sentences of ten years and under, prisoners serve approximately the same amount of time measured by their maximum sentence, under either form (remembering always that two-thirds of definite sentences are for under five years, whereas two-thirds of indeterminate sentences are for five years and over).

However, on sentences of ten years and over, prisoners under the definite form of commitment serve substaintially longer periods of time than under corresponding maximum sentences of the indeterminate form.

What is the reason? I had never encountered any explanation, and in fact had hardly thought about it until it was stressed by my colleague, Milton Rector. I suggest the following: The indeterminate sentences may be called "maximum sentences" in the sense that the judge is fixing a minimum-maximum in which the upper limit is higher than it is under the definite sentence, because the judge is taking into account that he is fixing a parole period also, and for the other reasons already stated. Of course, in the eight or nine states in which sentences are automatically fixed at the maximum provided by law, the concept of "maximum sentencing" is not only a tendency but a rigid requirement.

The indeterminate sentences, therefore, have a certain likeness or equality—that of being "maximum"—which does not apply to the definite sentences. In other words, a judge under a definite sentence system "means it" more than a judge under a indeterminate sentence system. The parole boards are aware of this and therefore while the longer-term indeterminate sentence prisoners spend more time in prison under their sentence, the boards are probably compensating for the excessively long maximums. Under the definite sentence commitments, where the psychology of "maximum sentencing" does not prevail, it may well be that the parole boards are somewhat more responsive to the maximum terms fixed by the judge than are the boards under indeterminate sentences.

In any event, the large number of sentences over ten years under both systems of sentencing—in fact, the huge number of sentences over five years—is the heart of the matter.

Question of Parole Flexibility

We have seen that parole boards can and do compensate for the extremely high maximum terms imposed under the indeterminate sentence. How far does this policy extend? As the question is often put: Aren't the parole boards more liberal under the indeterminate sentence? Aren't they more flexible?

Part of the answer has already been given, but it requires repetition. For most sentences of ten years or less, parole boards are *not* more liberal in the indeterminate sentence states than in the definite sentences states. The statistics (see table, page 123) show that prisoners under either form of sentence serve almost the same amount of time, according to the maximum term. Then is not the effect of the sentencing systems the same? No. It is necessary to repeat also: Two-thirds of the individuals sentenced under indeterminate sentences receive maximum terms of five years or more; whereas in the definite sentence states two-thirds receive sentences of *under* five years.

On the other hand the table is evidence that on maximum sentences of ten years and up to twenty-five years the indeterminate sentence prisoner is released substantially earlier than the definite sentence prisoner. We have already suggested that part of this behavior is a "holding action" against the many long "indeterminate" terms. It cannot be taken as evidence of greater parole flexibility. We know from study of state data that a substantial percentage of indeterminate sentences have an impossibly narrow range—three to four years, or four to five, even seventeen or nineteen to twenty.

By contrast, the most common formula where the definite commitment is used is for parole eligibility to occur when one-third of the term has been served. Furthermore, among the ten states which in general fix no minimum term—that it, which thereby provide the greatest flexibility for the use of parole—all but three are definite sentence states.

Persistence of a Cliché

The basic fact is that the indeterminate sentence form results in commitments longer than those under the definite sentence form. Furthermore, the indeterminate sentence system does not provide a more flexible setting for parole than does the definite sentence; it is less flexible.

With such an outcome, so far removed from the ideals and expectations of its early advocates, why is the indeterminate sentence still advocated? But perhaps it would be more fruitful to ask, "How strong in fact *is* the advocacy of the indeterminate sentence?" In *writing,* it is almost unanimously endorsed. The picture is quite different in practice. It is generally said that the indeterminate sentence has been endorsed to the extent that about three-quarters of the states use it. This is a distorted way of viewing sentencing practice. The way in which *National Prisoner Statistics* now refers to the forms of sentence is more realistic. The 1955 report states that "twenty-seven of the states and the District of Columbia have predominantly indeterminate-sentence systems, and twenty-one states retain predominantly definite-sentence systems." In other words, in practice the states are not far from evenly divided.

But it is odd that some of the best writers in the field make the astonishing error of stating that the indeterminate sentence facilitates parole, or even that parole depends on the indeterminate sentence. Of course it does not; every state has parole, the definite as well as the indeterminate states.

Why, then, the persistence of the view that the indeterminate sentence form is superior? One reason is the limited awareness of the actual effect of the indeterminate sentence, that of lengthening terms of commitment. I have asked a number of correctional people what effect they thought the indeterminate sentence had on length of terms. Most had the impression that it shortens terms, precisely the opposite of the actual effect.

Also, the original theory of the indeterminate-sentence—that it provided a superior mechanism for rehabilitation or that it was necessary for parole—continued to be repeated in spite of its increasing distance from the facts. No doubt, also, there are judges whose philosophy of correction is simply punishment; they know the indeterminate sentence is punitive and they prefer it for that reason. We have already referred to the same reason for legislative support of the indeterminate sentence.

More Effective Form of Commitment

Because of the common use of minimum terms, and because of its resultant pattern of long terms, the indeterminate sentence system as it has developed is destructive to many prisoners. The judge fixing a minimum-maximum sentence is, in part, controlling parole, and as we have seen, the effect is to limit parole flexibility. Also, because the judge controls parole eligibility under an indeterminate sentence, and since judges vary in their concept of treatment, punishment, and parole, there is a greater inequality of sentencing under the indeterminate sentence system than under the definite sentence. Under the form of indeterminate sentence in which the commitment is fixed automatically at the maximum provided by law, the judge exercises no discretion whatsoever.

By contrast, the judge who fixes a definite sentence is serving a clear-cut, important, and proper purpose. He does not control parole, because parole eligibility is governed by statute. Instead, he determines the outside limit of imprisonment, keeping in mind not only the constitutional protection of the prisoner against excessive punishment, but also his treatment prognosis. The presentence investigation is a tool of the judge in making such a decision. By *exercising* his discretion, rather than by abandoning or compromising it, as in the forms of indeterminate commitment, the judge is building toward equality of sentencing as well as contributing toward a plan of rehabilitation.

Indeed, paradoxical as it seems, a definite sentence—that is, a judge-fixed maximum but no minimum—together with a flexible parole authority probably better serves the goals of the advocates of the indeterminate sentence than does the indeterminate sentence in the forms it has developed in the United States. It provides greater individualization, does not overload our prisons with long destructive terms, does not hobble the parole board with long minimum terms. As I said in the earlier article:

> It is assumed that a competent, adequate probation staff would serve the court. A definite sentence law gives the judge greater responsibility to fix a sentence than the indeterminate sentence law, and the allocated responsibility is one of the things needed to avoid the automatic long terms. A parole law affording complete discretion, coupled with a definite sentence system, more truly meets the intent of the indeterminate sentence idea than an indeterminate sentence system, even with a flexible parole law. A four-year definite sentence combined with complete parole authority is in effect an indeterminate sentence with no fixed minimum but with a maximum of four years fixed by a court which knows it is responsible for considering the individual defendant in fixing that maximum.

Although I still prefer the definite sentence form with no minimum term, it is still true that even in the definite sentence states the sentencing form can stand improvement. It is still true that there, as well as in the indeterminate sentence states, far too many long terms are imposed. Out of 21,163 definite sentences imposed in 1951, there were slightly over 4,000 sentences of five years and under ten years, and 2,800 sentences of ten years and over. Out of 24,008 indeterminate sentences imposed in 1951, 7,400 were for five years and under ten years, and 8,500 were for ten years and over. Furthermore, on terms of over ten years, the definite sentence prisoner earns his release much later than the indeterminate sentence prisoner with the same maximum terms. Evidently both forms of sentence require marked improvement.

But the basic reform is that of the Model Sentencing Act, which unfortunately has not been adopted by any legislature to date. Besides the advantages of community treatment for the nondangerous offender, a therapeutic institution for dangerous offenders, there would be other advantages. Parole boards could more easily deal in treatment, free of the tyranny of rigid sentences and the need to save prisoners from the worst of long terms. The indeterminate-definite sentence controversy would become a matter of history.

The essence of the findings—*findings,* because I have been dealing with the *facts* of American penology—is that *today* the superior form of sentence (call it what you will) is a judge-fixed maximum, within the maximum allowed by law; no minimum term; and early parole eligibility so that a parole authority will have substantial latitude in which to work. But the definite sentence in itself, like the forms of indeterminate, does not meet the current needs. We need to reduce our unduly long terms for the great majority of defendants, as the MSA proposes.

I should like to refer to an analogy. In the years since the end of World War II a remarkable and greatly encouraging trend has occurred in the country's mental hospitals. In the face of a mental hospital population that had steadily risen for years, creating a health problem of major dimensions, rather suddenly the rise was halted, and in fact in some states the number of inmates in the mental hospitals actually dropped.

What was the reason? The principal ingredient in the event seems to be the introduction and widespread use of tranquilizing drugs. It makes patients more tractable and eases the relationship between patients and hospital personnel. It facilitates other forms of treatment, and thus in turn enables releases to be made earlier than would have otherwise been considered safe.

Would it not be wonderful if such a remedy were found for our prisons and their populations, so that the increase in the numbers of prisoners could be halted or even reversed! We need not look far; the remedy is there to be used. It needs only courageous enough legislators or public officials, unless the public can be educated and aroused to require that it be done.

Professor Henry Weihofen has written, "It is time we Americans realized that we have probably the most ferocious penal policy in the whole world." It is a galling accusation, but evidently true; and it is time. The quality and character of a culture are deeply affected by its major social institutions, including its penology. A callous penology is not only the product of a culture, it is also a brutalizing element in that culture. And so a culture which can replace an institutional penology by a community treatment penology is making an over all advance, and is not merely improving the lot only of criminals. This, too, I see as the inspiring reward of a change in sentencing policy such as has been suggested.

Notes

1 Simon E. Sobeloff, "Appellate Review of Criminal Sentences" (*American Bar Association Journal,* January, 1955).

2 "Sexual Behavior in Penal Institutions," Albert Deutsch, ed., *Sex Habits of American Men* (Prentice-Hall, 1948).

3 Clayton J. Ettinger, *The Problem of Crime* (Long and Smith, 1932).

4 *Third Report of the Prison Association of New York* (1847).

5 *Third Report of the Prison Association of New York* (1847), which included a survey of the number of convicts in thirteen states; see p. 358 of the report. See also Table CLXXIX, "Statistical View of the U. S., A Compendium of the Seventh Census."

6 An excellent account of how it happened is contained in *The Sutherland Papers,* the chapter entitled "The Decreasing Prison Population of England" (Indiana University Press, 1956). In England, Sutherland makes clear, "the decrease was not a direct result of a reduction in the general crime rate, but rather of changes in penal policies."

7 "Crime and Punishment," in *Recent Social Trends in the United States,* Vol. 2 (McGraw-Hill, 1933).

8 Sol Rubin, "The Indeterminate Sentence—Success or Failure?" (NCCD, *Focus,* March, 1949, p. 47).

9 Courtlandt C. Van Vechten, "The Parole Violation Rate" (*Journal of Criminal Law and Criminology,* January-February, 1937, p. 638).

References

This chapter is based on an article which originally appeared in the October, 1956 issue of the NPPA *Journal,* an issue entirely devoted to the subject of sentencing. The report on prison riots referred to at the beginning of the chapter is entitled "A Statement Concerning Causes, Preventive Measures, and Methods of Controlling Prison Riots and Disturbances," published in 1953. The quotation from Professor Weihofen at page 143 is from his book, *The Urge to Punish* (Farrar, Strauss, and Cudahy, 1956).

The United States government took a big step forward on behalf of scientific sentencing when it passed a law (in 1958) authorizing institutes and joint councils on sentencing under the auspices of the Judicial Conference of the U. S. The objectives of the institutes include the formulation of policies, standards, and criteria in sentencing. (The Act is Public Law 85-752).

Chapter 9

The Convict's Lost Status and Readjustment

Under our law an individual's rights may be taken away only by due process of law. Accordingly, it is also a basic tenet that the criminal laws, which authorize rights to be taken away from convicted individuals, are to be strictly construed. Punishments imposed may be only those allowed by law—usually imprisonment (which may be defined in terms of a right, deprivation of the right to liberty) ; fine (deprivation of a right to property) ; death (deprivation of the right to life) ; and certain others which our civilization accepts and our codes impose. Some barbarous punishments formerly imposed on persons charged with or convicted of crime are no longer allowed.

The foregoing punishments (lost rights) are imposed individually, more or less selectively, by a judge, or, less often, by a jury, through the sentence which follows conviction. But other rights are lost upon conviction of crime that are not referred to in the sentence and do not require the act of the judge. They are lost automatically upon conviction, or they are lost by act of some administrative agency or official, not the convicting court. They are mainly various rights that the unconvicted citizen exercises as a matter of course, referred to in the laws as "civil rights," and less importantly, certain property rights. In brief, the statutes declare that a person *convicted* of a felony, or, under some statutes, a person *committed* on conviction for felony, loses these rights. But—and it is important to remember—this is true in most states *but not all.* In Michigan, for example, none of these statutes exist; a conviction does not result in the loss of civil rights.[1] The number of states in which a particular right is lost varies from a large number for certain rights, to only a few for others.

The Rights Lost

Property rights are in general unaffected by a conviction. Usually a convict may take, hold and dispose of property by will, deed, or other method. But property and other rights are affected by the power to institute or defend suits. Where civil rights are suspended because of a commitment, the prisoner may not sue, although he may defend a suit against him. (However, he does not lose the right to a writ of habeas corpus to test the legality of his cutody.) It is hard to see why a prisoner should not retain the right to sue. It is no greater protection to the state or the public to limit suits. In fact, since almost all prisoners are sooner or later released, if suits were allowed the prisoner's affairs on release would be in better order, hence his rehabilitation would be assisted.

The loss of the right to vote is a statutory penalty for conviction of felony in three-fourths of the states. Should a convicted person retain the right to vote? Allowing a person with a criminal record to vote is no threat to the state, and may be a help in rehabilitation, affording the individual a greater feeling of restoration as a full-fledged citizen. Very likely little attempt is made to enforce this law. The right to vote would have an especially constructive meaning to a prisoner, who has few activities indeed that place him in touch with the world outside; this lack is destructive of morale and personal confidence.

Should a person who has been convicted be disqualified for jury duty? Any argument for such a position seems remote, and only in half a dozen states does a conviction so disqualify an individual. Although if a witness has a criminal record it may generally be used to affect his credibility, nevertheless the right of an individual convicted of a felony to testify is in almost all states preserved.

Conviction of felony and sentence to imprisonment is a ground for divorce under the statutes in 35 states. In several of these states the commitment is a ground only if a certain minimum term of imprisonment is imposed. In the remaining dozen or so states, the conviction is not a ground for divorce. Should sentence to imprisonment be a ground for divorce? It may be noted that the rationale of the statute is "practical" rather than moral; it is the imprisonment, not the conviction of a crime, that is the ground for divorce, presumably because the marital state is disrupted by separation. But the separation is temporary. The majority of prisoners sentenced to a state prison actually serve only a few years, or less. They receive their discharge through termination of sentence, good time allowance, parole, or clemency. To make their imprisonment a ground for divorce is obviously a harsh punishment without parallel in the law of divorce. An equally harsh family penalty is a provision, such as New York's, where under the statute the convicted felon loses his natural rights as a parent: assent to adoption is not required of a parent who has been deprived of civil rights through imprisonment, even though since released.

Statutes in some seventeen states provide that a defendant sentenced to a life term is deemed "civilly dead." In seven states the statutes provide that his property shall be distributed as though he were naturally dead. Civil death dissolves the convict's marriage, as would a natural death (although the prisoner's obligation to support wife and child continues). Except for the rights of a wife remaining, the children are subject to adoption as though the prisoner were naturally dead. Of all the laws depriving offenders of civil rights, this is the most backward, thoroughly outmoded and without value. If a life term meant permanent incarceration, the rule might be debated. But it does not. Most life term prisoners are eligible for parole and in practice often obtain parole. In any event any prisoner may be pardoned, and thus return to the community. The community derives no advantage or security by depriving the former prisoner of his rights.

Other penalties may also be imposed as the consequence of a conviction, again not through the process of sentencing but by a later decision, and typically not by the judge but by administrative officials or agencies. Within the general police power, the state legislatures may regulate the issuance of licenses of various kinds. Thus it requires that an individual meet certain conditions to be admitted to practice law or other professions. In the same way it may require the disbarment of an attorney who is convicted of a felony or misdemeanor that involves moral turpitude, and there are many such statutes.[2] Similarly, statutes in all states have established regulatory administrative boards to grant and revoke licenses to practice medicine. Generally, but not always, the authority is placed in a public board; in some jurisdictions the authority is conferred on medical societies. Although under the statutes conviction of crime, particularly one involving moral turpitude, is usually regarded as sufficient ground for revocation of a license, the statutes are not uniform in making revocation automatic; in some a hearing is required and the board has discretion. The other professions are similarly regulated.

The right to practice a trade or business, the exercise of certain individual rights of citizens, such as a license to drive a car, possess a weapon, or to fish, are often regulated by statute. The statutes vary from state to state, and may authorize administrative boards to revoke, or to deny to persons with a criminal record, licenses such as to sell or deal in liquor or beer, practice beauty culture or barbering, engage in nursing or real estate, serve as private detective or special policeman, undertaker or embalmer, notary public, insurance adjuster, etc.

What weight should administrative agencies be authorized to give to a record of a criminal conviction in the consideration of licenses or privileges? Should an individual convicted of a sex offense, or embezzlement, be denied a license to drive an automobile? For this particular license almost always the offense that serves as a barrier is an offense related to the use of the license, such as driving while intoxicated.

Should an engineer or accountant lose his license if he has been convicted of driving while intoxicated, or of negligent manslaughter by auto, or assault? There are two questions to ask: Is the public endangered by the grant of such a license to such a criminal? Second, does the conviction have any bearing on the qualification of an individual to perform the work? The administrative agency passes on the qualifications of an individual, and should not impose penal sanctions. A license should be granted where on the basis of reasonable tests or other proper qualification, an individual is competent to perform the duties and responsibilities of the license. If the criminal conviction is relevant, it should be weighed; if it is irrelevant, it should not.

Should a convicted burglar be permitted to practice medicine if qualified? If the conviction occurred at sixteen, should a youth be denied a professional career for the rest of his life? If the conviction has no bearing on the employment, the public is not safeguarded by barring such licenses to persons convicted of crime. Compare the fact that corporations rendering vital services may be conducted by persons who have a record of criminal convictions. Such persons are not barred and the corporate franchises are customarily not lost, even where the conviction is a violation involving the basic function of the business or service (fraudulent advertising by an advertising agency or company; adulteration of food by a food products corporation, etc.).

It is not only as the consequence of a conviction that an individual loses certain civil liberties. Loss of rights may also result from an arrest which does not eventuate in a conviction. Rights may be lost upon administrative discretion exercised under vague, loose statutes. For example, the licensing and employment statutes refer not only to convictions (as the occasion for denial), but (sometimes) to "disgraceful conduct" or some similar vaguely worded ground for denial. Under these provisions a record of an arrest may be ground for denying a license or a job.

Correctional agencies also act upon arrests which do not ripen into conviction. An arrest may be referred to in a presentence investigation (the statute in Massachusetts, forbidding reference to arrest not followed by conviction, is unusual). Probation and parole may be revoked following arrest of the probationer or parolee, even where the arrest is following by discharge. The rationale of this administrative behavior is that it is based not merely on the arrest but on the underlying behavior upon which the arrest was based, just as the administrative action could have been taken upon the behavior without arrest. This is undoubtedly sound, when borne out by the facts in a particular case. Conversely, where the behavior without arrest would not justify loss of liberties, or where discharge follows arrest, legislation should protect against the denial of a right or the imposition of punishment.

A criminal conviction may be the occasion for a special loss of a right by an alien. The United States Attorney General may deport an alien convicted of a crime involving moral turpitude committed prior to entry, or where the alien has been imprisoned for a term of a year or more for such a crime within five years after entry, or where he has been convicted twice for such crimes at any time after entry. We suggest that a distinction should be made between aliens who are *wrongfully* in the country and those whose original entry was lawful. For the former, deportation is restoration to legally pre-existing status. But not so for the latter. For the alien who has lawfully entered, this punishment for crime is a penalty not imposed on the non-alien. In such cases deportation is, in fact, a form of *transportation* as punishment for a crime, a punishment no longer permissible, being prohibited by constitutional provisions against cruel and unusual punishment.

The Number of People Affected

This brief review suggests that the whole structure of loss of civil and property rights other than those individually determined on the sentence is an illogical and harmful throwback. It appears to have only the effect of humiliating and declassing the offender.

But, a reader may ask, why this sympathy for criminals? Is it misplaced? What of public protection? The questions are proper, and the answers are sobering ones. First of all, we are talking mainly about people who have already returned to the community, discharged, having completed their sentence, and others who will be returned sooner or later. If they are a threat to the community, that threat is increased as their personal lives become disorganized; it is decreased to the extent that they can be helped to live successful lives as law-abiding citizens.

Secondly, it should not be thought that attention is being given to the welfare of a small group of individuals, hence not a very sizable problem. The facts are quite different: *there are many millions of people in this country with a criminal record,* affected by the things discussed in this chapter. Aaron Nussbaum, assistant district attorney in Kings County, New York, declares that 50,000,000 persons in the United States have a record of criminal conviction. This astounding figure is based on the Uniform

Crime Reports published by the Federal Bureau of Investigation. The data show over six and one-half million individuals arrested and held for prosecution in 1953. (The figure is typical for a year.) Approximately four and one-half million were found guilty and sentenced. Based on an assumed recidivist rate of 63 per cent (which is, if anything, too high), a total of 1,600,000 persons were *first offenders*. Using the figure as average for any year, each thirty years (a generation) produces a total of almost fifty million persons with a criminal record. Over ten million are convicted of major crimes.[3] We can find no error in the computation. Perhaps the underlying FBI data are incorrect, enlarged somewhat. But even based on a generation of twenty years, and lopping off some millions, the number of persons with a criminal record still would reach tens of millions—gigantic in its implications.

Nor should it be overlooked that an arrest without a conviction, affecting many more persons, sometimes has a serious aftereffect on a person's exercise of civil rights. And we have not mentioned those with a record of juvenile delinquency. Here, then, is a problem affecting a truly substantial segment of our population, whose welfare is a matter of concern to all.

Employment

The individual who has a record of a criminal conviction is more often than not denied public employment. Although the laws in the federal government and almost half the states do not prohibit public employment to persons with a criminal conviction, even in these jurisdictions the individual with a conviction may be barred by administrative action, generally taken by the examining and certifying agency rather than the employing department. Administrative rule may exclude are individual with a record of crime, or a crime involving moral turpitude, or such specific crimes as habitual drunkenness or drug addiction. Sometimes the record automatically excludes a convict from certain employments, particularly police or correctional or related positions (motor vehicle inspector, probation officer, conservation officer), or positions in which the employee regularly handles money. Sometimes particular offenses exclude certain positions. In some jurisdictions the decision to employ or not is an individual decision by the administrator in each case. Again, in these jurisdictions former offenders are generally never hired for such positions as police officer, prison guard, liquor control agents, etc., and certain offenses (habitual drunkenness, a recent offense, bribery to secure appointment, and others), are in some jurisdictions considered barriers to any positions. The number of ex-convicts in public employment is extremely low.

The foregoing summary is based on a survey among public personnel directors.[4] It brought from them the virtually unanimous view that each case should be treated on its merits—that is, by matching the candidate to the job. They felt that conviction itself should not be a barrier; rather, it is significant for what it tells about the qualification of the applicant for the job. Most stressed that the government must share with private employers the responsibility for the rehabilitation of former offenders. Several spelled out specific provisions which would encourage governmental employment of offenders, including counseling, setting aside a percentage or number of jobs for persons with convictions, applying special placement procedures to qualify such candidates. A philosophy of attempting to rehabilitate offenders is contradicted by statutes that prevent public employment of offenders. Where the statute permits employment, many public personnel administrators are personally opposed to hiring all, or certain, offenders.

Even in the states with liberal statutes, administrative rules are needed to establish the practice of hiring persons with a criminal record, where qualified. Certainly the decision should be made in each case on the basis of the individual's fitness for the job.

A corresponding problem exists with respect to private employment. A number of studies have made it clear that there is a significant amount of rejection or discrimination practiced against those with a criminal record (even where no license is required). In one study 16 per cent of the employers had a definitely negative policy, refusing to hire a former offender under any conditions. Typical was a banking company which thoroughly investigated every employee, and disqualified them for any evidence of guilt of any criminal offense. To 34 per cent of the employers, a man's past offenses were not important factors in hiring. A construction company was representative. It would not ask questions about the applicant's past, and would not disqualify him for employment if he voluntarily admitted an offense. The remaining one-half of the employers had no definite policy, either deciding each case on the merits of the individual applicant, or leaving the policy up to the personnel director or the person hiring.

But the picture is less favorable than this breakdown indicates. Despite a positive policy, where there was a choice between a man with a criminal record and one without, a majority would hire the latter. All of the employers stated that before hiring a man with a record they would consider the nature of the offense. Although 84 per cent of this group would consider a former offender for unskilled labor, only 64 per cent would consider him for skilled labor, 40 per cent for clerical positions, eight per cent for salesmen, and none of the position of accountant, cashier, or executive.

To what extent is this employment policy warranted? The same study recorded that none of the employers with negative policies had ever had any experience with people found guilty of a criminal offense. Of the twelve employers who had knowingly hired former offenders, five found their services satisfactory, four found them unsatisfactory, and two were noncommital. Only one maintained that employment of former offenders had a demoralizing influence on other employees. In other studies the performance of the former offenders is better than this, and the employment policy poorer.[5]

Many positions for which the former offender is qualified and is satisfactory to the employer are nevertheless barred to the offender where an employee bond is required. Companies issuing these bonds do not grant insurance where the employee has a criminal record; and some routinely require fingerprinting. The policy is a general one, and is uniformly applied, without consideration of its justification in individual cases. Low cost blanket bonds require an employer to report employees with criminal records, and failure to do so voids protection.[6] Another form of insurance that is often essential to employment may be difficult for a man with a record to obtain. Where the employment requires driving a car, and liability insurance is essential, the former offender may find that he either cannot obtain the insurance or must pay an increased rate. Almost all states have an assigned risk plan by which insurers are required by law or agree to accept higher risks for insurance as an increased rate, the insurers rotating in taking the risks. Former offenders are listed as risks. Although frequently the classification is illogical, the conviction having no bearing on the particular activity covered, nevertheless the plan gives the offender access to insurance, although at a higher rate. The success of the assigned risk plan for automobile insurance is clearly a pattern that is applicable to the issuance of surety bonds. The great hardship in readjustment of former offenders resulting from inability to obtain the bonds where it is needed for employment is unfair and unnecessary.

Offenders are not only rejected by employers, private and public, but also by certain community services, besides insurance. The data are sparse—perhaps another sign of rejection and lack of concern. One writer points out that voluntary family and children's agencies offer less help to former offenders than to others;[7] another says, "Many persons, agencies, and community centers have become infected by this fear-bred atmosphere which demands retribution against young offenders. Disruptive children who should be helped are being barred by community centers and child-caring institutions. Public housing projects have evicted whole families where one child had become a problem. The heads of some private schools exclude children if they are charged with delinquency. . . . Private agencies have become increasingly selective. More and more they reject the aggressive adolescent who has committed some seriously antisocial act. Some 60 per cent of such boys in New York must now be sent to the state training school because the private agencies tend to accept only the less seriously delinquent and emotionally disturbed children."[8]

Government's Role in Employment of Offenders

It is generally accepted, and indeed seems axiomatic, that regular employment is a basis for successful living for the former offender, just as it is for the individual who has never violated the law. It is so recognized by government in its efforts to deal with the problem of crime, and specific efforts are made to help the offender in his working career. To some extent they are effective, but they are also being undercut by half-heartedness or cross-purposes.

The government's first relationship to the employment problem of an offender occurs at the points of arrest and arraignment. For minor offenses, an individual may be summoned instead of arrested. Of course, avoiding taking the defendant into custody supports his continued employment, whereas arrest, even if not long continued, threatens it. But the use of summons to take the place of arrest is rare, except for trivial ordinance violations. Thereafter at the point of arraignment, the judge facilitates release or deters it, by his action. The use of release upon the defendant's own recognisance, or his attorney's or another person's, avoids a threat to his current employment. The fixing of low bail can have the same effect. Study after study has criticized the too limited use of release without bail, or low bail, but the fixing of unjustifiably high bail continues to be the usual practice, with the effect of delaying release pending trial, or of preventing it. Obviously the continuation in custody is a threat to the defendant's current employment, just as it is harmful to him in other ways.

The government's next point of relationship to the employment of an offender occurs at the time of sentencing. From this point of view there are two broad categories of sentence—dispositions that allow the defendant to remain in the community, and those which remove him from the community.The former are suspended sentence, fine, and probation; the latter, institutional commitments. We know from discussion elsewhere (chapter ten) that community treatment is not used sufficiently, and that imprisonment is used excessively. Of course, one of the factors supporting the use of community treatment wherever possible is precisely the fact that the existing relationships of the defendant, including his employment, may continue. The man on probation also has the advantage of the probation officers assistance in obtaining and keeping suitable employment.

If the defendant is committed to a correctional institution, although any employment is of course terminated, the state is nevertheless in a position of undertaking to build or restore the individual's capacities, including his vocational ability. Most prisons do undertake programs of labor and vocational training. However, the quality of the training and experience leaves much to be desired, and is often not acceptable outside. Perhaps this is one of the reasons (of which there are several) that there is greater reluctance to employ the former *prisoner* than the individual who has been convicted but not imprisoned. A "con" or "convict" is popularly one who has a *prison* record, rather than a record of conviction.

The correctional services can assist the discharged prisoner, whether on parole or not, with regard to employment placement, including obtaining any necessary bond. The parole service or the individual parole officer, like the probation office or officer, generally offers such help. State employment service staffs have assigned personnel to state and federal institutions for consultation and placement help to prisoners, and for training of prison personnel in such consultation. But there are no legal measures by which government supports the employment status of former offenders, as we observed above. On the contrary, there are in fact legal restrictions on their employment. In a number of states manufacturers or distributors of alcoholic beverages may not knowingly employ anyone who has been convicted of a felony. The act setting up the New York-New Jersey waterfront commission provides for administrative barring of former offenders from employment. It is doubtful that such acts have been adequately justified. They rely on the dubious proposition that such restriction on the individual workers is important in controlling rackets.

In recent years partciularly, statutes have come into existence protecting individuals from discrimination in employment because of race, color, or religion. We know of no such statutes protecting against discrimination against persons with criminal records, and probably such a law would face a variety of difficulties. But it would have a sound basis in social need. One does not often reflect that there are millions of people in America, probably tens of millions, as we have seen, who have a record of conviction, even more with a record of arrest, and who are living successful lives—employed, normal members or heads of families, average members of their communities. They are not a menace to anyone. It is likely that most of them secured employment through concealment of their record—perhaps even committing a "needless" perjury, but certainly making their social adjustment more difficult. Perhaps this kind of protective law is too advanced for our current attitude toward criminals. If so, it is the responsibility of the correctional administrators to attempt to solve the problem to the extent possible through administrative means.

Restoration of Civil Rights

The law provides methods of restoring the convicted offender's rights. Best known is the exercise of clemency by the head of a state. It may take several forms—pardon, commutation, amnesty, and others. But although it is the best known, executive clemency is perhaps not the most effective method of restoring these rights. It is often limited in effect and, being an extraordinary method, it is sparsely used in many jurisdictions.

The restoration of civil rights of offenders is in some jurisdictions simple, automatic, accomplished as a matter of law and as an incident of change in the status of the offender. In general these statutes provide that on completion of the sentence the rights lost by the sentence are restored. Completion of the sentence may occur at any of several points. Thus civil rights may be restored upon completion of a term of imprisonment. An equivalent status is reached when a parolee has completed his term of parole, either by expiration or discharge before expiration. This is in effect completion of the term and some statutes provide for automatic restoration of rights when it occurs. The statute may also provide for restoration of rights upon completion of probation. The civil rights lost upon conviction or sentence are in some jurisdictions subject to restoration at the discretion of an administrative agency, usually the parole board, or the court of conviction, acting administratively. The administrative restoration may come at the time of completion of sentence or at some later date.

The provisions for restoration are, in most states, inadequate to meet the offender's problem of readjustment. Restoration of rights generally does not include restoration of a license forfeited by the conviction. Administrative restoration may not restore the right to hold public office, while pardon may; but there is no uniformity in the effect of a pardon either. Restoration by administrative action is very spotty. In New York during 1954, 176 applications for certificates of good conduct were processed, of which only 67 were granted. But in New York over 17,000 persons are convicted, and over 9,000 are committed in a year. North Carolina reported that its use of the restoration procedure is rather limited, except for restoration of driver's licenses; North Dakota reported that less than ten per cent ever apply to have their rights restored; in Ohio some counties use the procedure to restore rights, others do not.

Whatever strength these is in the argument that the rights lost on conviction or commitment should be as few as possible, and only where clearly needed for public protection, it becomes increased where the same points are made with respect to the offender who has completed his sentence; that is, who has "paid his debt to society." It also appears that, to be practical, restoration of rights at this point must occur automatically. Where it now depends on administrative action, the procedure is applied unequally, and often the procedure is for all practical purposes ignored. The Standard Probation and Parole Act provides that defendants placed on probation or suspended sentence do not lose any civil rights. It also provides that discharge of a parolee or of a prisoner upon completion of his term shall have the effect of restoring all civil rights lost by operation of law upon commitment, and that the certification of discharge shall state this.

Annulling a Conviction

Aside from his loss of civil and property rights (and aside from punishment imposed on him individually through the sentence), the offender's *legal* status is also affected by a conviction. He has the status of a convicted person (which, as we have seen, entails legal and social strictures). Often no punishment is imposed on a defendant—sentence is suspended without conditions—and often such a dispositon does not carry any loss of civil rights, whereas punishment in addition to the conviction does. But even with this disposition, the individual is still a person who has the status of having been convicted of crime. He may be required to confess the fact under oath in a variety of judicial and administrative proceedings, in addition to being penalized for it in various ways which we have already seen. Accordingly this status, like the rights lost because of it, presents the issue of restoration.

But this is one consequence of the conviction that generally remains unrestored, both in the states in which the defendant who is convicted or imprisoned loses *no* civil rights, and in the states in which his rights have been restored under one of the procedures referred to above. But there are procedures in a few states by which the conviction may be annulled or expunged. In the main, the procedures are available to probationers who have successfully completed their probation periods, but they may also be applicable to persons who have completed a prison term. The logic of the procedures is pertinent to parolees and prisoners as well as probationers—they are an additional rehabilitative measure for a convicted person who is demonstrating that he can live a successful, law-abiding life.

With this line of reasoning, the 1956 National Parole Conference adopted the following recommendation: "The expunging of a criminal record should be authorized on a discretionary basis, with the authority to be vested in the court of conviction. Such action by the court may be taken at the point of discharge from suspended sentence or probation; it may be taken by the court on recommendation of the parole authority either upon unconditional discharge from parole or discharge upon expiration of a term of commitment.

The NCCD has published a model act and interpretive pamphlet implementing the foregoing recommendation. It is badly needed, as was made evident in a surprising and disappointing decision of the United States Supreme Court in 1960. A conviction appealed through the state and federal courts took so long to reach decision—five years—that the defendant had served his sentence and had been released when the Supreme Court considered it. Thereupon the Court dismissed the man's writ on the ground that the case had become moot.

Four judges dissented from the holding, Chief Justice Warren writing: "If the Court is right in holding that George Parker's five-year quest for justice must end ignominiously in the limbo of mootness, surely something is badly askew in our system of criminal justice. . . . Conviction of a felony imposes a *status* upon a person which not only makes him vulnerable to future sanctions through new civil disability statutes, but which also seriously affects his reputation and economic opportunities."[9]

But more than this, said the Chief Justice, "there is an important public interest involved in declaring the invalidity of a conviction obtained in violation of the Constitution." (Unfortunately, *no* member of the Court recorded such words when it dismissed another appeal as moot for another reason—the man, who had appealed his sentence of death, had been executed. For some reason, no stay of execution was asked in connection with the appeal, and the State of New York went ahead with the execution while the appeal was pending.[10])

Helping the Offender—Prisoners' Aid

As a consequence of their experience of community rejection, former offenders add their own forms of psychological rejection, of themselves and the community. To succeed they need special help rather than special rejection. This need has been recognized by a group of private voluntary agencies, the prisoners' aid agencies. Eligibility for help from these agencies is precisely the element that causes discrimination elsewhere—a record as an offender.

In modern times the use of imprisonment as penal treatment, sometimes barbarous, always punitive, has been accompanied by movements of reform or other activities by sympathetic or humanitarian individuals. The organized form of these actions has been the advocacy of prison improvement or abolition, and in more recent times the alternatives of community treatment, and assistance to individual prisoners to alleviate their problems. It was natural that both programs were commingled, prison visitors being advocates of reform, and reformers entering the prisons, sometimes as prisoners, to experience the conditions under which prisoners lived.

The prisoners' aid movement in the United States has been almost entirely local rather than statewide. The approximately two-score agencies coordinate their work through the International Prisoners' Aid Assocation. They continue to have the dual functions of prison reform and help to individual offenders and their families.

Many institutions have no social casework programs, and some of the counseling by prisoners' aid agencies deals with problems which could and should be handled by the institution staff. It is also true, however, that some needs of the inmates can be satisfied only by an outside voluntary agency. Many inmates are seldom or never visited by friends or relatives, and therefore have no contact with individuals other than inmates or custodial personnel. The repressive psychological effect of the disciplinary requirements of a large congregate high security institutions can be balanced to some extent by contact with the community outside. Visits of friends or relatives, or of the friendly voluntary agency worker, provides a new psychological experience to the inmate. It gives him a feeling of dignity and individuality withheld by the institution and its personnel by virtue of the custodial relationship; it gives him contact with a person who can receive his requests without the compromise of a disciplinary responsibility to the institution; it permits him to express a variety of needs, some of which may be too minor to be worthy of attention by institutional staff, and yet for that very reason of special importance to the inmate; it supports him by means of a sympathetic attitude and service by a person or agency with whom the relationship of the prisoner can be more open than it can be with institutional personnel.

To the offender released or discharged to the community the prisoners' aid agencies offer help of several kinds—assistance in employment, finding or providing a place to live, minor financial assistance, and casework counseling. Parole release plans for federal and some state prisoners require a lay adviser, a volunteer who provides advice and supportive supervision, with varying specific assistance (job, finances, etc.). The prisoners' aid agencies frequently serve as parole advisers.

To perform these various duties, the prisoners' aid agencies have staffs which typically are severely limited—two, three, or several workers. They can help only a small percentage of the hundreds of thousands of prisoners in federal, state, and local institutions. Of the steady flow of released offenders, similarly only a small percentage receive help.

A discussion of the loss of rights of an offender cannot conclude without reference to the help that can be provided only by the legal profession. Reference need not be made here to the considerable writing on the subject of legal aid, from which it is evident that the criminal branch of legal aid is woefully neglected. Nowadays the offender before conviction is entitled to the assistance of an attorney. It is evident, however, even without going beyond the corners of this chapter, that the conviction calls into play or is followed by many legal consequences on which legal counsel would be most advisable, or in which rights would simply be lost or defeated without legal help. But it is precisely after conviction, from the point of sentence onward, that legal aid for the individual without financial resources is practically nonexistent.

The public defender offices occasionally give such help, but the populations served by them are a small part of the total population. The public and voluntary defenders require strengthening in this regard. The local and state bar associations are woefully lacking in offering such help. Relatively few bar associations have criminal law committees; and almost none of them offer post-sentence assistance to indigent offenders. It is a serious gap in the service they owe the community.

Notes

1 "In Michigan a person loses no civil rights upon violation of a criminal offense, or upon sentence following conviction. . . . We have, of course, observed that the problem exists with some of the parolees we have supervised for other states, and we have felt that we were fortunate to be free of this added complexity. In our opinion, to cause convicted offenders to lose their civil rights is to add to the degradation or stigma that they already feel, and complicates further their readjustment," Gus Harrison, Director, Michigan Department of Corrections, in a letter to the author.

2 By virtue of its inherent power to conduct its affairs a court has jurisdiction to deal with misconduct by an attorney, and may suspend or disbar him. This authority of the court is subject to legislative control, which usually exercises it by placing supervision of attorneys in the hands of the courts, specifying the general criteria of punishment. Commission of a crime subjects an individual to the disciplinary jurisdiction, as exercised in a discretionary decision of the governing court.

3 "First Offenders—A Second Chance," by Aaron Nussbaum (privately published, printed by Case Press, New York City, 1956). Footnote 6 refers to another estimate.

4 "Public Employment of Persons With a Criminal Record," by Randolph E. Wise, NPPA *Journal,* April, 1960.

5 "Employment Problems of Former Offenders," by John Melichercik (NPPA *Journal,* January, 1956); "The Employment of Released Offenders," by Clem Wyle (*Probation,* 1946); "Job Adjustment for Probationers and Parolees," by Charles E. Odell (*Federal Probation,* June, 1951).

6 "The Treatment of Recidivists," by Marcel Frym (*The Journal of Criminal Law, Criminology, and Police Science,* May-June, 1956). The article deals particularly with the problems of employment and bonding of criminals. Frym estimates ten and one-half million persons with a criminal record, excluding traffic violations.

7 "Community Discrimination Against the Parolee," by Isaac Gurman, (*Focus* November, 1953).

8 "Back to What Woodshed," by Justine Wise Polier, Judge of the Domestic Relations Court of the City of New York (Public Affairs Pamphlet No. 232, 1956) p. 10.

9 Parker v. Ellis, 80 S. Ct. 909 (1960).

10 Dawkins v. People, 359 U.S. 970 (1959); New York Times, October 20, 1959.

References

The central organization of the prisoners' aid agencies is the Correctional Service Federation, U.S.A., in Milwaukee, Wisconsin. Its directory lists the following prisoners' aid agencies in the United States: *California:* Jewish Committee for Personal Services, Los Angeles; Northern California Service League, San Francisco. *Connecticut:* Connecticut Prison Association, Hartford. *Delaware:* Correctional Council of Delaware, Inc., Wilmington. *District of Columbia:* Bureau of Rehabilitation of the National Capital Area, Washington, D.C. *Hawaii:* John Howard Association of Hawaii, Inc., Honolulu. *Illinois:* John Howard Association, Chicago. *Maryland:* The Prisoners Aid Association of Maryland, Baltimore. *Massachusetts:* United Prison Association of Massachusetts, Boston. *Minnesota:* Correctional Service of Minnesota, Minneapolis. *Missouri:* St. Louis Bureau for Men, St. Louis. *New York:* Correctional Association of New York; Osborne Association, Inc.; Quaker Committee on Social Rehabilitation, Inc.; Special Social Service, Inc., New York City. *Ohio:* Correctional Association, Dayton. *Pennsylvania:* Pennsylvania Prison Society; Personal Aid Bureau of Jewish Family Service, Philadelphia. *Wisconsin:* Wisconsin Correctional Service, Milwaukee.

Information on legal aid may be obtained from the National Legal Aid and Defender Association, Chicago.

This chapter is a revised and condensed version of a chapter of *The Law of Criminal Correction,* written by the author (1963). The voluminous legal references for the latter work are omitted.

Part V

PROBATION AND PAROLE

Chapter 10

Drafting Probation and Parole Laws

In 1955 the National Council on Crime and Delinquency published a new *Standard Probation and Parole Act.* In 1940 it had issued a publication covering many of the same phases of correction unde the title *A State Administered Adult Probation and Parole System.* The changes appearing in the newer act were considerable. What were they, and what is their essence? In the years to come this act, like the 1940 act, would affect the selection of personnel, the procedures used, and the welfare of those convicted of crime. What did the 1955 act have to offer—to probation, to parole, to correction generally? What did it propose to the legislatures, which ultimately control the conditions of correctional life?

The Standard Probation and Parole Act defines probation as "a procedure under which a defendant, found guilty of a crime upon verdict or plea, is released by the court, without imprisonment, subject to conditions imposed by the court and subject to the supervision of the probation service." The act defines parole as "the release of a prisoner to the community by the parole board prior to the expiration of his term, subject to conditions imposed by the board and to its supervision."

These two key correctional treatment methods are the clearest opportunities in correction for the application of the individualized treatment. The quality of probation and parole officers, their supervision and sufficiency in numbers, are crucial in the success of these forms of treatment. So also is the wisdom of judges in sentencing, particularly in the choice of a proper disposition. So also is the wisdom of parole boards in their corresponding decision with respect to release of a prisoner on parole.

Just as crucial is the form of the probation and parole laws. The law poorly written may prevent the judge and board from using the proper method of treatment, or prevent him from using it at the optimum moment. The statutes govern the rights and status of the probationer and parolee. Hence it is of considerable importance in the treatment program that these laws be supportive of a rehabilitation program, rather than in conflict with it. The Standard Act provides the legislatures with a model upon which to draw in the writing of laws. The Standard Acts have in fact been very widely used, and few legislatures today write probation or parole laws without considering the model Act.

As is said in the foreward to the Act, "the proper development of probation and parole can make it possible for the correctional institutions to become, instead of mass custody centers, specialized and professionalized rehabilitation services for the relatively small number of offenders requiring institutional treatment."

A Philosophy of Community Treatment

Looking from the vantage point of the passage of 15 years between the 1940 and 1955 Acts, the earlier one appears more a tool than a philosophy. It offered legal techniques of a presumbaly improved order for the use of probation and parole. If it offered philosophy too, it was the philosophic stand that probation and parole are highly useful correctional tools. It would be a gross injustice to the distinguished committee which drafted the 1940 Act to minimize the importance of what they did to enhance these tools, and to prepare the way for the next steps. Yet a careful review of both Acts encourages one to feel that the 1955 publication represents a real advance philosophically, while at the same time proposing modified (and hopefully, improved) techniques.

The 1955 Act has a section on construction and purpose; there was no corresponding section in 1940. The 1955 section is worth quoting in full: "This Act shall be liberally construed to the end that the treatment of persons convicted of crime shall take into consideration their individual characteristics, circumstances, needs, and potentialities as revealed by a case study, and that such persons shall be dealt with in the community by a uniformly organized system of constructive rehabilitation, under probation supervision instead of in correctional institutions, or under parole supervision when a period of institutional treatment has been deemed essential, whenever it appears desirable in the light of the needs of public safety and their own welfare."

Two basic philosophic foundations are included here. The first is the preference for community treatment. How is this philosophic goal supported? It should not be overlooked that this very statement incorporated in the statute is a support to a judge and a parole board in liberalizing release practices. The goal is also supported by the provision in the sentencing section (section 12) that "the court may modify a judgment within 60 days after it is imposed." The comment to the provision refers to it as permitting a reasonable period of time "not so much for the correction of legal error as for further consideration by the court as to the social wisdom of the sentence imposed."

The 1940 Act provided for the use of fines as a sentence, but offered no comment. A fine may be used progressively in our penology, or not. The 1955 Act authorizes the judge to allow payment of a fine in installments. The comment on this reads as follows: "The same purpose is inherent in the provision authorizing payment of fines in installments. The fine is essentially a disposition looking toward community treatment. However, in many cases where the defendant cannot pay immedaitely, he is committed despite the court's confidence that he could be released without danger. The authorization of payment of a fine in installments, which may be combined with probation supervision, supports the disposition as a process of correction in the community. By avoiding commitment of an individual deemed not suitable for institutional treatment, it helps to ease the institutional problem with respect both to overcrowding and to rehabilitative processes. In England a most dramatic reduction in prison population was effected by the requirement, enacted in 1914, that time must be granted for payment of fines (except where special reasons make the granting of time inappropriate)." The Model Sentencing Act went even further, and authorizes a fine as the sentence for any cases, including all felonies (except murder, and those sentenced as dangerous offenders).

How can the philosophic concept be stated in a parole section? Section 18 of the Act declares that the board "shall release" on parole any person confined in any correctional institution administered by state authorities, when in its opinion there is reasonable probability that the prisoner can be released without detriment to the community or to himself. The comment to the section explains that although the term "shall" cannot require and does not require the board to release any prisoner at any time, it nevertheless "stresses the policy of the Standard Act that treatment in the community is to be preferred to institutional treatment, where it is feasible 'without detriment to the community or the prisoner himself.' "

These are a few demonstrations of a philosophy of community treatment of which there are in fact many more in the Act, as we shall see.

Individual Study

Individualized treatment based on a case study comes out much more strongly in the 1955 Act than it did in 1940. This is the second philosophic element in the construction and purpose section. It is principally evident in the provision relating to presentence investigation. In the 1955 Act a presentence investigation is mandatory on felony convictions. "No defendant convicted of a crime the punishment for which may include imprisonment for more than one year shall be sentenced, or otherwise disposed of, before a written report of investigation by a probation officer is presented to and considered by the court." The section continues with the provision that the court may in its discretion order a presentence investigation for a defendant convicted of any lesser crime or offense.

The 1940 Act had the very limited provision that "when a probation officer is available to the court" no defendant shall be placed on probation until a written report of investigation shall have been presented to the court. This does not really or necessarily encourage probation or presentence investigations. In fact the provision implied that for a commitment to an institution a presentence investigation is not necessary, and that in order to place an individual on probation the judge requires the security of an investigation. The 1955 Act makes clear that a presentence investigation is a prerequisite to a sound *sentence* and is not merely related to the use of probation or the suspension of sentence. It calls for a probation service adequate for this responsibility. The tenor of the comments, substantially expanded in the 1955 Act, is to stress individualization and the importance of the case study.

Probation

Several probation concepts are reconsidered. The 1955 Act condemns the practice of combining probation with a term of imprisonment. It does this through the definition of probation, declaring it to be a release *without imprisonment.* The comment states, "The probation definition is constructed to exclude the practice of some courts of combining a period of imprisonment with probation to follow. Such a disposition is a contradiction in terms and in concept and is condemned. The purpose of probation is to avoid, where it is feasible, the impact of institutional life."

The 1940 Act authorized probation before conviction. This provision was unanimously condemned by the 1955 committee, and does not appear. The reason was that probation on consent, it was felt, did not provide sufficient legal authority for the state, and was questionable legally since the consenting defendant had never been convicted. This was resolved in the Model Sentencing Act, which has a model section on deferred conviction, authorizing probation on consent only *after* a plea or finding of guilt, but without entering the judgment of conviction (unless there is a violation of probation). If there is no violation—no conviction is ever entered.

The 1955 Act expands the meaning and requirements of due process of law in probation and parole. The 1940 Act did not clearly establish the right of a probationer to a hearing on a charge of violation. The 1955 Act specifies that a hearing shall be had on the violation charged, although the hearing may be informal or summary. The hearing on the charge of violation must be had "without unnecessary delay." And, in this connection, the section on presentence investigation requires that it be made "promptly." Under the 1955 Act there cannot be a revocation without a violation being established (although revocation is not mandatory even where the violation is established). It authorizes the issuance of a notice to appear on a charge of a violation of probation; a warrant is not mandatory. Where a probationer is held in detention on a charge of probation violation, bail is authorized. All of these provisions are new in the 1955 Act.

Parole

How do the provisions of the two Acts compare with respect to parole? The "mandatory" language in the parole authority has already been referred to. Under the 1940 Act a prisoner could be placed on parole only when arrangements had been made for the proper employment or for his maintenance and care. These specific features of a parole plan are not mandatory in the 1955 Act. The mandatory aspect of what is essentially a wise procedure is undesirable because often the requirements are burdensome for the prisoner and the board. Flexibility is gained and nothing is lost by making these features of parole planning permissive. The 1940 Act prohibited attorneys from presenting oral arguments to a parole board, but required that statements be filed. This is continued in the 1955 Act, but the board is also empowered to permit an oral statement to it.

The 1955 Act introduces a new section, providing for conditional release; that is, for the supervision, as though on parole, of a prisoner who has been released prior to the completion of his term on the basis of good time credits. The section it patterned after the United States and Wisconsin conditional release statutes, and brings us closer to the goal of every released prisoner being supervised for some period of time.

Potentially, perhaps the most important parole provision in the new Act is that relating to parole from local (municipal and county) institutions. In the 1940 Act the authority of the board to release applied equally to state and local institutions, but the board was not required to consider the cases of those serving sentences of less than a year. In practice, of course, few prisoners in local institutions, even those serving over one year, are released by state parole boards. This is one of the many phases of neglect in the correctional treatment of misdemeanant offenders.

The 1955 Act introduces a remedy for this situation. It includes a section requiring the state parole board to "promulgate regulations regarding and shall direct, control, and supervise the administration of a system of parole from correctional institutions administered by county and municipal authorities." The section recognizes that parole from local institutions will and probably should remain a local responsibility. Nevertheless local parole systems as they are presently constituted call strongly for efforts by the state to standardize, improve, and regulate the procedures.

On a charge of parole violation, procedure by way of notice (rather than arrest) is authorized (corresponding to the provision for procedure on probation violation, referred to above). On arrest on a charge of violation of parole, the prisoner may be lodged in a local jail; the 1940 Act required that he be returned to the penal institution from which he was paroled. The 1955 Act requires that a violation be clearly established (as it correspondingly requires for a probation violation); this was not clearly set forth in the 1940 Act. In the 1955 Act, on a violation of parole the time which elapses between the issuance of the warrant and the time of arrest may be credited on the sentence by action of the board. Under the 1940 Act the time could not be credited.

Supporting Community Treatment

Additional new measures in the 1955 Act support community and individualized treatment, affecting probationers and parolees, persons under suspension of sentence, and those discharged from prison. The exercise by convicted persons of ordinary civil rights is legally limited in a variety of ways, as we saw in the previous chapter, and the limitations are often an impediment to successful community living. The 1955 Act committee considered most limitations to be unnecessary, and the act therefore provides, first, that dispositions other than commitment to an institution shall not entail the loss by the defendant of any civil rights. Then, discharge from parole and the discharge of a prisoner who has served his term of imprisonment have the effect of restoring all civil rights lost by operation of law upon commitment.

It is hoped that more tangible support for successful community living by offenders will come from another provision which is new in the 1955 Act. The Act would authorize the board to establish and maintain residence facilities for the housing of probationers or parolees, or to contract for such housing in facilities approved by it. The board would also be authorized to establish and maintain diagnostic and treatment facilities for persons under presentence investigation, or on probation or parole, or may contract for such facilities.

Administrative Provisions

The 1940 Act generally and in its title supported a combined probation and parole system. The 1955 Act continued the recommendation of the combined organization. However, the position was not that this is the only sound administrative form. But where probation service is separate, state responsibility is still stressed. The Act, and particularly the comment to the sections, emphasizes that the best fulfillment of the potentialities of a probation service may be obtained only with the support of a suitable state organization. Accordingly, where a combined board does not exist, tht Act proposes a plan for a state probation commission. The Act also calls for state subsidy to local probation where probation service is not provided entirely by the state.

The 1955 Standard Act adopts the plan of a merit system of selection of board members, through selection by a panel. It also places the director (as well as other personnel) under civil service, which was not done in the 1940 Act. Personnel are examined and appointed under the state merit system, rather than by the board, as in 1940.

One other important proposal should be listed here. It is a sad and shameful truth that some of the most elementary facts in correction are not really available for use. In few jurisdictions do the correctional workers (or the general community) have available the data of judicial criminal dispositions, that is, the number of sentences of each type imposed, for the different offenses, with necessary analyses. In most places this information exists only in the individual docket entries.

The 1955 Standard Probation and Parole Act proposes that the board be given the responsbility and authority to make and publish research studies, specifically including "a compilation and analysis of dispositions by criminal courts throughout the state." It is important to note that the Act declares that where there is not a combined probation and parole board the appropriate agency to perform those duties is the state *probation* agency. This provision goes back to the requirement of a presentence investigation in all felony cases. In other words, the probation service is (or should be) the agency with information *before* sentence on each felony defendant, and is, therefore, a natural agency to compile statistics of dispositions in all cases.

Commitments

The foregoing is not an exhaustive statement of all of the changes made or the new positions taken by the 1955 Standard Probation and Parole Act. But it is evident that they were numerous and important. In the light of these many changes it is remarkable that with one important exception the committee which drafted the Act took virtually unanimous positions on all of these things. On only one aspect of the 1955 draft is there a division, and in this the division is substantial and meaningful.

The one issue on which the 1955 Act committee divided is the form of a commitment, this important technicality that makes an enormous difference in the term of incarceration for defendants. No doubt it makes other differences as well, in administration of both prisons and parole. No doubt it has something to do with prison riots.

In the 1940 Act where there was a commitment to an institution, the provision was for an indeterminate term—the court fixed no maximum term but in each case the maximum was the maximum provided by the statute for the particular offense. In all cases there was to be no minimum term. The parole board could therefore release at any time, and the prisoner in every case could be held to the maximum provided by law. The 1955 Act changed this by authorizing a minimum term. The provision is that a judge may, but is not required to, fix a minimum term. If he does fix a minimum, in no case may it exceed one-third of the maximum term and in no case may it exceed seven years, whichever is less. In addition, the court may reduce the minimum term on the recommendation of the board. With respect to the maximum term, the 1955 Act continues to provide that the maximum term provided by law for the offense shall apply in all cases.

It was the provision for a maximum term in all cases, as well as on the provision for minimum sentence, that there was an even division in the committee. The comments in the 1955 Act reproduce some of the statements of committee members. No attempt is made here to summarize the various positions. What is being emphasized at this point, rather, is that the division in the committee signifies that a great deal more truly exploratory research and study remained to be done in these areas of the sentence.

For many years the "indeterminate sentence" was accepted as an untouchable standard in our penology. Yet while this position was taken theoretically, the actual indeterminate sentence in practice was not at all the indeterminate sentence of the theory. We ought to look hard at what it has really meant. As already pointed out, almost always in the United States an indeterminate sentence has meant a minimum term (as well as maximum), and very frequently the minimum term practices were a mockery of any treatment concept. Very often the minimum term was fixed to be very near the maximum, depriving parole of most of its meaning; frequently the minimum term was exceedingly long, often leading to irretrievable demoralization or a spirit of revolt.

The position taken in 1955 was a compromise, deemed to be a practical approach to coping with both of these elements in the use of the indeterminate sentence. The new position on minimum sentence assumes that courts properly staffed and serviced for thorough presentence study will use institutional commitments only when community treatment is not indicated. The court should at this point be in a position to determine that the committed defendant requires a certain minimum period of incarceration. If subsequent experience shows the minimum sentence to be too long, the Act provides that the parole board may recommend to the court a reduction of the minimum.

But all this doubt and conservatism were overcome in the Model Sentencing Act, which came out clearly against any minimum term of parole eligibility, whether fixed by law, by the judge, or by the parole board. Parole, under the MSA, may be granted at any time in the discretion of the parole board.

What of the maximum term? Should it be the maximum of the statute, or should the judge be authorized to fix a lesser maximum term? The committee divided on this. With the division also as to a minimum term, the division in the committee is not so much between forms of the indeterminate sentence, as between the indeterminate sentence and the definite sentence. We have seen that this in fact is the division in the country, in practice.

Taking the federal sentence as a form of the definite, it is a maximum term fixed by the judge (not automatically the maximum of the statute), no minimum term, and parole eligibility determined by the statute.[1] Almost half the states use such a sentence. Yet surprisingly little writing has appeared analyzing the forms of sentences. The present writer several years ago compared the effects of the definite and indeterminate sentences, and took up the cudgels for the fixed maximum without a minimum (i.e., definite sentence); but better forms still are undoubtedly available (and, in chapter 8, we have attempted to explore them).

Dynamic Standards

This summary directs attention to the main differences between the two Standard Probation and Parole Acts. Of course a totally different statement could be written, one which pointed out the many basic features of the 1940 Act which were retained.

A great deal could be said about the many merits and values of the 1940 Act. So also proposals for probation and parole reform antedating the 1940 Standard Act remind us not only that we have made many advances, but also that some recommendations, which none deny have to be implemented, must be made over and over again.[2]

But this is not such a comment. The stress here is on the proposition, applicable to so many other aspects of correctional work as well as other fields, that we ought not to feel that any of the standards we advocate or the procedures we use are ever beyond reexamination; indeed that generally we shall profit from examining them. Therefore it is also true that the one thing that cannot be done with the 1955 Act is to consider it fixed or static. Beyond all other things, the committee for the 1955 Act deserves praise for instilling this point of view in all of its work. It was a committee principally of practitioners, yet they were people who saw well beyond what they themselves were doing.

There is one other general statement which should be made, characterizing the underlying approach in the 1955 Standard Act. Although the Act suggests standards as ideals ond goals, the committee in drafting it never lost sight of the fact that it would have to be applied in the kind of administrative reality that exists and that we recognize will exist for some tme to come. Because the committee kept in mind that mortal men of all sorts will be applying the provisions, the Act is a necessary mixture of provisions which reach out for finer work in correction, and yet hold on to cautions and limits at many points.

Notes

[1] The federal law was liberalized in 1958, authorizing a sentencing judge in his discretion to fix the minimum term of parole eligibility at less than one-third of the maximum, or to declare the prisoner eligible at the parole board's complete discretion.

[2] "Recommendations for Legislative Reform in Prison, Parole, and Probation," by O. L. Harvey, *Journal of Criminal Law and Criminology* (November, 1936), considering various reports between 1913 and 1932.

References

The most comprehensive legal analysis of probation and parole laws is to be found in the volumes of *The Attorney General's Survey of Release Procedures* (Government Printing Office, 1939). Rubin, *The Law of Criminal Correction* (West Pub. Co., 1963), includes chapters on probation and parole. Each year the statutes and appellate court decisions of general interest are digested in an article appearing in the NCCD quarterly, *Crime and Delinquency.*

An interesting account of the invention of probation over 100 years ago, is *John Augustus, First Probation Officer,* containing a reprint of his original report published in Boston in 1852 (NCCD, 1939). The most comprehensive general account, for layman, student, and professional, is *Crime, Courts, and Probation,* by Charles L. Chute and Marjorie Bell (The Macmillan Company, 1956). A British account of its service is given in *The Probation Service,* edited by Joan F. S. King (Butterworth and Co., Ltd., London, 1958).

In addition to publishing the Standard Acts and other books, pamphlets and periodicals, the NCCD provides technical advice to legislatures and other groups in drafting and reviewing bills and laws in its fields. The Standard Acts are the product of nationally representaive committees working with the staff of the Council.

The present chapter is based on an article that appeared in *Federal Probation* in December, 1956.

Chapter 11

The Man on Probation or Parole

The individual on probation or parole is, as we observed earlier, still subject to supervision. Furthermore, his release into the free community is conditional, and may be revoked. If revoked, he is usually committed to prison. Under what circumstances may probation and parole be revoked? If it is established that a condition of release has been violated.

It is thus evident that the conditions are an important part of the framework governing probation and parole. They are important, however, not only as the legal basis of the supervision, but also as setting the tone for the supervision process and the relationship of the officer to the offender. If the conditions are negative and punitive in spirit and in control, the officer is handicapped in rehabilitative efforts and the individual under supervision is handicapped in his community existence. Although they need not be negative, unfortunately in most jurisdictions they are, being a list of forbidden behavior (not to drink, not to associate with certain persons, not to change residence or employment without permission, etc.).

A few jurisdictions have broken away from this traditional pattern. Their conditions are very few, and approach the minimum conditions which can be as low as two in number. One—not to commit a crime; two—to consult with the supervising officer regularly, and always before making an important change in the pattern of living. In some jurisdictions this cannot be achieved without a change in the law; in these states a list of conditions is required by statute. In most states, however, the conditions could be readily simplified through administrative decision.

The supervision process involves other problems. What are the relative rights and responsibilities of the individuals involved? Where does discretion enter and how should it be exercised?

We are accustomed to speak of probation and parole supervision as being *authoritative,* implying that the probationer and parolee are markedly subject to stringent legal requirements and strict administrative control. We are often apt to say that this is an aspect of probation and parole that should not be stressed, the preferred emphasis being on the casework relationship which should exist between the officer and the individual under supervision—or, even—the "client." On the other hand, probation personnel are probably not unhappy that the law and the court or agency they are serving give them a good deal of security in the authority inhering in them through the law. The legal problems involved in probation and parole supervision are, in fact, problems of *authority:* What is the extent of the legal authority involved in supervision, and what are limitations, from the officer's point of view? From the point of view of the probationer or parolee, what rights does he have, if any, which must be respected by the officer, and what are his obligations under the law?

Two Statuses

There are, then, two statuses to be taken into consideration—first, the status of the probationer and the parolee, and second, the status of the officer. Basically, these statuses are determined by the probation and parole laws which create the authority of the officer (and of the court and parole board) and which subject the offender to certain conditions of living.

What is the status of the probationer and parolee? Although the penal laws attach certain variable or unvarying sanctions as consequences of a criminal conviction, the probationer and parolee are not without rights. In fact, the legal situation is often defined as being a quasi-contractual one—the probationer or parolee is entitled to liberty so long as he does not violate the law or the conditions which are imposed on him. This means that the officer, as well as the offender under supervision, is bound by the conditions imposed.

There is another point to remember, and that is that penal laws are strictly construed against the state. The law favors the liberty of individuals. Applied to probation and parole supervision, the appellate court decisions hold that where doubt exists the behavior of the offender will be interpreted as not being a violation.

What of the status of the probation or parole officer? We may say generally that he is a peace officer, but not a police officer. In one sense his duties are narrower than those of a police officer—he is not called upon and does not have the authority to enforce the law generally. On the other hand, his powers are wider than those of a police officer by virtue of the special authority given him to supervise individuals, and he may control the lives of individuals under his supervision to a far greater extent than may a police officer.

The Guiding Legal Element

The conditions of probation and parole are the guiding legal element in supervision. What does the law say about the kind of condition that may be imposed upon a probationer and parolee? The general statement is that a condition may control behavior in any respect, except that it may not require behavior which would be illegal, immoral, or impossible.

Undobtedly, however, this is a power broader than is wanted or needed, and in fact even legally the range is narrower than the general rule indicates. For example, sometimes the condition imposed is exile of the offender from the jurisdiction. It has been condemned by some courts as constituting cruel and unusual punishment; some constitutions forbid it. But probably the issue is not so much a legal one as it is one of the wisdom or propriety of "solving" the problem of the offender by banishment.

Undoubtedly another limitation is that a condition may not enlarge the sentence of the court, nor may a revocation result in enlarging the sentence. An ancient Virginia case held invalid a condition that the convict labor for three years in such a manner as the majority of the directors of public buildings might require. Perhaps, in fact, the rule should be—perhaps, inherently it is—that a condition of probation or parole must be framed within the purposes of the statute and must be reasonably related to the treatment needs of the individual, in the light of his offense.

Some formality is required in imposing the conditions. The probationer or parolee must have been definitely advised as to the conditions, preferably in writing, in order for a violation to be validly established.

We have said that the officer as well as the probationer or parolee is bound by the conditions imposed. The conditions of behavior are set by the court or parole board, not by the officer, and the power cannot be delegated to the officer. Where the condition of release subjects the offender to the direction of the officer, no doubt the orders of the officer must be within the context of the conditions laid down by the court or board. For example, the officer could not independently order restitution or support. And since the court or board may not delegate its authority, it may not *give* the officer authority to fix an amount of restitution, if the court or board orders it in general terms. It is questionable whether the kind of condition which *apparently* gives the officer the widest latitude in supervision—subjecting the offender to the general direction of the officer—secures it in fact. It may have the opposite effect, since if it amounts to an attempted delegation of authority, that would not be valid. The offender then would be subject to little more than visitation and reporting requirements.

The officer exercises "general supervision" over the offender's behavior. He has the right to visit the offender's home and to require an accounting of behavior. But we have already implied that there are legal limits to the control the officer can exercise in this way. No hard and fast rule can be stated, but the general guide is the line between friendly oversight and delegation of higher authority. For example, does supervision include the right to intervene in the offender's life in such matters as control of his finances? It would not seem so, except insofar as a condition spells out a monetary obligation on the part of the offender (restitution, fine, support). Even here, the officer "enforces" the condition not by taking control of the offender's finances but by existence of the sanction of revocation for a violation.

Again, how far does the officer's right of visitation extend? Does it include the right to search the residence of the offender? Probably not. A search for evidence of a violation of law may be made only pursuant to a search warrant, which may be issued only by a magistrate. The situation is different when an arrest is being made for a violation. The officer has limited power of arrest, spelled out in the probation and parole laws. An officer making an arrest has authority to search the person of his prisoner, and any dangerous weapon or anything else may be taken away when such action is reasonably deemed necessary for the safety of the officer or the public.

Something more before the arrest, however. If the officer has knowledge of a violation of a condition of probation or parole, what does the law require him to do? The law gives the officer discretion as to whether the violation will be brought to the attention of the court or board; the law does not require that every violation be reported. On the other hand, the officer is subject to the direction of the court or board in this respect, and the kind of violation to be reported is governed by the administrative policy of the court or board. The important thing, however, is that there is no legal requirement—in most states, and in the Standard Probation and Parole Act—that every violation of a condition be reported by the officer. And it may be noted also that when a violation is reported administratively, the court or board may decide to take no further action, just as it may continue probation or parole after the violation is established.

As a practical matter, the offender is not protected by the legal limitations on authority unless the officer (and the department) see to it that they are made effective by not overstepping the limits. An officer can, if he chooses, exercise authority with a heavy hand, in effect imposing his own conditions of behavior, and the man under supervision has no effectual way of protest. At the present time in most departments he can challenge this kind of supervision only by submitting to a violation hearing. Some administrative review should be permitted the offender who questions the directions he reecives from his officer, and the availability of such a review should, in appropriate cases, be interpreted to him by the court or probation department.

On violation of a condition the authority of the officer to arrest is governed by the probation or parole statute. If the act does not constitute a crime authorizing arrest by a peace officer, the conditions of which are so carefully spelled out in the law, the officer should return to the court or board for the issuance of a warrant. The offender must be informed of the violation charged, and this is one of the functions of the warrant. The warrant may authorize any peace officer or the probation or parole officer to make the arrest, or the law may authorize the probation or parole officer to issue authorization to any peace officer to make an arrest.

If a warrant has been issued to the officer he has no further discretion, but must execute it, and the statutory procedure on arrest must follow. The jailing of a probationer or parolee as a disciplinary measure, followed by release without court or board action, is therefore a questionable procedure.

Authority in Balance

The foregoing are some of the principal legal rules involved in working with probation and parole conditions. It is not difficult to anticipate mixed feelings about them. On the one hand, we might feel that, having wide authority, we must be cautious about exercising it to retain a casework approach. On the other hand, if the limitations of authority described are greater than we had thought, are we unhappy at seeing how our authority is curtailed?

Possibly there is still another feeling—that the authority is broad, but not wide-open; that it is sufficient for the purpose of protecting the community; that the limitations are quite acceptable in the light of the effort to work with the offender on a casework basis. I assume most professionally (casework) trained officers would state it so; authority is needed, but it is a burden as well as a resource; and a balance between these two aspects of authority requires definite limits on the powers of probation and parole officers, and on courts and parole boards. The practical casework problem in probation and parole supervision is cooperation and rapport between offender and officer; and the basic tenet held to this is that this is to be obtained *voluntarily,* and cannot be compelled.

Does this mean that all is in balance in the legal phases of supervision? That may depend on how we look at the rules. I have referred to the rights of the probationer and the parolee, the legal rules of strict construction, favoring liberty—and I see these as authority impinging on the officer *constructively,* pushing in the direction of permissiveness, underscoring the need for understanding. I have quoted the general statement of the rule regarding conditions of probation and parole, the wide-open rule that any condition is valid if the behavior required is not illegal, immoral, or impossible. But I have suggested that there are limitations on this general statement, and have implied that they are healthy and desirable, compelling the court and board to recognize the offender as an individual with rights. Do we not *have* to recognize him as an individual with rights, if we expect him to succeed later, when all the controls have been taken off? If so, the direction ought to be toward supporting limitations of authority, and not toward increasing authority.

This leads to recognizing that with respect to authority, responsibility is not only toward the offender, but toward the law. Probably the answer to the question of whether the law is in balance regarding authority is in the attitude of administration. Does it really see the merit in limitations of power, and are they made real in everyday administration? Probably in the long run the law will respond to this administrative attitude in action. But the law is slow, administration is swift, and in many ways—for the individual—its action is irreparable.

A practical paradox results, which potentially makes the power of the officer *greater* than the authority of the law. The law can be frustrated, or "added to," by the officer and supervisor, by the court and board. We come round to the realization that, in not a remote sense, the law is the officer's authority, but that the administration of the law is a higher authority still. It is this which makes the working attitude toward the law decisive, this which is the double responsibility of probation and parole staffs.

A Maryland court recently made an observation that not only states a legal rule but suggests a viewpoint toward rules that seems eminently realistic. It said: "A parolee is not expected or required at once to achieve perfection. If his conduct is that of the ordinary well-behaved person, with no more lapses than all people have, with no serious offenses charged against him, and with no indication that he intends in the future to pursue the course which led to his original conviction, the courts and probation officers should not seek for unusual and irrelevant gounds upon which to deprive him of his freedom."

References

This chapter is based on an article that appeared in the January, 1956 issue of the NPPA *Journal*, an issue devoted to the subject of probation and parole conditions and violations.

Chapter 12

Probation and Due Process of Law

The early history of probation is a story of the efforts of humanitarian volunteers and courts which, however reluctantly, were willing to experiment with new legal procedures. In time of course the statutes regulated the procedure, and public officers were paid to do probation work. The system of probation for both juvenile and adult offenders spread to every state. But none of it came into being full blown. It had to be developed in struggles with state legislatures, encouragement and disappointment in the attitudes of judges, and slow but steady development of the casework process and its introduction into probation work.

Although in its beginnings probation was based on the traditional, that is, the common law right of the court to suspend sentence during good behavior,[1] its legal development has been principally a statutory one. All the probation systems in the United States are statutory. The most basic element in modern probation, its indispensable component—supervision by a public officer during the period of "good behavior"—is strictly a statutory establishment. The paradox of the famous Killits case[2] is that although it invalidated early federal probation, based on indefinite suspension of sentence under common law, it directed probation decisively into the statutory field. "It cannot now be doubted," the United States Attorney General's Survey declared, "that both Federal and State probation have enjoyed a growth which might well have not occurred but for a definite and authoritative statement that further development must be sought within the framework of permissive legislation."[3]

Nevertheless the courts still have an important creative contribution to make to probation law. They have on occasion expressly or impliedly pointed out limitations in the statutes. Perhaps their most natural contribution is to the components that make up due process of law, although ultimately due process in probation law must remain essentially a statutory deevlopment, as we shall observe.

Claims of due process cannot be permitted to paralyze probation. It was inevitable that the U.S. Supreme Court would uphold a statute which provided for a presentence report to the court based on information given by persons outside the courtroom not confronted by the defendant or subjected to cross-examination by him.[4] The court said, "Most of the information now relied on by judges to guide them in the intelligent imposition of sentences would be unavailable if information were restricted to that given in open court by witnesses subject to cross-examination. . . . Such a procedure could endlessly delay criminal administration in a retrial of collateral issues."

The termination of the trial ends the defendant's protection by the rules of evidence. It is interesting, however, that the Supreme Court relied on common law sentencing practice rather than on the probation statute, despite its tribute to the modernity of probation laws. In its opinion the court said—and it appears the precedent cited is sufficient to justify the holding—"Before and since the American colonies became a nation, courts in this country and in England practiced a policy under which a sentencing judge could exercise a wide discretion in the sources and types of evidence used to assist him in determining the kind and extent of punishment to be imposed within limits fixed by law. Out-of court affidavits have been used frequently and of course in the smaller communities sentencing judges naturally have in mind their knowledge of the personalities and background of convicted offenders."

The decision, like most due process decisions, is a negative one, ruling that a particular practice, restrictive of the defendant's right, does not violate constitutional and statutory due process requirements. Within the limitations of the decision a great deal can be procedurally required for valid and due probation process. A statute which expanded the present rights of the defendant would of course not violate the constitutions, but would add to the meaning of due process in probation. If, for example, a statute provided—as one or two do—that the defendant to be sentenced *has* the right to confront and cross-examine informants, the defendant would be entitled to the benefit of such procedure.

Developments under Probation Statutes

Due process today is what we have considered to be necessary to protect individuals against arbitrary, oppressive and unjust procedures. Probation is a new statutory procedure which imposes obligations and grants rights to courts, administrative officers, and defendants. New concepts of due process must develop to accompany the newly provided authority in the court and probation department. In fact the probation statutes have already established protective rules beyond the common law of sentencing.

The Illinois probation law requires that "Before granting any request for admission to probation, the court shall require the probation officer to investigate *accurately and promptly* the case of the defendant making such request," and it proceeds to specify some of the particulars of information to be included in the investigation.[5] The New York statute requires that probation officers shall "fully" investigate, and that the report shall be made promptly.[6] Is it not inherent in the concept of probation that the probation officer's report shall be accurate and promptly made? It would seem, indeed, that a court could read into the probation law a requirement of public policy that the probation officer's performance under the law shall be in accordance with some minimum standards. The statutory provision, however, is preferable.

It is the law, under such a holding or such a statute, that due process requires a probation investigation to meet the specified standards. To insure that the investigations shall conform to the legal standards, there must be provided a staff with the necessary ability, time and facilities. There must also be provided a means of scrutinizing the investigation to determine whether the required standards have been met. Is any scrutiny of the probation investigation other than by the sentencing judge permissible?

An Illinois case says such scrutiny can be made by a court higher than the sentencing court. In People v. Adams,[7] on a plea of guilty and application for probation, a presentence investigation was ordered. The report of the probation officer recommended that Adams not be admitted to probation, and probation was denied. Defendant filed a motion in arrest of judgment, seeking to change his plea of guilty to not guilty, and filed objections to the report of the probation officer, supporting the objections by affidavit. The motion to withdraw the plea of guilty was denied, and this was the error urged on the appeal. The Supreme Court of Illinois pointed out that the report of the probation officer was not filed and sentence was not imposed until more than a year after the case had been referred to him. It considered the affidavits presented by the defendant of disinterested persons familiar with the facts who denied the imputations of a bad past record on the part of Adams. It was clear, said the Supreme Court, that the trial judge in denying probation and in denying leave to withdraw the plea of guilty, was infiuenced by the report and recommendations of the probation officer. Then, citing the statute, the court said, "It cannot be said in this condition of the record that the report of the probation officer was either of that accurate or prompt character which the statute requires." The court thereupon reversed and ordered a new trial.

In short, affidavits contradicting the presentence report were submitted to the trial court and were weighed against the probation officer's report. Furthermore, said the Illinois Supreme Court, the probation officer's report is not a document inviolate in the bosom of the trial court. On the contrary, it is subject to the scrutiny of the appellate court, and if it is found not to be sound, the defendant's rights are held to be infringed. In other words *due procress did require a proper probation report.*

A more recent federal Court of Appeals case takes the same position. In Klingstein v. United States, the court states: "Appellant makes an attack on the [presentence] report, but *we have examined it carefully and have had it made a part of the record on appeal,* and we think the attack thoroughly unjustified." (Our italics; the opinion continues with an analysis of the presentence investigation to consider the question of its fairness.) [8]

Due process requires something else. In another case, where no referral for investigation was made and no report submitted by a probation officer, the Illinois Supreme Court similarly directed the trial court to permit withdrawal of a plea of guilty.[9] The court said: "The discretion the court may exercise upon an application for probation is not an arbitrary discretion to be exercised at the mere will or whim of the court, but is a sound legal discretion dependent for its exercise upon the facts shown. It is obvious that where the facts are not shown and are not inquired into, the denial of probation is an arbitrary and unauthorized exercise of the power." Here the court had heard evidence in aggravation of the offense but no testimony in mitigation was heard. "From the record in this case," said the appellate court, "we are not satisfied that plaintiff in error did not plead guilty under a misapprehension that the court would admit him to probation." Even an authority which enjoys the exercise of an untrammeled discretion must exercise its discretion soundly, must not abuse it.

Police records, other than those concerned with arrests leading to convictions, are a part of a presentence investigation. Should they be included in the report? In the light of the great procedural care surrounding a trial, it is perhaps inconsistent to use allegations of other crimes never proved in court, for sentencing purposes. Minimum protection to the defendant would be the opportunity to rebut such accusations. Possibly the greater protection of barring reports of other crimes attributed to the defendant, but not culminating in conviction, or at least arrest, is needed. Massachusetts law provides that the report to the court shall not contain information of prosecutions resulting in a finding of not guilty.[10]

Hearing on the Presentence Report

"The essential elements of due process of law are notice and an opportunity to be heard and to defend in an orderly proceeding adapted to the nature of the case."[11] How should this general concept be applied to the sentencing process short of confrontation and cross-examination by the defendant of those who have supplied the probation officer with information?

The defendant prior to sentence is always given the right to speak on his own behalf. Where the court has a presentence report by a probation officer, the defendant's statements are addressed to a judge who will rely heavily on the report. Should the defendant be given access to the report before his own address to the court? This is the law in Alabama, where the probation law provides that "in no case shall the right to inspect said report be denied the defendant or his counsel after said report has been completed."[12] It is the law in California,[13] and well established as the rule in England and Canada.[14] In the other states the probation law is silent on this point; the judges may authorize inspection of the presentence report by the defense, or may deny it. In People v. Adams, cited above, the defendant Adams presumably knew the contents of the presentence report.

Should the statute give the defense the *right* to see the presentence report, or should this right be denied? This troublesome question has many facets, and requires full discussion. It is separately treated in the chapter following.

Revocation Procedure

Both statutes and courts have more or less forthrightly guarded due process in the procedure to revoke probation for a violation of conditions imposed. Most statutes require that before revocation is ordered for a violation of probation, the accused probationer shall be given due notice and an opportunity to be heard. Specifically or impliedly most statutes authorize a summary hearing. In a few states the court may revoke without notice and hearing, it being held that revocation under such circumstances violates no constitutional right or privilege. These decisions have been criticized. "The reasoning upon which this procedure has been sustained is not particularly clear," says the Attorney General's Survey. "If a constitutional right is involved, it seems unduly technical to sustain a revocation without a hearing on the ground that the probationer accepted the probationary release subject to the possibility of being committed without an opportunity to explain."[15]

Contrary holdings appear to be based on concepts of due process. For example, the federal probation law provides that following arrest for an alleged violation of conditions, the probationer shall be taken before the court, but nothing is said of a hearing. The Supreme Court has construed this to provide the probationer with an opportunity to explain. Although the court rejected the contention that the privilege of a hearing had a basis in the due process clause of the Fifth Amendment, it said, "Clearly the end and aim of an appearance before the court must be to enable an accused probationer to explain away the accusations. The charge against him may have been inspired by rumor or mistake or even downright malice. He shall have a chance to say his say before the word of his pursuers is received to his undoing. This does not mean that he may insist upon a trial in any strict or formal sense. . . . It does mean that there shall be an inquiry so fitted in its range to the needs of the occasion as to justify the conclusion that discretion has not been abused by the failure of the inquisitor to carry the probe deeper."[16]

Other courts have held similarly. The Utah Supreme Court, interpreting a statute which said nothing of a hearing, nevertheless required the safeguards of a hearing.[17] The Washington statute said nothing about notice and hearing, but its Supreme Court supplied this requirement. It held that a substantial right of the defendant was involved and that to enter a revocation without giving the defendant an opportunity to be heard "is to disregard a principle as old as the law itself."[18] The court quoted with approval and adopted the reasoning of the New Mexico Supreme Court which declared that "it would seem that due process of law would require notice and opportunity to be heard before a defendant can be committed under suspended sentence."[19]

Other than the gradual spread to more and more states of due process requirements recommended here, the one important development came in 1967 from the Supreme Court of the United States (after several states led the way) in providing that on the revocation hearing the probationer is entitled to be represented by counsel, and if indigent, the state must provide him with counsel.[20]

It cannot be doubted that the due process developments, some solidly established, others less well accepted, are contributing to the growth of probation generally, as well as reflecting its growth. This progress is most immediate for the probation statutes themselves. It is probably equally true that the definition and clarification of due process contributes to the development of probation casework. A factor of difficulty is the authoritative setting of the probation status. An awarenes of rights of the probationer is a compensation for the hand of authority, lying heavy on the probation officer and the probationer.

Probation has often been said to be the correctional procedure most worthy of a democracy, principally because it recognizes the value of each individual and attempts to conserve the individual in the community. "Probation and parole," said Walter C. Reckless, "constitute a democratic faith which the people have in the ability of the average offender to come to grips with himself." Non-punitive and humanitarian probation best typifies the modern approach of individualized treatment. Our statutes and the courts in their decisions have been and should be moving forward consistently with this philosophy, to provide suitable legal protection to the defendant who is the subject of probation.

Notes

1 *Attorney General's Survey of Release Procedures,* Vol. II, Probation (Government Printing Office, 1939, p. 8).

2 Ex parte United States, 242 U.S. 27 (1916).

3 *Attorney General's Survey,* supra, p. 10.

4 Williams v. People of the State of New York, 337 U.S. 241, 69 S. Ct. 1079 (1949).

5 Jones Illinois Statutes Annotated, Section 37.773

6 Code of Criminal Procedure, Section 931.

7 People v. Donovan, 379 Ill. 323, 40 N.E. 2d 730 (1942).

8 Klingstein v. United States, 217 F. 2d 711 (1954).

9 People v. Donovan, 376 Ill. 602 (1941).

10 Session Laws 1950, Chapter 145.

11 American Jurisprudence, title *Constitutional Law,* Section 648.

12 Code of Alabama 1940, Title 42, Section 23.

13 California Penal Code, Section 1203.

14 For a thorough review of the English and Canadian rule, based on the statutes and cases, see Rex v. Stevenson, Court of Appeal of British Columbia, 3 Western Weekly Reports (new series) 29 (1951).

15 *Attorney General's Survey,* supra, p. 329.

16 Escoe v. Zerbst, 295 U.S. 490, 493 (1935); cited *Attorney General's Survey,* p. 330.

17 State v. Zolantakis, 70 Utah 296, 259 Pac. 1044 (1927).

18 State v. O'Neal, 147 Wash. 169, 265 Pac. 775 (1928).

19 Ex parte Lucero, 23 N.M. 433, 168 Pac. 713 (1918). This group of cases cited in *Attorney General's Survey,* supra, pp. 330-332. See also, holding similarly, Lester v. Foster, Sheriff, 207 Ga. 596, 63 S.E. 2d 402 (1951).

20 Mempa v. Rhay, 389 U.S. 128, 88 Sup. Ct. 254 (1967).

References

This chapter is based on an article published in *Focus,* March, 1952.

Chapter 13

Presentence Reports

Most of our discussion of probation thus far has dealt with probation as a disposition by a court, and the process of supervision which is the inherent element in it. But probation includes two functions, and the other function is no less important than probation as a disposition. The second function is that of the presentence investigation. The investigation is almost exclusively the means by which the judge obtains the kind of information upon which he can base a scientific judgment, that is, the formulation of the sentence best suited for the rehabilitation of the defendant, without sacrifice of public protection.

The discussion in the previous chapter considered briefly the hearing on the presentence report, leading to the policy question of whether or not the defense should have a right, under the statute, to see the presentence investigation report before offering a statement or evidence on the defendant's behalf. We noted that in the United States only two states give this right, and that in the others the question is within the discretion of each sentencing judge.

This is one of the plainly controversial issues in correction, and admittedly the position which urges that the defendant have a right to see the presentence report is a minority position. Most probation administrators support the practice of denying the defendant a right to access to the report—neither he nor his attorney is permitted to see it, unless the judge in a particular case authorizes access to the report, or himself discloses the information contained in it.

Yet among probation people there are also many who consider it important to acquaint the defendant with any material in the report which is adverse to their interest, to provide them with an opportunity to controvert any factual material. There are judges who regularly permit defendants to examine the presentence investigation reports, and hear their testimony on it. There are others who regularly reveal adverse material; and some judges reveal much or all of the report where they consider it necessary in the interest of fairness. Few probation administrators or criminal court judges would support a rule of denial of the defendant's access to the report under any circumstances.

The limits of the issue should be made clear: it is whether or not the defendant (and counsel) should be entitled to see the presentence report which is seen by the judge, so that they may be better prepared to make the statement on behalf of the defendant prior to the imposition of sentence. It does not suggest that all information obtained by the probation officer be shown to the defendant; nor is all this information shown to—or should it be shown to—the judge. And it is not a rule giving access to the record of *supervision* of a probationer. It is *not* a proposal to make the presentence report *public*.

Presentence reports, particularly the social investigation, are properly private to a certain degree. The *public* should be denied access to these records. Thus in Alabama the statute provides that all data assembled by the probation officer and referred to the court shall be "privileged," by which it proceeds to explain is meant not available for public inspection except upon order of the court. It is then added, as we noted in the previous chapter, that in no case shall the right to inspect the report be denied the defendant or his counsel. So other probation statutes when they speak of confidentiality do not discuss disclosure to the defendant but protection against public disclosure to other agencies and courts.[1]

It has been said that to argue for access to the report is legalistic, and that the contrary argument is the casework point of view. Not necessarily. A rule denying access to the report, or making access discretionary, is just as much a rule of law as granting access. The heart of the discussion is, in fact, to discover which rule better supports probation and the correctional process as *treatment,* although the concept of due process requires fairness to parties as a goal in itself. As pointed out in the previous chapter, appellate courts may have access to presentence reports, in order to be able to pass on their competence. If we were to make a legal argument, it could be suggested that, therefore, the defendant below needs access to the report in order to exercise his right to decide intelligently whether to take an appeal. This is arguing for the rule on the basis of legal logic rather than wisdom. Correspondingly, the argument *against* disclosure sometimes goes that the defendant's procedural rights which existed during the trial are at an end; hence he is not *entitled* to see the report, as a matter of right, but only as a matter of discretion. This, too, is simply a legal argument (that incidentally begs the question), not going to the wisdom of the rule. Or, that if the defendant was fairly convicted (as he must be), he has no further rights.

Legal logic aside, then, what the the effects of a rule of disclosure? The effects are two—possible limitation of available data and the effect on the attitude of the offender and his relationship to the court, probation officer, and, if incarcerated, the correctional process in general.

Limitation of Available Data

The advisory committee which drafted the Rules of Criminal Procedure for the federal courts, prior to revision and promulgation by the United States Supreme Court in 1945, proposed that the presentence report should be available, on such conditions as the court might impose, to the attorneys for the parties and to other persons or agencies having a legitimate interest in it. The Supreme Court, exercising what was in effect a legislative function, rejected this recommendation, thus making the granting of access to the report discretionary with the trial court in all cases. It repeated this rule in a later revision. The opposition to the proposed rule appears to have been based principally on a desire to protect the privacy of the presentence report. In an article which appeared prior to the promulgation of the rules, federal District Judge Carroll C. Hincks pointed out that presentence reports draw freely on the files of social agencies and information given by individuals, both of whom would hesitate to provide information if it were to be disclosed, and particularly if the source were disclosed.[2]

Presumably there would be no oppositon to giving the defendant the right to access to the report if it were felt that doing so would not damage the presentence investigation. A great deal of information comes from public records and from sources indifferent to disclosure to the defendant. Much information in the presentence report comes from such public records as vital statistics, physical and mental examination, school and employment data. The Supreme Court, elsewhere in the Rules of Criminal Procedure, shows no hesitancy about disclosing prosecution evidence to the defendant. A defendant in a federal court may obtain an order requiring the government to permit inspection before the trial of papers and other tangible evidence. It has been held that documents of an evidentiary character furnished the government *by voluntary and confidential informants* are subject to inspection.

Where for one reason or another an informant's identity must be protected, the court may determine that material shall be disclosed without disclosing the source. The Supreme Court added, "Where the court concludes that such materials ought to be produced, it should, of course, be solicitous to protect against disclosures of the identity of informants, and the manner and circumstances of the Government's acquisition of the materials."[3]

United States District Judge Charles E. Wyzanski, Jr., in a comment supporting a rule giving the defendant access to the presentence report, writes regarding the problem of confidential information, "In those situations where a wife, a minister, a doctor or other person is willing to give confidential information to the judge provided that the defendant does not hear it, this information ought to be revealed to the defendant's counsel for scrutiny and reply."[4]

Some psychiatric material might be destructive if disclosed to the defendant. The British Columbia Court,[5] while holding for a general rule of disclosure, considered that excepting such information would be proper. It suggested that "the examining doctor would be the best judge as to whether or not the result of his examination should be fully disclosed to the convict." Consideration might be given also to disclosing information to the defendant's counsel where it is withheld from the defendant for special reasons.

What about the information from general sources, making up the usual report? There is needed a study of a large number of presentence investigations to test the alternative rules. No such study has been made, and there are few published reports. Starting in 1950 *Federal Probation* has from time to time presented analyses of probation and parole reports. Two of these[6] are presentence reports. These are typical, containing information regarding the offense, the prior record of the defendant, the family history, and present conditions. The information is obtained from official sources, members of the family, the defendant himself, friends, neighbors, employer. Is there any suggestion that these reports could not with perfect safety be shown to the defendant, or that the obligation to show them would require the repression of any material? There does not appear to be anything of the kind in these reports.

Related to the consideration of whether material would be inhibited by a rule of disclosure is the whole matter of the value of the material obtained, particularly from collateral sources. Helen H. Perlman recently wrote, "Largely within the past ten years, . . . pushed by our heightened awareness of the client as a personality, by our deepened convictions about maintaining democratic principles, by our growing competence in purposive interviewing, there have risen a number of provocative questions to challenge this practice [use of the social service exchange]. These questions have centered on the ethics of exchanging information allegedly given in confidence and the actual usefulness of such data."[7] Most of such discussion has been focused on use of the social service exchange, coming in for more and more question. But the principle is involved of keying the casework practices to the values they have for the client, rather than convenience to the agency.

"Finally, and perhaps of most importance," says Mrs. Perlman, "the way that will insure maximum value in the use of collateral information is by the caseworker's open sharing with the client himself the purpose for which it is sought and the value which it may have for him. Nobody wants to be 'checked'; and nobody wants another person to 'find out about him' just in general. But if what is to be found out or even checked can be shown to have a relationship to promoting our welfare or meeting our needs, there is scarcely one among us—unless we have something to hide—who would object to such an inquiry."[8]

In the authoritative setting of probation, of course, the defendant with "something to hide" could forestall an inquiry. But the path of this thinking is on the one hand interpretation of the investigation to the client and consideration of his response in the quest for material and, on the other, an evaluation of the material.

The debate should not be made in a vacuum. We have not buckled down to examine how much our sources are injured, or would be, by a rule of disclosure, and how we could handle such a rule. Do we know how much really vital information would be withheld by a social agency which was informed that it might be revealed to the defendant? Can we not constructively use a preliminary discussion with the defendant as to the sources being contacted? Can we not profit from the discussion, discovering the defendant's reactions to the plan of the investigation? Where closeness of relationship to the defendant makes an individual reluctant to give information, is it not generally possible either to interpret the process or, as a last recourse, adopt Judge Wyzanski's suggestion of making it known only to the attorney? Judges who do disclose the report to the defense do *not* find the sources of information drying up.

The other consideration urged against disclosure to the defendant is that disputed matters would require a hearing by the court, with consequent delay in disposition. The argument based on delay at this stage of the proceeding does not seem a strong one. One of the unhappy aspects of sentencing is haste, the offhand imposition of sentence. On the other hand a defendant is frequently held for a considerable period before trial, or even before arraignment, through no fault of his, an experience which contributes nothing to the treatment process. Yet delay may have value if it is due to a careful approach to the sentence, as in the process of an investigation. If still further delay is introduced by the defendant in controverting material in a presentence report, it is a privilege for which he, not the court, pays in time.

But is the delay likely to be considerable? There is no problem if, after seeing the probation report, the defendant challenges no part of it. The report of a skilled probation officer in a competent department will not frequently be controverted. Some cases in which the probation report is challenged may require no more than the submission of affidavits.

If a hearing is required on a report the manner of conducting it is at the discretion of the judge. No formal evidentiary rules apply, unless the judge desires them. Judge Hincks pointed out that "It is always possible and generally desirable for the judge to inquire in open court whether any items which he considers controlling are disputed. If so, the judge can either disregard the item in dispute, or, if he deems it of sufficient importance, call for more information or evidence." This closely approaches the English rule, which requires disclosure of the report, and opportunity to the defendant for denial of evidence regarding personal history, with presentation of evidence. Controverted allegations unsupported by proof may not be relied upon.

The Challenge of a Rule of Disclosure

What effect would a rule disclosing the report to the defendant have on his attitude? It has been debated whether or not probation is casework. Perhaps it is not far from the mark if we say probation is casework where casework methods are used in dealing with a defendant being sentenced and with a probationer; it is not casework if they are not. If the defendant being sentenced is excluded from the sentencing process, does it not correspond to supervision as surveillance rather than as an interpersonal process? When do we exhibit a casework approach to the investigation—when we refuse to disclose the report which is the basis for the sentence, or when we permit disclosure? Is not disclosure an occasion and an opportunity to interpret the report, so that the disposition will be better understood and a mutually open relationship begun? Departments which make it a practice to disclose unfavorable material to a defendant do so not merely to be fair, but to know and understand the response of the defendant to it.

It has been said that to suggest a rule of disclosure implies lack of confidence in the probation officer. On the contrary; we presuppose an objective and competent report. Is it not well for the attitude of the defendant that he see the report is an objective one? The element of fairness does not stand in isolation. *Fairness is a positive, constructive element in the success of the probation process.*

Not only are there positive values to disclosure, there are negative values to withholding. Practically all the material supporting the denial of access is negative—it points out the harmful aspects that may flow to the relationship of the probation officer to the defendant and to those who provide information to the probation officer.

But if the report is not shown to the defendant, whether he later becomes a probationer or prisoner, what is the effect on his attitude of the realization that he was not trusted, that an account and evaluation of his own history was concealed from him? What of his feeling of unfairness that the crucial matter of sentence has been done without his knowing the basis for it, without an opportunity to contribute to it with knowledge of what it contains?

If it is not shown to him the defendant-probationer speculates as to what is known—or may endeavor to discover it. On probation he may be on guard because the court and probation officer have not trusted him with information he feels should be his.

A comprehensive presentence report is the mainstay of any claim to scientific sentencing. An advocate of probation must face the disagreeable aspects of reality. The United States Attorney General, on the basis of the most comprehensive study made of national probation practices, declared, "If, however, there is any general sttaement that this study can offer without hesitation as to the faults of modern probation, it is that records of probation work are inadequate, unreliable, and for the most part nonexistent . . . Observation of probation investigative practices throughout the country reveals that only in the Federal probation service and in no more than three states is there a uniformly fair investigation system within the jurisdictional boundaries."[9] The situation has improved only moderately since this 1939 report.

Giving the defendant access to the report and opportunity to comment on it, even to controvert it, is not only a protection to the defendant against error, it is also a degree of protection to the court. Furthermore, disclosure to the defendant who is the subject of investigation would be an influence against laxity in the investigation, carelessness in the writing of the report, and rubberstamping of the report by the judge.

The sentence is an important step in treatment, not only in the obvious sense that it determines the basic mode of treatment as between incarceration or release in the community, but also for its immedaite psychological effect on the defendant. The defendant should be helped to understand the sentence imposed, a vital consideration if he is to have any feeling of being fairly treated. Giving him access to the report helps the defendant to understand the sentence.

In a recent article federal Judge Theodore Levin wrote of the importance of disclosure of judicial reasoning. "The sentencing process," said Judge Levin, "should include the transmittal of information to the prisoner, his family, and to the public so that variations in sentences may be understood to be due to the individualization of punishment and not to mere whim or caprice on the part of the judge; to the extent possible, the conviction should be induced in the minds of the public that the administration of justice is a democratic process applied cautiously and carefully by the agents of the Government, in the interest of and for the protection of the whole body of the people, without discrimination and without vengeance."[10]

For a presentence report to serve as the basis of a just and rehabilitative sentence it must be relied on by the court in systematic fashion. Giving the defendant access to the report also gives the appellate court access to it, a necessity if there is to be assurance that, in the words of the Illinois Supreme Court in People v. Donovan,[11] the report is to be handled not arbitrarily but with a sound legal discretion dependent for its exercise upon the facts shown.

Finally, the considerable authority given by statute to court and probation department imposes a corresponding responsibility. Probation officers must counteract the authoritative setting in which they work by a nonauthoritative attitude. Such an attitude is not supported by concealment of the contents of the presentence report; it is supported by frankness in revealing what the court knows about the defendant. There is a further obligation. Authority means not merely authority to decree, but the *noblesse oblige* of an authoritative procedure which suggests surrounding itself with precautions against abuse.

A rule giving the defendant access to the report will in some measure inhibit the officer in preparing his report, and in obtaining some information. The issue is presented as to whether the advantages of disclosure, and the requirement of fairness to the defendant being sentenced, outweigh the disadvantages. One writer has said: "At these relatively infrequent times [when proof becomes necessary] the risk of injustice to the defendant would seem to outweigh contrary consideration of administrative convenience. . . . The possibility of a partial drying up of sources of information is an unavoidable consequence of any system of criminal administration which requires that the defendant be informed of the evidence against him, and would seem to be no more than one of the many burdens imposed on the state in any such system because of the overriding importance of avoiding falsity and oppression of the individual."[12]

A Safe Rule—Or a Dynamic One

If we examine the basis for resistance to disclosure, do we not find there a tendency to choose a supposedly "safe" way—*perhaps* we can disclose with profit, but *certainly* we can withhold with safety. Immediately that kind of "safety" recalls another kind of "safety" which is one of the deadliest obstacles to a proper increase in the use of probation. This other "safe" decision is made at the time of sentence, when the judge considers probation, but is not sure it will succeed. He therefore does *not* place on probation, but commits to prison. Is he confident that prison treatment will be successful? Oh no. But with the defendant in prison *the judge* is safer—prison failure is not his. Unfortunately it is this "safe" policy that results in our present institutional situation—a great percentages of prisoners, people who would probably have succeeded on probation, creating problems of overcrowding and demoralization for themselves and the institutions.

Of course there is a risk in placing on probation; but we know that prison is not the superior alternative. Of course there are risks in a rule of disclosure! of course a rule of privacy safeguards our sources of information. But there are risks also in a rule of privacy; the values of disclosure are lost—of a certainty. It is suggested that we learn to handle the problems of disclosure, and by this rule can retain the benefits of a casework attitude.

One of the great issues of the day, in America as elsewhere, is the winning, protection, and strengthening of civil liberties. The question of secrecy of accusation (to which our present discussion is highly relevant), is coming time and again before our courts, which have repeatedly repudiated the idea of secret evidence or secret accusations. In 1957 the United States Supreme Court ruled that where a police informer's testimony was relevant and helpful to the accused in preparing his defense, the government had no right to withhold it. The struggle goes on in many fields, perhaps less in the field of correction of offenders than in other activities, but it is alive here too, and correction is bound to be affected by trends in other parts of American life.

Notes

[1] Code of Ala., 1940, Title 42, Section 23; N.C., Laws of 1937, Section 15-207; Ky., Revised Statutes of 1942, Section 439.210; Md., Laws of 1931, Chapter 132, Section 1.

[2] "In Opposition to Rule 34 (c) (2), Proposed Federal Rules of Criminal Procedure," by Carroll C. Hincks, *Federal Probation,* October-December, 1944.

[3] Bowman Dairy Co. v. U.S., 341 U.S. 214, 71 S. Ct. 679 (1951).

[4] Judge Charles E. Wyzanski, "A Trial Judge's Freedom and Responsibility," (*Harvard Law Review,* June, 1952, p. 1291). "Despite the latitude permitted by the due process clause, it seems to me that a judge in considering his sentence, just as in trying a defendant, should never take into account any evidence, report or other fact which is not brought to the attention of defendant's counsel with opportunity to rebut it. *Audi alteram partem,* [hear the other side] if it is not a universal principal of democratic justice, is at any rate sufficiently well-founded not to be departed from by a trial judge when he is performing his most important function."

[5] Rex. v. Stevenson, Court of Appeal of British Columbia, 3 Western Weekly Reports (new series), 29, 1951.

[6] *Federal Probation,* March, 1950 and December, 1950.

[7] "The Case Worker's Use of Collateral Information," by Helen H. Perlman (*Social Casework,* October, 1951).

[8] See also, "The Client's Rights and the Use of the Social Service Exchange," by Charlotte Towle (*Social Science Review,* March, 1949).

[9] *Attorney General's Survey of Release Procedures,* Vol. II, Probation (Government Printing Office, 1939, p. 180, 181).

[10] "Sentencing the Criminal Offender," by Theodore Levin (*Federal Probation,* March, 1949).

[11] Cited in the previous chapter.

[12] "Right of Offenders to Challenge Reports Used in Determining Sentence," Note (*Columbia Law Review,* April, 1949).

References

Writing taking more or less the opposing point of view, arguing for privacy of presentence reports, are these: "Confidentiality of Presentence Reports," by Albert W. Roche (*Focus,* March, 1953); "The Confidential Nature of Presentence Reports," by Louis L. Sharp (*Catholic Law Review,* May, 1955); "Shall Presentence Reports be Made Available to Defense Attorneys?" by Judge Carroll C. Hincks (*Federal Probation,* October, 1944). An article with more sympathy for the point of view of our chapter, is "Due Process and Legislative Standards in Sentencing," Note (*University of Pennsylvania Law Review,* November, 1952).

The Probation Officer Investigates, by Paul Keve (University of Minnesota Press, 1960), deals incidentally with the subject of this chapter, and generally with the preparation and use of the presentence investigation. On use of the presentence investigation in arriving as a disposition: *Guides for Sentencing* (Advisory Council of Judges of NCCD, 1957); *The Selection of Offenders for Probation,* Prepared by Dr. Max Grünhut (United Nations, Department of Economic and Social Affairs, 1959).

This chapter incorporates material previously published in two articles, one in *Federal Probation,* December, 1952, and the other in *Focus,* March, 1952.

Part VI

RESEARCH

Chapter 14

Research for a Scientific Criminology

Is criminology—the study of crime and the treatment and control of criminals—a science? The question falls into two parts—one, the social and individual nature of crime and its causation; and two, the nature of administrative action in dealing with criminals.

If we look at the many available discussions of what causes crime and delinquency we must conclude that thus far criminology is not a science. At the moment we have at best not more than debates between different "schools of thought." Two thoughtful writers, for example, discuss this situation.

Albert K. Cohen in his fine book, *Delinquent Boys—The Culture of the Gang,*[1] discusses the theory of those who argue that delinquency is a result of some attribute of the child, an attribute which the non-delinquent child does not possess, or does not possess in the same degree; and the more or less conflicting theory that delinquency may be the behavior of any kind of personality if circumstances favor intimate association with delinquent models.

Frank E. Hartung writes in the *Journal of Criminal Law, Criminology, and Police Science*[2] that he regards "the social-psychological approach to criminality as being the most reasonable," but he also refers to the social disorganization hypothesis, the rationalistic hypothesis, and several varieties of psychiatric hypotheses. These probably refer to most of the theories going the rounds today. They are competing theories, in the main.

The plane upon which we question whether criminology today is scientific is in the broad sweep of the theories, in relation to the data they purport to cover. Compare the beginnings of astronomy and the other sciences of the cosmos. "Before the time of Copernicus," wrote William Kingdom Clifford, "men knew all about the Universe. They could tell you in the schools, pat off by heart, all that it was, and what it had been, and what it would be. There was the flat earth, with the blue vault of heaven resting on it like the dome of a cathedral, and the bright cold stars stuck into it; while the sun and planets moved in crystal spheres between. Or, among the better informed, the earth was a globe in the centre of the universe, heaven a sphere concentric with it; intermediate machinery as before. At any rate, if there was anything beyond heaven, it was a void space that needed no further description. The history of all this could be traced back to a certain definite time, when it began; behind that was a changeless eternity that needed no further history. . . . Now the enormous effect of the Copernican system, and of the astronomical discoveries that have followed it, is that, in place of this knowledge of a little, which was called knowledge of the Universe, of Eternity and Immensity, we have now got knowledge of a great deal more; but we only call it the knowledge of Here and Now."

The early history of astronomy (like the beginnings of other sciences) by analogy tells us the kind of thinking, or research, which is too speculative for a science of criminology. It is theorizing constructed without adequate accounting for the facts we have, and that does not test itself by exposure to new data. It is a broad generalizing that jumps long distances between facts, and falls into error because of the mass of speculation between them. There are those who are quite convinced of an individualistic origin of criminal behavior. To them crime stems from the formation of character in the family setting. The relationship of parent to child is fairly decisive. To others, crime is mainly to be explained in sociological terms—somehow, crime is a product of society. But these theories do not take us very far. If we ask—if it is the family, *how* does the family produce crime?—replies may forthcoming, but they are just so much more speculation. Or, *how* does crime develop in society? What is the mechanism, the step-by-step process? It is not explained.

And so it has been. The many doctrines of causation of crime and delinquency have had their day time and again, and all of them marched up the hill and down again, either ending in invalidation, or remaining partly suspended above the undigested facts. For a while the "best" scientific thought worked around the thesis that anomalous and degenerative physical conditions, particularly in the skull and brain, were the chief characteristics of the criminal and the key to his behavior. A little later, in the early decades of this century, considerable respect was paid to the thought that there was a basic relationship between defective mentality and crime. Then emphasis was based on the psychopathic criminal and on the neurotic or emotionally disturbed. And so it was with a series of varying statements of social or environmental theories (poverty, "delinquency areas," or other aspects of social disorganization).

Although these studies revealed much worthwhile data, because so much remained unexplained they have not resulted in a solid foundation for a scientific criminology. Each researcher started out on a practically new path, using little of what others have done. One did not build on the other.

If the sweep of the successive theories is too broad, we have to focus them. A popular newsweekly carried a special nationwide survey on the problem of parental responsibility for juvenile delinquency. A colleague told me about it, and I asked whether there was anything new in it. "No," he said; "what could be new?" What could be new on this subject, or ony any subject in our field, is, *one, facts,* and *two, finding reliable relationships among facts.* The facts would be events, changes, influences, responses, in the lives of delinquents, shown to have a relationship to the delinquent act or behavior. It is premature (unscientific) to argue the reasons *why* a thing is so, until we can show or know *how* it is so, through convincing explanations of the data. Until then we may not really know *whether* it is so. The theories might be narrow rather than broad, but would account for facts specifically enough to be capable of demonstration and proof.

The ancient Greek philosopher Anaximander taught that life arose from mud warmed up by the sun's rays. Plants came first, then animals, and finally man; and he further reasoned that since a child is unable to feed or to take care of himself he must have arisen from another animal. Not bad; but it took a new era to produce a Darwin to demonstrate far less, and far more—*how* creatures evolved in their biological forms.

Seeing the Facts of the Delinquent and Criminal Behavior

This is the first problem then for any "school" of criminological thought: to marshal the facts that are significant to the criminal and his criminality, and to track the step-to-step action of one thing upon another, leading to the delinquency and beyond. To avoid high-flying speculation, the facts about delinquents and criminals that we have to look at closely are those facts that we can relate to their behavior, whether they be facts about the individual or facts around him. We have many life histories of delinquents and criminals, and in this day of casework and psychiatry we are producing them prolifically. What do we have to do to tie the facts together scientifically?

Isn't there something else axiomatic? That in each individual, there are factors that push him toward delinquency, and factors pushing to law-abiding behavior. The life of a delinquent or criminal, like the life of anyone else, is a development, a history. A delinquent act is related to many things that went before, not all of equal weight of course, but many that are significant and that depend upon one another as do the events in a nation's history. No individual, no matter what his personality or family background, is predestined for crime. It is a life history that ordains it.

The culture presses upon the individual (the individuals and his drives) in ways supporting behavior that is lawful, and supporting behavior that is unlawful. The relationship of forces varies with time and place in society and differently in different individuals. We can undoubtedly enumerate these factors, and we can see them operate in a life history or in a group.

What do these axiomatic statements lead to? I should think they lead to the need, now, for clear sight in describing and analyzing life histories, many of them, in terms of two main streams of force and their elements. Description and analysis must be keen and convincing in evaluation of the relative weight of the factors, and must demonstrate their influence in the life. With a number of such analyses of life histories one could proceed to classify the facts, and their effects on different kinds of individuals in different settings or situations. Nor do we have to study only entire lives. Those who are in contact with individuals for an appreciable period can analyze wisely on that basis.

Something else would be accomplished in this way. Crime is frequently referred to as though it were a solidly uniform concept. But of course each crime is not like every other; each crime is different from others. Crime is the product of all sorts of forces and attitudes, moving from all sorts of ethical motivations, sometimes representative of an individual's general outlook, and sometimes not. In the life history of an individual who has committed a crime, the crime does not represent the end of the life, but an incident in relationship to others.

Thus this kind of life history study would comprehend the meaning of the particular criminal or delinquent act; it would avoid the error Professor Cohen referred to: "How perfunctory has been our concern with the delinquent action itself, that with which these 'correlates' are presumably correlated. In what passes for a 'thorough' report on a delinquent child, we can often learn more about his pre-natal care and the condition of his teeth than about his delinquent behavior itself. The assumption seems to be common that delinquency, like measles, is a homogeneous something that people either have or have not and that it is sufficient, therefore, simply to note that a person is or is not a 'delinquent.' "[3]

In a paragraph above I have suggested as axiomatic that in each individual case, in the course of history of a life, there are factors pushing to delinquency, and factors pushing to law-abidingness, the weight of the forces varying with time and place in society and in the individuals. This is somewhat different from Sutherland's "differential association" concept, but it is also very much like it.[4] As little as it says, it is a notch above the common expression that crime is the product of a "multiplicity of factors," which contains no guide at all as to how the factors are to be distributed or classified.[5]

But it undoubtedly says little about causation. Like "differential association," it is not a theory; rather, both are suggestions of techniques of investigation, based on the natural development of lives. Yet it is this technique of life history analysis, with its classification of crime-encouraging and law-encouraging elements, that has its own great importance, and it is this path that can be taken to a scientific criminology.

Life History Studies

Several criminologists represent this point of view consistently. Edwin H. Sutherland placed great reliance on this method, undoubtedly formed many of his ideas about crime causation from it, and repeatedly referred to it as a reliable method. *The Professional Thief,* written ("annotated and interpreted," he said) by Sutherland in 1937,[6] is based on a single life, that of a professional thief. Sutherland submitted the manuscript to four other professional thieves and to two former detectives. He discussed the ideas and problems with several other professional thieves, with several other representatives of municipal and private police systems, and with clerks in stores. In general these supplementary sources did not even hint at disagreement with the manuscript on fundamental issues. Most of the book, it is true, is given over to an account of the professional life of a thief, rather than to the things that made him a thief. But the latter is not omitted, and Sutherland suggests the living course of development.

It has considerable interest and a reliable ring. His study leads Sutherland to suggest that to a certain extent, so far as the development of the thief goes, the course is accidental. He suggests that the individual is *selected* for his career, rather than that he does the selecting: "The selective action of the professional thieves is probably more significant than the selective action of the potential thief. An inclination to steal is not a sufficient explanation of the genesis of the professional thief. Everyone has an inclination to steal and expresses this inclination with more or less frequency and with more or less finesse. The person must be appreciated by the professional thieves. He must be appraised as having an adequate equipment of wits, front, talking ability, honesty, reliability, nerve, and determination. The comparative importance of these several characteristics cannot be determined at present, but it is highly probable that no characteristic is valued more highly than honesty. It is probably regarded as more essential than mental ability. This, of course, means honesty in dealings within their own group.

"An emergency or crisis is likely to be the occasion on which tutelage begins. A person may lose a job, get caught in amateur stealing, or may need additional money. If he has developed a friendly relationship with professional thieves, he may request or they may suggest that he be given a minor part in some act of theft. He would, if accepted, be given verbal instructions in regard to the theory of the racket and the specific part he is to play. In his first efforts in this minor capacity he may be assisted by the professional thieves, although such assistance would be regarded as an affront by one who was already a professional. If he performs these minor duties satisfactorily, he is promoted to more important duties. During this probationary period the neophyte is assimilating the general standards of morality, propriety, etiquette, and rights which characterize the profession, and he is acquiring 'larceny sense.' He is learning the general methods of disposing of stolen goods and of fixing cases. He is building up a personal acquaintance with other thieves, and with lawyers, policemen, court officials, and fixers. . . . As a result of this tutelage during the probationary period, he acquires the techniques of theft and consensus with the thieves." Etc.[7]

Very likely such a pattern is similar to other underworld careers, but not to that of the casual offender. The lives of casual offenders would reveal other typical sequences leading to their crimes. The pattern of crimino-genesis would be different again for white-collar criminals.

There is little on the early development history of the thief. "He was born in Philadelphia about fifty years ago. His family was in comfortable circumstances. In adolescence he was ushering in a theater, formed an attachment for a chorus girl, married her, began using narcotic drugs occasionally in association with her, left home, and became a pimp. In that occupation he became acquainted with thieves and through them learned to steal." Obviously much more was warranted, although Sutherland must have felt the preeminence of the sociological process which he presented in summary.

There are other merits of the study, from our point of view regarding life study. The life of a criminal may represent not only *entrance* into crime, but *exit* from it. How does it come about? The vast majority of juvenile delinquents "outgrow" delinquency; by what process? Sparse as Sutherland's statement on it is, we rarely see such a thought related at all. He writes: "A person who is a professional thief may cease to be one. This would generally result from a violation of the codes of the profession or else from inefficiency due to age, fear, narcotic drugs, or drink.

Because of either failure he would no longer be able to find companions with whom to work, would not be trusted by the fixer or by the policemen, and therefore he would not be able to secure immunity from punishment. He is no longer recognized as a professional thief, and therefore he can no longer be a professional thief. On the other hand, if he drops out of active stealing of his own volition and retains his abilities, he would continue to receive recognition as a professional thief. He would be similar to a physician who would be recognized as a physician after he ceased active practice."[8]

What impact does law enforcement have on a professional thief? It represents hazards in his profession, not at all insurmountable, and sometimes supportive of the career. Without belaboring the matter, it is evident that the thief's life went on professionally, and that the efforts of the law were incidents in that life.

Sutherland plainly advocates this type of study in his critique of *Later Criminal Careers,* by Sheldon and Eleanor T. Glueck. "The most significant conclusion, in my opinion, which emerges from this study is that those who ultimately reformed differed from those who remained to the end almost entirely unreformed in their pre-Reformatory characteristics. The characteristics of those who reformed changed while the characteristics of the unreformed remained relatively constant. This indicates that reformation is a process, a growth involving many aspects of life. In order that research on this subject may be effective, it is important to secure an organic picture of the process. This could be done by asking reformed ex-prisoners why they reformed and unreformed ex-prisoners why they did not reform. Categorical answers to these questions would, of course, be of little value. But if answers could be secured in the form of detailed and intimate descriptions, it would be possible to form a picture of the process of reformation as a whole. At that point statistical studies might be developed on the crucial problems, and a schedule with hundreds of questions, such as that used by the Gluecks, would not be needed."[9]

Elsewhere Sutherland suggests study of the lives of prisoners: "A study of them will result," he writes, "not in a statistical conclusion regarding the importance of intelligence as a factor in the causation of crime, but in a description of the process by which intelligent persons become criminals. Feebleminded criminals can be studied in a similar manner. Again, 'organized criminals' are less likely than others to be committed to prison, but even Al Capone has been incarcerated once, and most of his lieutenants and many other gangsters and racketeers have served prison terms.

"Comparable studies are conducted in medical clinics. It is not necessary that the proportion of persons with typhoid fever who appear in the clinic should be the same as the proportion of persons with scarlet fever in order that the physicians in the clinic may make studies of the patients. If each prisoner is regarded as a representative of a 'species' of criminals, he can be studied as such, even though some species may not be represented in prison in proportion to their crimes."[10]

Clifford R. Shaw made a major contribution in his life history studies, *The Jack-Roller: A Delinquent Boy's Own Story,*[11] *The Natural History of a Delinquent Career,*[12] and *Brothers in Crime.*[13] A summary here of equal length to that given of Sutherland's work would be warranted; but perhaps the point is well enough made for the present discussion. And there are others; for example Dr. Frederic Wertham's *Dark Legend,*[14] and *The Show of Violence.*[15] Some keen and sensitive novels provide excellent life histories in our field.[16] The autobiography of Caryl Chessman, whose execution in California aroused world-wide protest, is a goldmine, both as to development of criminal careers and as to the impact of correctional treatment.[17]

Nor is it only complete life histories which can serve. Life *experiences, incidents,* carefully observed and associated, tell us a great deal. The social work journals, and somewhat less, the correctional journals, have such material, at various levels of insight.

These, then, seem to me to be the beginning of the facts and analysis which can serve as the core of a scientific criminology. But we have hardly used these materials. Sutherland himself did not give sufficient recognition to his own (as well as other's) life histories and the life history approach. In the latest (fifth) edition of his *Principles of Criminology* (with Donald R. Cressey) under a brief section headed "Methods of Studying Crime," the "individual case study" is treated briefly and without great emphasis. "Life history" is not indexed. The fourth edition, by Sutherland alone, is about the same.

The textbook writers, who are a great link between basic findings and transmission of their significance, pay scant attention to these works. We have many excellent criminology and juvenile delinquency textbooks, but they would be enormously more valuable if the writers undertook to provide their own analyses of the life history materials already produced and those the writers have themselves observed.

In an established science there is a constant building up of accepted knowledge and theory that serves as an ever growing base for new research and theories. But this has not happened yet in criminology, each writer dwelling very much in the house of his own beliefs.

Correctional Treatment and Administration

The second part of criminology is the treatment of criminals. How scientific are we here?

We sometimes talk about correctional treatment in the life of the offender as though we had two quite separate operations. The life of the offender is thought of as though it inevitably pursues a course to crime; and the life of correction as though it ineluctably pursues the effort at his rehabilitation. Neither of these concepts is true. We know that correction generally has not achieved more than a low estate. With some exceptions, its personnel are insufficient, poorly trained, with hardly any clinical resources. With few exceptions, the judiciary are not specialists in either juvenile court or criminal court work. But even if this were not so, and in the few places where standards in correction are fairly high, it is still true that the life of the individual under correctional treatment may remain essentially what it was before, that the efforts of the law were merely incidents in the thief's life, and the same can be said of the lives told by Clifford Shaw.

The realities of administration in law enforcement and correction are facts in the world of delinquents and criminals, perhaps affecting their behavior and development, perhaps often being swalllowed and assimilated into the individual's basic patterns.

Correctional treatment may not have as great an impact as we think, and perhaps in some ways it furthers criminogenic factors.

The correctional experience may verify for the offender his view of the world. In his study of an army disciplinary barrack, Richard Cloward found that many military prisoners gradually lost interest in becoming rehabilitated. Their anti-social attitudes were fostered by the inconsistencies of the military prison.[18] It has frequently been observed that our prisons and jails actually serve as schools of crime and delinquency.

It is at this point that despite many studies, the critical facts are poorly known. We have not adequately studied administration as it affects the lives of offenders. Surveys in the correctional field commonly evaluate a court, institution, probation department, with reference to some generally accepted standards, rather than with reference to what impact they have on individuals. This occurs also in other fields, and to an extent it is good and worthwhile. The method is a tool in improving administration. When the most thoughtful, experienced people in a field concur in defining standards, we are justified in relying on them. But they do not contribute to criminology as a science.

First, then, in correctional studies, we ought to observe the impact of treatment on the lives of the people involved. And in examining these things, we should look not so much for a follow-up study in which the individuals are found, say, after five or ten years. Perhaps such follow-up studies have their uses, but they are far from a reliable test of correctional practice to which individuals were earlier exposed, whether for long or little. It seems much more sensible to see what were the immediate or presently observed effects.

What are some illustrations? What sort of facts do we need?

An Ohio study drew a useful picture of institutions for delinquent children through an analysis of the answers of the children in them to numerous questions about how they felt about various aspects of their treatment.[19] The extended and organized use of the "worm's eye view" method proved to be fresh and productive.

A New York City study examined the case records of 200 children and youths in courts and institutions, to determine what had happened to them in the hands of community agencies, what plans were made for them, whether the dispositions were wise, whether the children received the help they needed. The results were gloomy. Most agencies performed their functions on a minimal basis; the dispositions were quite often not adequate to change a course of conduct or deal basically with a problem. Probation was more often a promise and a gesture than competent supervision. In many of the places available to the courts, children were as likely to be indoctrinated in anti-social patterns as to be helped.[20] Both of these studies are unorthodox; but that is not what is being stressed. Rather, we are pointing to their emphasis not on what the agencies did, but on what the effect was on the child.

The British courts use fines for children; and the judge fixes a commitment not over 3 years, in contrast to the universal use in the United States of the commitment which is indeterminate, with an outside limit of the child's twenty-first year. Do these methods work well or poorly? Can they be adopted here to advantage? How does the effect on the children compare with other forms of disposition? It was logic that led the Standard Juvenile Court Act committee to adopt for the 1959 Act the plan of a three year commitment for juvenile courts, as we noted in chapter 4. It would be wise, and not difficult, for a jurisdiction that adopts this feature of the Standard Act to be attentive to the differential results of the change in the form of commitment.

Such studies, like life history studies of individuals, must be closely factual, expertly descriptive, so that a reader may apply his own analysis, testing that of the author's (or researcher's).

Seeing correction as part of a life history has a meaning for the understanding of causation. The point has been made by Walter C. Reckless, who wrote: "It has already been suggested that studies of response to treatment can throw considerable light on etiology and that such studies properly manipulated can approximate experimental conditions. For example, it is possible to subject homogeneous groups of offenders to certain severe and liberal disciplinary rules within an institution or homogeneous groups of parolees to intensive and minimum supervision and to other permissible variations in treatment, in order to discover differential response to situations demanding conformity to conduct rules. By such means, it should be possible to obtain insight into factors determining an offender's ability or inability to take a period of supervision, treatment, or training as a constructive experience."[21]

But Professor Reckless' comment still suggests emphasis on studying the response of the offender to a correctional methodology of one calculated form or another. In addition to that we have to see the correctional service not as an abstraction, a summary, a set form; but rather as a living institution, that is in terms of the personalities, attitudes, lives, if you will, of the people performing them; and the process, manner, of its application. This, I suggest, is the second vital element commonly ignored in correctional studies. Through its use we can better judge how "objective" a treatment procedure is; we obtain a deeper understanding of it, so that we can more readily discern its merits and faults; we can better judge the impact upon offenders, knowing the attitudes and motivation which are affecting them—for they react not to an idealized service, but to its flesh and blood application.

Second, then, in correctional studies we ought to study, discover, and analyse not only the nature of the correctional services, but their living constitutions, the attitudes, personalities, of the people performing them, and the manner in which the acts are done. Dr. Sol Wiener Ginsberg has written; "The thesis of this discussion is that the personality that the social worker brings to his job is a complex resultant of many forces and that in the development of this personality, cultural factors have played a vital role; that his attitudes toward himself, his clients, and his job reflect his own life experiences, his values and goals, his expectancies and ambitions, and his image of himself as a person in a social setting; that these experiences will reflect not only the worker's racial, economic, and religious background and upbringing, but also his social class status and that of his family, his class allegiances and awareness and, especially in our country, practices and habits of thought and behavior which are native to the particular region in which he spent his formative years; that these attitudes and goals and needs may conflict with those of his clients who are also materially influenced by the impact of their own culture; that even when there is no conflict, the worker's own culturally influenced attitudes must inevitably play an important role in his understanding, handling, and treatment of the client's problems; and finally, that this interaction is not by any means always conscious and recognized but often, as with other human attitudes, may be active entirely at an unconscious level, disguised in rationalization, and rationalized in theoretical assumption and technical procedures."[22]

The same is true of our correctional institutions. I would only add that human beings (persons receiving correctional treatment) react not only to the thing—the service—offered them, but also—and perhaps more so—to the attitude and manner in which it is done. That is, we will actually have more *objective* studies, if we include awareness of the actors as well as the act performed.

A shorthand term for correctional research utilizing these approaches might be "psychological-administrative" research.

What illustrations are there of such research studies needed today?

If there is one underlying concept in penology it is the considered application of punishment. Yet there is hardly any study of the subject of punishment and its effects. When and under what circumstances, how applied, is punishment constructive—or hurtful? What, in fact, do we mean by punishment? Is it the thing that is done? Often it is; but often it is the way a thing is done. How much punishment is there in the probation setting; or in fines; how evaluate it and deal with it?

The phenomenon of prison riots has been studied, but we have not begun to penetrate the opportunity they present of learning broadly about correction. We have paid some attention to their causation; but not to the effect they have had, on prisoners, prison personnel, legislators. Lloyd Ohlin, after referring to administrative changes resulting from prison riots, made these apt observations: "Similar administration action may be observed during the occurrence of so-called 'parole scandals.' At such times of crisis, newspaper criticism creates a flurry of administrative activitiy to alleviate the situation. Such an incident occurred in Illinois in 1936 when a parolee, in the act of committing a crime, killed a policeman. The newspapers seized this opportunity to launch a bitter attack on the parole system. As a direct consequence a sharp reduction occurred in the number of paroles granted. Whereas in 1936 over 1400 paroles were granted at the Joliet-Stateville and Menard branches of the Illinois State Penitentiary System, in 1937 the paroles granted were cut to more than one-third of that number. A change also took place in the readiness to revoke parole for rule violation. Prior to this incident, there were nearly as many parolees returned for new felonies as for violating the parole rules. After this incident, there were over twice as many parolees returned for technical violation of the parole regulations as were returned for committing new crimes. . . . The stricter selection and revocation policies were gradually relaxed in succeeding years, until again in 1941 nearly 1400 parolees were released from Joliet and Menard. The relative proportion of minor and major violators again approached equality."[23] In brief, how has correction really reacted to the prison riots, what are the immediate as well as the persistent effects?

In an earlier chapter I discussed the problem of long prison terms, suggesting that a needed reform is the sharp reduction in their length as well as number. But what studies have we made of either long term or short term treatment methods, with respect to their effects and uses? What are the possibilities of short term treatment? What really is the curve of adjustment in an institution? When does adjustment in the institution represent actual maladjustment to life? The average sentence being served by prisoners in the Federal penitentiary at Alcatraz was over 22 years. On what basis were these sentences warranted? Were all or most of these prisoners really dangerous?

We know very little about sentencing by criminal court judges. Uusually at best we know what dispositions a court has made—what number and percentage of offenders were placed on probation, committed, fined. Occasionally studies go a little further, comparing the dispositions of different judges. What of the court behavior of judges, their attitude toward defendants, the manner of conducting sentencing hearings, of imposing sentences? What of the psychology of judges, as it affects their reaction to crimes? What kind of sentencing does it result in, with what effect on defendants? It appears that girls in juvenile court are committed in a greater percentage of cases than boys. Why is this? Is it related to sex bias of judges? What can we learn about the soundness or error of this judicial practice? It appears that girls are held in institutions longer than boys. What does it mean?

One could go on with suggesting such studies, because the approach is almost universally applicable. One could approach an understanding of the psychology of the legislative process. In an earlier chapter I discussed the forms of commitment; what factors, motivations, governed legislative behavior in adopting one form or another, giving up one form for another? What is the effect of the form of sentence, or other legislative mandate, on the attitude of the judge? What form elicits a rehabilitative rather than a punitive attitude? The same questions may be raised as to effects on parole boards (I should say: parole board members). . . . We could examine our attitude toward security in prison, and even toward escape. We are highly security-minded, and we are abnormally alarmed by the thought of a prisoner escaping. . . . A number of prisoners end their terms by dying. What sort of prisoners do we keep until death? . . . In another chapter we have talked about youth authorities. Here is an important new structure that should be explored dynamically. How has the existence of a youth authority affected the attitudes of the community in which it exists? How has it affected the judges? Is institutional treatment used more loosely or more precisely, where a youth authority exists? How does that come about? . . . What are the effects on the family unit of imprisonment of a member, or his being placed on probation, or otherwise dealt with? . . . Out of the problems dealt with in this book alone, innumerable research problems arise or are implied, which would lead to knowledge of the most practical application.[24]

We have asserted that the rate of use of probation can be substantially increased. Here, at least, we have new proof through research. A first report on the "Saginaw Project," the three year demonstration in this county in the State of Michigan, conducted under the auspices of the Michigan Crime and Delinquency Council of NCCD, accomplished these things: (1) The rate of use of probation in felony cases was increased from 61 to 68 per cent. (2) State prison commitments were reduced from 34 to 17 per cent. (3) Commitments on revocation of probation were reduced from 32 to 17 per cent. The research staff report promises to be more than a statistical accounting.[25]

Prospects for Scientific Criminology

Is this "mere" administrative research, action research? In any event it is useful. But I suggest it is more basic than that. In other fields we learn about the "cause" and nature of phenomena not only by an examination of the event and its antecedents, but also by a study of what happens in the study of our subject as we do things with it—analysing it by its after-history, or subjecting it to heat or dyeing it. Correspondingly, what happens to an individual subjected to six months in idleness in a local jail; or 6 years in a penitentiary; what difference if he labors in prison; and what difference if he labors and is paid for it; what is the effect of probation with incompetent supervision; etc.

Progress in the science of criminology, with respect to the causation and nature of criminal and delinquent behavior, is not particularly a problem in the unearthing of facts, so often (but by no means always) the problem in the natural sciences. Rather it is a matter of (1) looking at the facts dynamically (an analytical study of life histories, and the patterns of "psychological-administrative" research); and (2) proper systematization of facts. In the theories we suggest to account for data, we must reach only as far as we can see, but that is far enough, for then we have begun to build, with the first small skeins of relationships sweeping in more facts, and reaching out for the next connecting links.

Perhaps the struggle to claim and systematize the proper facts is going on even now, but I believe the contending schools have not yet come to close enough quarters with the facts. With the increasing professionalization of the correctional field, now going on, we can look forward to this development, I believe. Perhaps when it is done it will not be with the noise of thunder. Probably not. But then later we will look back and find that we have come a long way, and will not doubt that criminology is a science.

Notes

1 Albert K. Cohen, *Delinquent Boys—The Culture of the Gang* (The Free Press, Glencoe, Ill., 1955). See especially chapter 1.

2 Frank E. Hartung, "Methodological Assumption in a Social Psychological Theory of Criminality" (*Journal of Criminal Law, Criminology, and Police Science,* March-April 1955).

3 Op. cit. n. 1, at p. 172.

4 *Principles of Criminology,* by Edwin H. Sutherland and Donald R. Cressey, (J. B. Lippincott Co., 1955, fifth edition; p. 77).

5 See, ibid, pp. 59-62.

6 Edwin H. Sutherland, *The Professional Thief* (University of Chicago Press, 1937; 1956 printing).

7 Ibid., pp. 212-214.

8 Ibid., p. 215.

9 *The Sutherland Papers,* edited by Cohen, Lindesmith, Schuessler (Indiana University Press, 1956; p. 304).

[10] Ibid., pp. 249-250. The paper originally appeared in the *Annals of the American Academy of Political and Social Science,* September, 1931.

[11] Clifford R. Shaw, *A Delinquent Boy's Own Story* (University of Chicago Press, 1930).

[12] Clifford R. Shaw, *The Natural History of a Delinquent Career* (University of Chicago Press, 1931).

[13] Clifford R. Shaw, *Brothers in Crime,* (University of Chicago Press, 1938).

[14] Frederic Wertham, *Dark Legend* (Duell, Sloan and Pearce, 1941).

[15] Frederic Wertham, *The Show of Violence* (Doubleday & Company, 1949).

[16] There is, of course, Dostoevski's classic, *Crime and Punishment.* But there are many others. Among modern novels, I would use as illustrations *Knock on Any Door* by Willard Motley; *Mrs. Party's House,* by Caroline Slade; and *Out of the Burning,* by Ira Henry Freeman (1960).

[17] *Cell 2455, Death Row,* by Caryl Chessman (Prentice-Hall, Inc., 1954; Permabook Edition, Pocket Books, Inc., 1956).

[18] *New Perspectives for Research in Juvenile Delinquency,* ed. Helen L. Witmer and Ruth Kotinsky (U.S. Children's Bureau, 1956).

[19] *An Evaluation of the Services of the State of Ohio to Its Delinquent Children and Youth,* by H. Ashley Weeks and Oscar W. Ritchie (Bureau of Educational Research, The Ohio State University, 1956).

[20] *For Children in Trouble,* by Alfred J. Kahn (Citzen's Committee for Children of New York City, Inc., 1957).

[21] *Etiology of Delinquent and Criminal Behavior* (Social Science Research Council, 1943, p. 86).

[22] Sol Wiener Ginsburg, "The Impact of the Social Worker's Cultural Structure on Social Therapy" (in *Social Casework,* October, 1951, p. 320).

[23] Lloyd Ohlin, "The Routinization of Correctional Change" (in the *Journal of Criminal Law, Criminology, and Police Science,* November, 1954).

[24] Compare several of the problems suggested for study in "Problems in Social Work Practice, Organization, and Knowledge Needing Evaluative Research," Appendix A in David G. French, *An Approach to Measuring Results in Social Work* (Columbia University Press, 1952). For example: "What is the effect, in terms of modifying behavior, [a child's? cottage parent's?] of a policy in a boys' training school which removes from the hands of cottage parents the administration of disciplinary measures and puts it in the hands of a cottage-life supervisor? Does the distance thus created between the commission of an act and the consequences of that act reduce significantly the learning value of the discipline? What is the effect of this policy on the role of the cottage parent as a substitute parent to the boy in the institution? A correlated question raised was whether, given the kind of cottage parents frequently found in a public correctional school, some means other than such a rigid rule was available for protecting boys in the institution from physical brutality?" (Page 128).

[25] "The Saginaw Project," by John B. Martin (NCCD Journal, *Crime and Delinquency,* October, 1960).

References

Two articles by Alfred J. Kahn, "Facilitating Social Work Research" (*The Social Service Review,* September, 1956); and "Sociology and Social Work: Challenge and Invitation" (*Social Problems,* January, 1957), discuss the social work setting for research. Provocative thoughts on delinquent behavior and delinquency research are contained in Fritz Redl's "Research Needs in the Delinquency Field" (*Children,* U.S. Department of Health, Education and Welfare, January-February, 1957).

A British study of probation is disappointing in its exclusive concern with statistical correlations, whose implications are not examined; *The Results of Probation*—A Report of the Cambridge Department of Criminal Science, edited by L. Radzinowicz (Macmillan and Co., London, 1958). Compare a study in which the dynamics are considered, *Probation and Social Adjustment,* by Jay Rumney and Joseph P. Murphy (Rutgers University Press, 1952).

The NCCD has established a research and information clearing center to obtain and disseminate research findings and other information on crime and juvenile delinquency, as well as conducting its own research and provide consultation. The center's service as a clearing house will focus on the practical utilization of research findings by control and treatment agencies.

Chapter 15

Illusions in a Research Study —

Unraveling Juvenile Delinquency

An arduous, expensive piece of criminological research, supported by numerous foundations, utilizing a large, distinguished staff under the direction of one of the most eminent American research teams in the field of criminology, made its appearance in 1950. Its goal, as stated by Sheldon and Eleanor Glueck in the author's preface to the study, *Unraveling Juvenile Delinquency,*[1] is to study "causation, with a view to determining the bases for truly crime-preventive programs and effective therapy." Their intention is to be eclectic rather than particularistic.

To question the validity of such a study is not a casual undertaking. The criticism is given, however, in the spirit of the Gluecks' own words: "Our exploration of the causal mechanisms of persistent delinquency is still in process. This book represents the first analysis of the data; further reflection, particularly examination of more intimate inter-correlations of the constituents of the various levels of exploration, will very probably bring about deeper insights and some modification of present conclusions." The present writer finds illusions in the plan of the work, in the method employed, in its findings, and in its interpretation.

Illusion in the Plan

The authors strive to avoid what they consider a basic weakness in sociological explanations of crime: the assumption that "the mass social stimulus to behavior, as reflected in the particular culture of a region, is alone, or primarily, the significant causal force." The area studies reveal "crude correlations between the gross physical makeup and composite culture of different zones of a city, on the one hand, and the incidence of delinquency and other aspects of social pathology on the other"; but "they do not reveal why the deleterious influences of even the most extreme delinquency area fail to turn the great majority of its boys into persistent delinquents."[2] The authors claim that the sociological explanation fails to answer the question, Why in the same environment do two individuals behave differently, one becoming delinquent or criminal, the other law-abiding? Elsewhere Sheldon Glueck observes: "Obviously, whatever be the element of social disintegration we are concerned with its influence makes itself felt only on a *selected group of individuals.* It must therefore be the physical and mental makeup of offenders, as compared with non-offenders, that presents the crucial and practical issue in the study of crime causation."[3]

But must it? It is erroneous to dismiss social causation by pointing out that many slum dwellers are law-abiding; why? The slums are characterized not only by strongly criminogenic elements but also by forces strongly supporting lawful behavior. The latter are positive community attributes and family, group, and individual resources, which operate to protect some individuals better than others. Chance, too, plays a part in the selection of youngsters fated to be delinquent: the separation into delinquents and non-delinquents is not always a basic separation, not the sharp differentiation which the categories imply. A change in administrative policy may mean a change in a delinquency rate. In a slum, delinquent behavior for some may frequently be not unnatural, but rather a natural choice; it is not the only choice; and lawful behavior is likewise not the only choice. But, in fact, the very data contained in *Unraveling Juvenile Delinquency* provide unmistakable clues as to why not all slum children become delinquent—if, as will be shown, the data are properly interpreted.

Certainly, it must be granted that slum areas produce relatively high delinquency and crime rates. Then, perhaps, *Unraveling Juvenile Delinquency* is a study of causation within that primary fact? For that to be so, we would expect the study to seek the mechanism by which slums produce delinquency. One way to do that would be to contrast the behavior and conditioning of children in slums and children in good neighborhoods, or in some other way to pursue the clues; but, as will be shown, that was not done.

The method was to select 500 institutionalized delinquent and 500 nondelinquent children, matched as closely as possible with respect to age, general intelligence, national (ethnico-racial) origin, and residence in underprivileged neighborhoods. What is the significance of controlling the pairs as to residence in underprivileged neighborhoods? It means that the attempt is made *to exclude residence in underprivileged neighborhoods as a causative source* for purposes of the study. As the Gluecks say: "A comparative study of delinquents who have been paired with nondelinquents in respect to certain factors can throw little light on the very factors that have been controlled."[4] The findings of such a study could easily be predicted. This artifact of crime causation can be characterized by suggesting another study: match delinquents and nondelinquents as to the characteristics found by this study to be significant; then whatever differences were demonstrated to exist between them would be, automatically, factors *other* than those found significant in this study!

Illusion in the Method

The most elementary caution in criminology research is the recognition that an examination of institutionalized offenders (or delinquents) will provide information about *institutionalized offenders* and *not* about offenders in general. An institutionalized offender is characteristically an institution product, in part.

It is, of course, valuable, particularly as a guide to administrative reform, to understand clearly what happens to an individual in an institution not only socially and physically but psychologically. But *Unraveling Juvenile Delinquency* says nothing about the effect of institutional life on the inmate. Its purpose is to comprehend the causal pattern as it presents itself *at the time of entrance into public school.* The outcome of the study is a prediction table to be used at that stage of a child's life. Yet the institution children selected were not six, seven, or eight years old. They averaged in age fourteen years and eight months at the time they were selected for study,[5] ranging from eleven to seventeen years of age.[6] They have spent an average of 7.12 months in correctional institutions.[7] Their average age at the time of first commitment to a correctional school was thirteen and nine-tenths years.

What can be discovered by examining children at that age, in a correctional institution for such a number of months? Can we discover their characters and personalities as of the age of eight years, a time when they had no contact with courts, probation, police, or institutions? To suggest that we can is a hazardous surmise, not one to be relied on without justification and discussion. To rely on the probability that their personalities and characters *had* changed, at least in so far as character and personality are related to their criminal behavior, would be less hazardous.

Furthermore, is it not probable that the judge, at the point of disposition, considers the personality of the child and selects for commitment the less amenable delinquent? Very probable. Then we would be constrained to recognize that there may be a difference between a delinquent child released on probation and a delinquent child who is committed. If *three* groups were compared—institutional delinquents, noninstitutional delinquents, and nondelinquents (noninstitutional)—it is possible that the noninstitutional delinquent would be found to be more like the nondelinquents than like the institutional delinquents.

The nondelinquents told the psychiatrist who interviewed them on behalf of the study of their peccadilloes, as the authors call window-breaking, truck-hopping, occasionally sneaking admission into a movie theater, and occasional stealing from a five-and-ten-cent store.[8] What if children committed for peccadilloes were compared with these nondelinquents—might they not be similar to the children committed for more serious acts, rather than to the nondelinquent but peccadillo-committing boys? And might it not be found, then, that the difference between commitment and noncommitment of a boy guilty of a peccadillo is the resources available to the family rather than the personality or character of the boy?

Illusion in the Findings

Although delinquents and nondelinquents had been matched as to general intelligence, some differences in intelligent-test results were found. The delinquents showed less aptitude in vocabulary, information, and comprehension. The authors recognize that these results are related to the delinquents' lesser amounts of schooling and the inferior cultural atmosphere of their homes. In the performance of intelligence tests the delinquents and nondelinquents resemble each other closely. What do the Gluecks say about this? "Although it may be a fact that the way in which individuals score on intelligence tests is to some extent affected by cultural opportunities, it must be kept in mind in interpreting these findings that in the general sources of the culture-complex—ethnic derivation and residence in underprivileged areas—the two groups under comparison were closely matched. It is therefore reasonable to assume that there may be some fundamental residual difference between the delinquents and nondelinquents in their variability in test scores."[9] But what, in fact, are the literal findings with respect to social background? They are that *there in a greater difference between the delinquents and the nondelinquents in the quality of their social background than in their intelligence* scores.

More than half (55 per cent) of the delinquents as against 34.2 per cent of the nondelinquents live in blighted tenement areas;[10] 27.2 per cent of the homes of the nondelinquents are described as *good,* compared with 11.4 per cent of the homes of the delinquents, while 33.9 per cent of the homes of delinquents are extremely *poor* (overcrowded, lacking in sanitary facilities, filthy, etc.), compared with 19.8 per cent of the homes of nondelinquents in equivalent conditions.[11] The parents of the delinquents are markedly overburdened, as compared with the parents of nondelinquents, by serious social, physical, and psychological difficulties.[12] Naturally, then, the delinquents moved about more than the nondelinquents, and a considerably higher proportion engaged in the street trades, while more nondelinquents were in jobs in which some supervision was provided; a far larger proportion of delinquents hung around street corners, played in vacant lots, on waterfronts, and in railroad yards, frequented cheap poolrooms and dance halls; the delinquents were considerably involved in gang membership, while the nondelinquents avoided gangs almost entirely.[13] What, then, becomes of the "close matching" relied upon by the Gluecks for their assumption of "fundamental residual difference" between the two groups? How can one avoid seeing the effectiveness of these factors in the natural selection of delinquents?

Rorschach test and psychiatric findings indicate important differences between delinquents and nondelinquents. The delinquents are found to be more socially assertive, defiant, hostile, more impulsive, vivacious, and extroverted. They also suffer less from anxiety and are more independent.[14] The delinquents are said to be less adequate than the nondelinquents in deep-rooted emotional dynamics. On the other hand, they are more dynamic and energetic, more aggressive, adventurous, and impulsive.[15]

There are many other such findings, which we do not stop to summarize or evaluate. But, as has already been pointed out here, both these tests were made in the correctional institutions and hence are findings which compare not two groups from depressed neighborhood differentiated as to delinquency and nondelinquency but two groups from markedly different total social backgrounds, one group being an institutionalized group, the other with no experience in the institution.[16] There is a strong possibility that institutional life contributed to the greater display among delinquents of social assertiveness, defiance, ambivalence towards others, hostility, suspicion, destructiveness, less submisiveness to authority—to mention most of the characteristics noted by the Rorschach test. As for the psychiatric characterizations of the delinquents, much is said of the *cause* of the greater emotional tension of the delinquents than of the nondelinquents; but no attempt is made to show that these emotional differences are a *cause of delinquency* or to explain why they were *not* a cause of delinquency in the nondelinquents who also exhibited them.

Illusion in the Interpretation

In the concluding chapters of *Unraveling Juvenile Delinquency,* the authors derive from the findings (*a*) a tool for "practical crime prevention efforts" and (*b*) a proposed *law of crime causation.*

(*a*) THE PREDICTION TABLES

"The selection of potential delinquents at the time of school entrance or soon thereafter," the Gluecks point out, "would make possible the application of treatment measures that would be truly crime preventive."[17] (For the sake of accuracy this statement should in any event speak of "delinquency" prevention, not "crime" prevention.) Three prediction tables are therefore constructed and are proposed as aids in this selection. The first table uses five *social factors:* discipline of boy by father (over-strict or erratic; lax; firm but kindly) ; supervision of boy by mother (unsuitable; fair; suitable) ; affection of father for boy (indifferent or hostile; warm, including overprotective) ; affection of mother for boy; cohesiveness of family (unintegrated; some elements of cohesion; cohesive).[18] The second prediction table uses *character traits* determined in the Rorschach test: social assertion (marked; slight or suggestive; absent) ; defiance; suspicion; destructiveness; emotional liability. The third prediction table uses *personality traits* determined in the psychiatric interview; adventurous (present in marked degree; not prominent, or noticeably lacking) ; extroverted in action; suggestible; stubborn; emotionally unstable.

Are the prediction tables validly established?

1 . It is not at all clear that the table based on "social factors" is a true reflection of the useful data contained in the findings. Both delinquents and nondelinquents were seelcted from poor neighborhoods, for a simple reason—these are high-delinquency areas. The social factors table, however, says nothing about areas! Is this table applicable to *all* kinds of areas? One could, for example, select from good and poor neighborhoods children who meet the conditions of overstrict or erratic discipline of boy by father, unsuitable supervision of boy by mother, indifferent or hostile father and mother, and unintegrated family. Would this test be equally effective in predicting delinquency for both groups? Possibly not. But perhaps the test can be used for underprivileged neighborhoods? If the test is said to apply to the limited social setting only, then one concedes the effect of environment! But, if one overcomes the logical inconsistency of denying the prime importance of social causation while at the same time relying on it, and the prediction table is applied to the poor neighborhood, we find that only some of the factors are used. In the prediction table based on "social factors" no account whatsoever is taken of extra-household social conditions. As to the "under-the-roof" environment, for specific social facts interpersonal effects are substituted, [19] without its being established that the interpersonal effects are, in fact, causes rather than, like delinquency, *effects.*

2. As has already been noted, the psychiatric and Rorschach findings do not *provide* an explanation of anything; on the contrary they *require* an explanation. Did the differences noted between delinquents (*institutionalized*) and nondelinquents result mainly from experiences connected with court and institution for the delinquents? Did they result in great or little part from the role in which they were placed as delinquents? Or did they, in fact, exist earlier? Are there differences between these institutionalized children and the child delinquents in a modern camp or in a cottage institution with a small population or in an institution with adequate psychiatric service? Are there differences between these children and delinquent children from rural areas? The psychiatric study was neither prolonged nor intensive enough to answer these questions; it consisted of a single interview.

3. The psychiatric and Rorschach findings regarding children of the average age of almost fifteen years, within a correctional institution, cannot be used with confidence to "predict" what these children, or other children, were like at the age of six. It is awkward, to say the least, to call this "prediction." The social factors, by contrast, *are,* in all probability, relevant as of the time these children entered school; but, as seen, the prediction table based on "social factors" is a pale list of the social factors which are discernible in this study.

(*b*) THE LAW OF CRIME CAUSATION

The Gluecks tentatively formulate a "causal formulation or law." The great mass of delinquents, says the proposed law,

> as a group are distinguishable from the non-delinquents (1) *physically,* in being essentially mesomorphic in constitution (solid, closely knit, muscular); (2) *temperamentally,* in being restlessly energetic, impulsive, extroverted, aggressive, destructive (often sadistic)—traits which may be related more or less to the erratic growth pattern and its physiologic correlates or consequences; (3) *in attitude,* by being hostile, defiant, resentful, suspicious, stubborn, socially assertive, adventurous, unconventional, non-submissive to authority; (4) *psychologically,* in tending to direct and concrete, rather than symbolic, intellectual expression, and in being less methodical in their approach to problems; (5) *socio-culturally,* in having been reared to a far greater extent that the control group in homes of little understand-

> ing, affection, stability, or moral fibre by parents usually unfit to be effective guides and protectors or, according to psychoanalytic theory, desirable sources for emulation and the construction of a consistent, well-balanced and socially normal superego during the early stages of character development. While in individual cases the stresses contributed by any one of the above pressure-areas of dissocial-behavior tendency may adequately account for persistence in delinquency, in general the high probability of delinquency is dependent upon the interplay of the conditions and forces from all these areas.
>
> In the exciting-stimulating, but little controlled and culturally inconsistent environment of the underprivileged area, such boys readily give expression to their untamed impulses and their self-centered desires by means of various forms of delinquent behavior. Their tendencies toward uninhibited energy-expression are deeply anchored in soma and psyche and in the malformations of character during the first few years of life.[20]

It is a daring thing to formulate a law of crime causation—particularly so when the correlation which serves as the basis of the law is an untested one. The law is untested; it can be said to be *derived* from data, but not *tested* by them. (The law *has* not been tested. It is the efficacy of the prediction tables that has been tested; we discuss this below.) But how well, in fact, *is* the law derived from the data? A hypothesis and, even more so, a law, like a hypothetical question to an expert witness in a court of law, must be true to the facts.

1. The law is not limited as to place, age, or administrative policy, to accord with the limitations of the sample.

2. The law applies to the "great mass" of delinquents characteristics observed only in an institutionalized group of delinquents and only in a part—sometimes a very small part—of those delinquents. For example, as to the characteristics of temperament, the "great mass" of the institutionalized delinquents are not aggressive—only 15.1 per cent are (as compared with five per cent of the nondelinquents); 41.4 per cent of the delinquents are characterized as stubborn (Table XIX-1), 13.7 per cent are egocentric, 28.8 per cent are uncritical of self (Table XIX-3); etc.

3. The law declares, in its first clause, a definite physical characteristic for delinquents. But the physical differences had earlier been rejected by the authors for predictive purposes because, they

said: "As regards physique, we are dealing with a discipline as yet highly controversial because physical anthropologists have not yet answered a major question, namely, whether or not the somatotype remains constant and, if it does, whether, in the formative years of growth around the age of six or seven, when children normally enter school, the physique type is as yet reliably distinguishable.[21] Then what justification is there to include physique in the "law"?

The Gluecks had characterized as "crude correlation" the findings of the area studies which noted high rates of delinquency in regions of economic and cultural disorganization.[22] Here physique finds its way into the "law" as a sheer correlation rather general, without a guess as to a causal relationship. Although called a "causal law," *none* of the law goes beyond mere correlation.

4. Clause four similarly includes characteristics which were rejected for predictive purposes. "The possibility of a predictive device to be applied at school entrance derived from the differential findings of the Wechsler-Bellevue and Stanford Achievement tests was also ruled out, because Dr. Wechsler had suggested to us 'that the scale not be used with children under ten years.' "[23]

5. Clause five is the translation of social factors. What has been done here, however, as pointed out earlier (above, page 219, at section a, paragraph one, in the discussion of the prediction tables) has been to translate the data into a generalization which uses only *part* of the social factors, which uses the *effects* of environment rather than the environment itself, as if a chemist were to talk only of *properties* rather than substances.

Reinterpreting the Data

Two outstanding facts emerge from *Unraveling Juvenile Delinquency*: (1) in place of a study which sought steadfastly to eliminate environmental factors as well as to eliminate them from a causal law, *the force of social (or environmental) causation of delinquency proves irrepressible.* (2) Institutionalized children differ from children who have not been institutionalized.

Unfortunately, the study has not explored these facts. In what ways do rundown neighborhoods cause delinquency? Why do institution children differ from children who have not been institutionalized?

Although the authors determined to be *eclectic* in relation to the disciplines used in this study, they appear to have achieved the result of being *fractional with* regard to the child. Compare, for example, the following statement taken from the report of another kind of delinquency study:

> The project accepted the philosophy that each child must be treated as a whole and his problems as a unit regardless of the number of problems or the areas of his life affected. The experience of the project shows that minor and incipient problem behavior in children can be identified by the community and that if adequate community services are effectively coordinated much of this problem behavior can be corrected and modified or, if not susceptible to correction, prevented from developing into more serious forms. Its experience further emphasizes the fact that the community services called up to work in a coordinated program must include not only the social agencies, which are primarily concerned with the neglected, dependent, and delinquent child or the child in need of special care, but also the health and law-enforcing agencies and the agencies established to serve all children, such as the group-work agencies, the recreational agencies, and the schools. The acceptance of this philosophy of treating the child as a whole and of its corollary of including all services affecting children either directly or indirectly is of primary importance to the community interested in developing a program to prevent problem behavior in children and to identify and treat such behavior early in its development if it does appear.[24]

The foregoing are attributes of a rational preventive program, preventive of the varied problems of children, "problem behavior," delinquency or not. It takes the child's behavior as sharing in and reflecting his own, his family's, his community's life; it recognizes that he may develop critical difficulties at any time—at or before school entrance or at any time thereafter. His conduct is determined not only by his own attitudes and character and those of his family and companions but, not least, by the attitudes and character of the community and its agencies. A flexible plan of detection of incipient behavior problems is projected and tested sucessfully.

Serious questions may be raised as to the very concept of the prediction tables. The direction of a child's behavior depends not only on what he is but on how he grows and on how the community and its services behave and grow. Prevention is in the community more than it is in the child. It looks to the present and future rather than to the past. It strives to control adverse conditions which contribute to difficulties in children. Prediction tables do not assist in this broad approach to prevention.

Prevention also takes a more limited form in work with individual children, How practical are validly produced prediction tables at this level? The base of the prediction tables is in the past. Their concept is continued uniformity of the process which brings a child to the point of difficulty. Without such uniformity between past and future, the prediction tables are invalid. The larger prevention effort, the more important prevention effort, is therefore at work to produce changes which will affect the basis of the prediction table. Environment is not static; normal social change will in time render the prediction tables less and less reliable. The psychological framework of prediction tables is condemnation of the community and its services to unvarying persistence in a current course. The prediction tables are difficult and expensive to produce and to use, require extensive testing to confirm their validity in the first place, and continual retesting to reaffirm their validity thereafter. At best, they have an ephemeral life as a subsidiary tool in a delinquency-prevention program,

The analysis of the study speaks for itself, but (assuming the validity of our analysis) when one stops there, another interesting question arises: Why is the study in error, how did it come about? A complete answer is not being suggested by the present writer, but one of the factors would seem to be the goal that was set for the project—that of developing a prediction table. There is nothing wrong in the effort to obtain such a tool, but it does set a trap. The trap is that one may accept as cause a mere correlation between an early fact and a later result, without discovering whether there is a sufficient link between them.

For example, there was the professor whose demonstration to his class involved a frog. Holding the frog in one hand he commanded it to jump. It leaped into his other hand. Next he severed the frog's legs. Then when he called "Jump!" the poor frog did not move. "And so," concluded the professor for his class, "you note that when you sever the legs of a frog, he grows quite deaf."

Another factor probably relates to the current thinking in the field of behavior generally, which puts a major emphasis on the early parent-child relationship in the formation of character. Whatever validity there may be in this theory, it has yet to be established accurately in the setting of delinquency, although the family setting and delinquency are often said to be correlated. What is the relationship of character structure to delinquency? If it is said that the parent-child relationship of a certain kind impels a child to delinquency, how *does* it do it? What are the steps by which it is observed? Can we demonstrate it?

These questions (which go back to our early chapter, "Are Parents Responsible for Juvenile Delinquency?" go to the heart of the validity of *Unraveling.* The answers are not given by *Unraveling*; and they cannot be assumed.

"But the Prediction Table Works"

But must not the many critics of the Gluecks' study be silenced, when it is found that the prediction table works? By 1960 Eleanor T. Glueck was able to refer to a dozen validations of the predictive ability of the principle table.[25] They include demonstrations in Japan and France, as well as about ten in the United States. Furthermore, Mrs. Glueck points out, "worldwide interest is reflected in a resolution presented and passed at the Third International Congress of Criminology held in London in September, 1955," adopted, it is added, by a vote of 260 to 10.

Evidently the most impressive report on the success of the prediction tables developed in *Unraveling Juvenile Delinquency* is that of Richard E. Thompson, in his article "A Validation of the Glueck Social Prediction Scale for Proneness to Delinquency."[26] Mr. Thompson analyzes the predictive efforts involved in the "Cambridge-Somerville (Massachusetts) Youth Study," in which an attempt was made to choose pre-delinquents from among school boys and treat them to ascertain the extent to which the project staff could succeed in preventing the development of delinquent careers. Mr. Thompson concludes that the Glueck prediction table developed in *Unraveling Juvenile Delinquency* if applied to the boys in this project would have achieved a better predictive score than was achieved by the means used in the project. The project used an "informed guess" by a selection committee consisting of a psychiatrist and two social case workers, based on social and personal data obtained by the project staff and supplied by parents, teachers, police and others.

What would such a result mean? Would it validate the "findings" and conclusions of *Unraveling*? No; it would simply mean that the predictive device developed in *Unraveling* worked rather well. It would *not* mean that the analysis of what really happened to the boys was the analysis suggested in *Unraveling* as a "causal law." The frog no longer jumped; why?—not for the professor's reason.

What happens to the analysis if one adopts an *altogether different* prediction table, and it works? In *Unraveling* the Gluecks point out that other factors could have been used for prediction purposes. But the Gluecks themselves give the game away entirely in their later book, *Physique and Delinquency* (based on the same groups of boys as is *Unraveling-*. In *Physique* they find all sorts of correlations between physical characteristics and future delinquency. For example: "Delinquents as a group are more enuretic than non-delinquents"; "extreme restlessness in childhood is substantially more characteristic of delinquents as a group than of non-delinquents"; "the difference between delinquents and non-delinquents in [strength of hand grip], though slight, is significant"; etc. *There is no doubt that the Gluecks could select among these characteristics and develop another successful prediction table.* What does this prove as to the so-called causal law of *Unraveling*? It undoes it, and it is further undone by the latest new predictive device, based now on differences in response to certain intelligence tests, and described in *Predicting Delinquency and Crime*, the 1959 publication based on the same boys as is *Unraveling*.

The relatively successful prediction is not the feat it appears to be. It is not surprising that the examination of a great many possible correlations produces half a dozen which, taken together, have a rather accurate predictive result, better than the guesses of three individuals using a common sense estimate of delinquency. The feat would be important if it told us something about either causation, prevention, or treatment, but it does none of this.

Mr. Thompson presents this table:

ACTUAL SUBSEQUENT CONDUCT OF 100 CSYS CASES AS RELATED TO THE PREDICTED RESULTS OF GLUECK PREDICTION SCALE AND THREE-MEMBER CSYS SELECTION COMMITTEE

Actual Subsequent Conduct of 100 Boys	*Glueck Prediction Scale*	—*CSYS PREDICTIONS*—		
80 remained non-del.		Member 1	Member 2	Member 3
Number accurately predicted	73 (out of 80 cases)	44 (out of 75 cases)	38 (out of 71 cases)	37 (out of 65 cases)
Percent accurately predicted	91.3%	58.7%	53.5%	56.9%
20 became delinquent				
Number accurately predicted	18 (out of 20 cases)	18 (out of 20 cases)	18 (out of 20 cases)	17 (out of 18 cases)
Percent accurately predicted	90.0%	90.0%	90.0%	94.4%

That is, each of the CSYS members did *as well as* the Glueck table in predicting the delinquents. True, it is not a great achievement since they did less well in predicting non-delinqueny—that is, they "predicted" *that more* boys were potential delinquents. Is it possible that CSYS had a broader view of delinquency, and were not so much "predicting" as declaring that at the moment of study a number of boys presented problems sufficiently serious that their futures would probably be marked by delinquency or other behaviorial or psychological difficulty? Is this less valuable or more valuable than predicting delinquency?

Alfred J. Kahn, one of the reviewers critical of *Unraveling,* said this: "One must ask whether we need a means of identifying potential *delinquents* at an early age, or rather vulnerable *children* likely to develop a variety of forms of disturbance and maladjustment and in need of help. A strong case can be made for attempting to screen out a broader group, particularly since the Gluecks' non-delinquents show many evidences of needing help."[27]

There may be another, more foreboding, reason to be wary of the prediction tables. The prophecies may be fulfilled because they have been made, that is, the school system, particularly the teachers, "find" the expected to occur. This has been shown with respect to expected success—and expected failure. The reasons for these results are complex, but one feature is that unconsciously teachers assume different attitudes toward students, depending on what they think of them and their abilities.[28]

Notes

1 Sheldon and Eleanor Glueck, *Unraveling Juvenile Delinquency* (New York: Commonwealth Fund, 1950).

2 Ibid., p. 5.

3 Sheldon Glueck, "Crime Causation" (NCCD *Yearbook,* 1941, p. 90). This position has been taken by some others. A psychiatrist, Dr. Ralph S. Banay, writes: "Sociological causation, the existence of slums, deprivation, poverty . . . as criminogenic elements . . . [do] not stand up under statistical evaluation. The fact is that in identical bad environments relatively few succumb to antisocial drive. Most of them make an adequate adjustment" (NCCD *Yearbook,* 1949, p. 59). A penologist, Donald Clemmer, writes: "There must be some differences between the average run of mankind in the street who never becomes involved in conventional crime, and the bulk of these men in our institutions" (*Federal Probation,* March, 1949, p. 32).

4 *Unraveling Juvenile Delinquency,* p. 15.

5 Ibid., p. 37.

6 Ibid., p. 260.

7 Ibid., p. 28.

8 Ibid., p. 61.

9 Ibid., p. 206.

10 Ibid., p. 79.

11 Ibid., p. 83.

12 Ibid., p. 107.

13 Ibid., p. 167. The results of the intelligence tests were, like the findings in respect to bodily constitution, not used for predictive purposes, as being inaccurate or unsound when applied to children under ten. The foregoing cited treatment of these findings, however, illustrates the manner in which the raw data were weighed.

14 Ibid., p.240.

15 Ibid., pp. 251, 252.

16 To demonstrate the objectivity of the parts of the research, the authors point out that the psychiatrist, for example, did not have before him, prior to an interview, the findings of the psychological tests, the Rorschach test, or the social history. But, of course, the more important source of bias, if there were any (which is not suggested here), would be the knowledge of the history and the situation of the boys; the fact is that the delinquent boys were interviewed in the institutions.

17 Ibid., p. 257.

18 Ibid., p. 261.

19 Compare the items in the "social factors" prediction table, with the "under-the-roof" social conditions listed in our text in connection with nn. 11 and 12.

20 Ibid., pp. 281-82.

21 Ibid., p. 258.

22 Above, n. 2.

23 Ibid., p. 259.

24 Sybil A. Stone, Elsa Castendyck, and Harold B. Hanson, *Children in the Community: The St. Paul Experiment in Child Welfare* (United States Children's Bureau Publication No. 317, 1946, p. 158).

[25] "Efforts to Identify Delinquents," by Eleanor T. Glueck (*Federal Probation*, June, 1960).
[26] Richard E. Thompson, "A Validation of the Glueck Social Prediction Scale for Proneness of Delinquency" (*Journal of Criminal Law, Criminology, and Police Science*, November, 1952).
[27] Alfred J. Kahn, "Analysis of Methodology of Unraveling Juvenile Delinquency," in David G. French, *An Approach to Measuring Results in Social Work* (Columbia University Press, 1952).
[28] "Teacher Expectations for the Disadvantaged," Robert Rosenthal and Lenore F. Jacobson (Scientific American, April, 1968), v. 218, p. 19. A British study found the same to be true of delinquency; M. J. Power and others, in New Society, Oct. 19, 1967, reported in Trans-Action, October, 1968, p. 6.

References

One of the attempted validations of the prediction table is the still continuing study by the New York City Youth Board, started in 1952. In 1960 it endorsed the use of the table for broad use in the city schools. The Citizens' Committee for Children of New York, Inc., published an analysis questioning the validation of the table by this study. It declared:

"Of 186 boys predicted as future non-delinquents, 176 are non-delinquent, 2 are pre-delinquent, 8 are delinquent. *Of 37 predicted likely to become delinquent, 20 are non-delinquent, 4 are pre-delinquent and 13 are delinquent.* The Youth Board Report calls this a predictive accuracy of 86.5 percent. This is technically correct if the non-delinquency predictions and the delinquency predictions are added together. In the context of public evaluation of the scale, the claims are questionable.

"But much more crucial in considering the use of a scale of this sort in schools is the fact that thus far only *13 out of 37, or 35.1 per cent, predicted delinquents are actually showing delinquent behavior.*"

The Citizens' Committee statement said also: "More than a generation ago, educators discarded the view attributed to the Commissioner of Youth Services by the *New York Times* . . .: That we should seek to separate the delinquent from the simply neurotic child because, 'The neurotic ... does not commit crimes and is, therefore, not a public problem.' If the schools were to adopt only a device so limited as to find delinquency, we would need separate prediction scales for many other problems, such as potential mental illness, neurosis, learning difficulties, and so on. . . .

"This specialized scale poses an additional problem. Delinquency is a stigma-bearing legal adjudication, not a specific disease or diagnosis. A child labeled as a potential delinquent may well suffer consequences in teacher attitude, school program and in his own self-respect which will contribute to maladjustment and delinquency. To label a child as a 'future bad boy' (*New York Times* report of press conference) may help make him one."

The U.S. Children's Bureau states: "The evidence available thus far does not suggest that a large group of children should be tagged pre-delinquent, even though it is very likely that the majority of delinquents will come from their ranks. It should be remembered that this majority of delinquents may be only a minority of the children for whom delinquency is predicted by the scale. These children are rated pre-delinquent because of their family misfortunes. All children whose families show the index traits are likely to be in need of services and should get them according to and because of their need. It seems unfair and unnecessary to compound their misfortunes by branding them on the basis of statistical computations which, however worthy the intentions, are 'off the beam.'" (*Juvenile Delinquency Facts/Facets,* Identifying Potential Delinquents; 1960, No. 5.)

This chapter is based on an article published in the *American Journal of Sociology,* September, 1951).

TABLE OF CASES

Index